The State
as Terrorist

Recent Titles in
Contributions in Political Science
Series Editor: Bernard K. Johnpoll

Neighbors Across the Pacific: The Development of Economic and Political Relations
Between Canada and Japan
Klaus H. Pringsheim

International Dynamics of Technology
Ralph Sanders

Party Politics in Israel and the Occupied Territories
Gershon R. Kieval

The Strange Career of Marihuana: Politics and Ideology of Drug Control in America
Jerome L. Himmelstein

French Communism in the Era of Stalin: The Quest for Unity and Integration, 1945-1962
Irwin M. Wall

North Korea in Transition: From Dictatorship to Dynasty
Tai Sung An

The Harmonization of European Public Policy: Regional Responses to Transnational
Challenges
Edited by Leon Hurwitz

The Press and the Rebirth of Iberian Democracy
Edited by Kenneth Maxwell

Domestic Policy Formation: Presidential-Congressional Partnership?
Steven A. Shull

Communications Policy and the Political Process
Edited by John J. Havick

Abortion: A Case Study in Law and Morals
Fred M. Frohock

Minority Rights: A Comparative Analysis
Jay A. Sigler

Controlling Regulatory Sprawl: Presidential Strategies from Nixon to Reagan
Howard Ball

THE STATE AS TERRORIST

The Dynamics of Governmental Violence and Repression

EDITED BY
Michael Stohl and George A. Lopez

PJCS 68

CONTRIBUTIONS IN POLITICAL SCIENCE, NUMBER 103

GREENWOOD PRESS
WESTPORT, CONNECTICUT

Library of Congress Cataloging in Publication Data

Main entry under title:

The State as terrorist.

(Contributions in political science, ISSN 0147-1066 ;
no. 103)
   Bibliography: p.
   Includes index.
   1. Internal security—Addresses, essays, lectures.
2. Civil rights—Addresses, essays, lectures.
3. Terrorism—Addresses, essays, lectures. 4. Violence
—Addresses, essays, lectures. I. Stohl, Michael,
1947-   . II. Lopez, George A. III. Series.
JC571.S785   1984   323   83-5631
ISBN 0-313-23726-3 (lib. bdg.)

Library of Congress Catalog Card Number: 83-5631
ISBN: 0-313-23726-3
ISSN: 0147-1066

First published in 1984

Greenwood Press
A division of Congressional Information Service, Inc.
88 Post Road West
Westport, Connecticut 06881

Printed in the United States of America

10 9 8 7 6 5 4 3 2 1

To my parents
    Jean and Martin Stohl

To my family
    Cathy, Tom, and Marty Lopez

Contents

Acknowledgments

This volume had its genesis in the May, 1982, meetings of the Midwest Political Science Association in Milwaukee, Wisconsin, where eight of the essays contained in this volume were first presented. During two lengthy sessions the authors debated the contours of state terror and the level of specification necessary to move beyond the mere counting of human rights violations. If this volume has succeeded in developing a scholarly understanding of state terror, it is due to the forthrightness of that dialogue in Milwaukee and, during the months that followed it, the contributors' revisions and the suggestions of the editors for further revision. We would especially like to thank Ray Duvall and Terry Nardin for their contributions during the Milwaukee meetings and the early phases of this book. We appreciate the enthusiasm of Jim Sabin of Greenwood Press for the project and the patience and competence of the editorial and production staffs, most notably Maureen Melino and Louise Hatem. Last-minute research assistance and index preparation were provided by Cathy Lopez and an outstanding group of Earlham College students, including Anne Hayner, Tom Thornburg, Eric Garner, Melissa Moye, Fred McClure, Bob Schultz, and Diane Campbell.

The State
as Terrorist

Introduction

Michael Stohl and George A. Lopez ⸻

Political terrorism, it has been argued, has grown dramatically in the past decade and one-half. Accompanying that growth, the systematic study of that phenomenon of political violence that has been labeled "terrorism" has also greatly increased. This increased scholarly concern has concentrated primarily on the problem of insurgent and anti-state terrorism. Relatively little recent work has focused concern on the problem of terrorism as it relates to the activities of nation-states in forms other than what has been labeled counterterrorism.

This introductory chapter and the chapters that follow examine the use of violence, repression, and terrorism by the state in the pursuit of domestic and international interests. That political scientists should consider it worthwhile to study the role of violence by the state and in particular the systematic use of violence should come as no surprise. In fact, as we survey the literature, the truly astonishing fact is that it has taken scholars so long to "reinterest" themselves in state terrorism as a problem for study. It is a problem that requires investment in theory building and analysis and not simply description and condemnation.[1]

A CONTEXT FOR THE STUDY OF STATE TERRORISM

Sources for an investigation of state terrorism abound, but it is important to note at the outset that there are those who would seek to denounce a focus on state terrorism as "skewed," "biased," "ideological," "not in the mainstream of the literature," and "out of touch with real political events." These sources, or rationales, as they might more appropriately be cast, include the evidence of political history that irrefutably demonstrates state terror, the tensions existing in international legal discussions over the definition of *terrorism*, the scholarly literature on state terror that emerged before definitional debates came into vogue, and selected patterns of analysis of scholars of group-based terrorism.

The most sobering source justifying the study of state terror is political history. The Jacobin "Reign of Terror" introduced Western societies to unprecedented levels of government violence against such a wide array of nationals that its victims numbered about 17,000 and included atheists, orthodox clergy, nobles and beggars, the Queen, and ultimately Robespierre himself. This century alone has witnessed numerous purges by post-revolutionary governments. Western analysts have focused mainly on the institutionalized systems of terror that developed under Stalin in the Soviet Union and Hitler in Germany. Sean MacBride has pointed out that there have been many recent cases of "massive massacres amounting to genocide" including Indonesia, 1965-1967; Chile, 1973; Kampuchea, 1975-1976; East Timor, 1975-1976; Uganda, 1976-1978; Argentina, 1978-1979; the Central African Empire, 1978-1979; and Equatorial Guinea, 1977-1979. As Leo Kuper noted, MacBride omitted the cases of Bangladesh in 1971 and Burundi in 1972-1973, where the killing was on a much greater scale.[2] Arguments abound about the causes of state violence in contemporary societies, but the preceding list of government killing stands as overwhelming empirical evidence that state violence is a standard operating procedure of numerous contemporary regimes.

A focus on the state as terrorist in the 1980s also emerges from a survey of the tense discussions of the rule of law that developed in the midst of the international organizational debates a decade ago regarding what governments might do to deal with nongovernmental terrorism. In assessing the character and direction of United Nations discussion on terrorism we can now note that the stalemate in that body occurred due to disagreements that cut across regional and ideological lines. Simply expressed, the conflicts entailed three legal claims:

1. The position that *terrorism* is defined and constituted by the "criminal acts" taken against governments by individuals or groups. This position was supported by most of the advanced industrial Western states and some Latin governments.

2. The position that *terrorism* should be defined by acts, but in a broader context than 1. above so as to include acts of governmental groups that violate human rights and reinforce policies such as apartheid. This position was advanced primarily by the African states.

3. The position that the definition of *terrorism* resides in the motivation of the actor and the context of the act. This argument claims that to consider terrorism narrowly, outside of national liberation movements, is to label inappropriately a freedom fighter as a "terrorist." A variety of developing nations and Arab states held this view.

Reflecting on the lack of U.N. consensus due to these positions, many analysts asserted that the collective encounter with the phenomenon of terrorism had brought to the surface what policy and academic discussion up to that date had not: that governments on practical, political, and legal grounds could be considered terrorists. In analyzing the character of this debate in light of the larger dimensions of the Charter, W. T. Mallison and S. V. Mallison wrote:

Charter obligation is as applicable to the avoidance of discriminatory concepts of terrorism as it is to other fields. It is clear that no act of terror should be excused because of the identity of the terrorist; and it is equally essential that no act of terror be excused because of the identity of the victim. Thus, terrorism directed at Asians and Africans must be as effectively reduced as terrorism directed against Europeans and North Americans. The protection of diplomats and members of other elite groups may be most effectively achieved along with the protection of members of the mass. It is an elementary practical reality that preferred groups or individuals, according to a discriminatory value orientation, are not likely to be immunized from terror unless the less favored are immunized along with them. The result of terrorism is to deprive its victims, whoever they are, of their most basic human rights.[3]

U.N. Ambassador Charles Yost put it even more bluntly: "The fact is, of course, that there is a vast amount of hypocrisy on the subject of political terrorism. We all righteously condemn it—except when we ourselves or friends of ours are engaging in it. Then we ignore it or gloss over it or attach to it tags like 'liberation' or 'defense of the free world' or 'national honor' to make it seem like something than what it is."[4]

The final impetus from considerations of law and political history that gives weight to the focus on governmental terror unfolded during the early stages of the U.S.-Iranian hostage epoch and the irony of the logical conclusion and legal recourse that the incident presented to the United States. In November 1979, when "students" seized the U.S. embassy compound in Teheran, nations began to position themselves for analysis and interpretation of this "typical" terrorist event according to the three aforementioned predispositions.

The United States claimed the action was a clear violation of international law and called it criminal. In doing so, it also rearticulated its traditional policy of non-negotiation with terrorists. Other states, when pressed on the issue, claimed the incident was unfortunate, if not illegal, but also noted that the crimes of the Shah were equally repugnant. Still other states associated themselves with the claims of the militants that the action was a legitimate part of the Iranian Islamic revolution and that the issue of terrorism should be focused on the atrocities of the Shah and SAVAK, if not also on the Washington regime that supplied the repressive tools for these surrogates.

But beyond these fairly predictable disagreements, most international actors initially considered the Khomeini regime as caught somewhere in the middle of the situation. That is, it was not quite a hostage and not quite a "go-between" for the students and the United States. This had been the typical position of governments faced with such situations. But in its endorsement in late November of the embassy takeover, the Khomeini government changed the nature of the discussion of terrorism for this case and perhaps for the international system in general.

Although developing and developed states had disagreed about the motivation of groups, about the link between terror and revolution, and about whether South Africa was a human rights or a terrorist issue, these parties had always viewed acts of states as distinct from those of groups. The Iranian situation had "joined" (in a legal sense) all of the issues. What was originally a nongovernment act became a government act. What was first terrorism became surrogate warfare. What had placed the West, and particularly the United States, in yet another position of condemning group terrorism now lent itself to the West taking a strong position against state terror. What had been a fairly typical embassy-hostage-bargaining situation to some developing states now became a situation all too closely linked to the state-sanctioned activities they had vigorously condemned.

The dynamics of state terror in recent times and within diverse states also warrants consideration, because such study can be assessed against classical analyses in the field of terror and political systems. E. V. Walter's anthropological study of terror in primitive African communities stands free of contemporary definitions, ideologies, and political constellations.[5] Yet his concentration on the "process of terror," which includes a focus on the particular tactics of terror, the agents of state terror and their societal position, the reaction of the wider social system participants, and ultimate results of such a process, provide important descriptive and comparative categories for the study of contemporary government.

Similarly, Alexander Dallin and George Breslauer, in studying the use of terror in Communist systems, have placed such government activity in the wider context of political development.[6] They emphasized the importance of questions beyond those of the tactics, ideology, and motivation of the state in this area to a focus on the relationship of terror to elite values and perception, to the progress of the ideals of the political system, and to the dictatorial, authoritarian, or totalitarian tendencies of persons or groups.

Despite the continual growth in various approaches to the group-terrorism phenomenon, some of the premier scholars of the group approach are themselves more cognizant of the state terror dynamic and the need for its incorporation into "legitimate" inquiry into terrorism. Brian Jenkins, of the RAND Corporation and author of dozens of studies of group terror, noted in discussing the problem of the overworked assertion that "one man's terrorist is another man's freedom fighter":

The phrase implies that there can be no objective definition of terrorism, that there are no universal standards of conduct in peace or war. While recognizing the diversity of views on terrorism, this is a notion we must fight.

Most nations have identified, through law, modes of conduct that are criminal, among them homicide, kidnapping, threats to life, the willful destruction of property. Even war has rules outlawing the use of certain tactics.

If we define terrorism by the nature of the act then, not by the identity of the perpetrators or the nature of their cause, an objective definition of terrorism becomes possible. All terrorist acts are crimes. Many would also be violations of the rules of war, if a state of war existed. All involve violence or the threat of violence, often coupled with specific demands. The targets are mainly civilians. The motives are political. The actions generally are designed to achieve the maximum publicity. The perpetrators are usually members of an organized group, and unlike other criminals, they often claim credit for the act. (This is a true hallmark of terrorism.) And, finally, it is intrinsic to a terrorist act that it is usually intended to produce psychological effects far beyond the immediate physical damage. *One man's terrorist is everyone's terrorist.*[7]

In a recent book review essay, Paul Wilkinson drew attention to the heart of the matter:

A particularly thorny problem in all the major contributions to the literature on terrorism has been the relationship between terrorism by factions and state acts of terror. It is interesting to note that most of the recent academic literature has sought to avoid getting bogged down in this aspect: in general all the authors of the works reviewed below accept that it is unreasonable to insist on encompassing analyses of the complex processes and implications of both regimes of terror and factional terrorism as a mode of struggle within the same covers. There is a rich and growing literature on what most authors now term state terror, but the term terrorism is now widely used to denote the systematic use of terror by non-governmental actors.

Nevertheless we should not lose sight of the fundamental truth that one cannot adequately understand terrorist movements without paying some attention to the effects of the use of force and violence by states. Indeed some of the best historical case-studies of the use of factional terrorism as a weapon vividly demonstrate how state violence often helps to provoke and fuel the violence of terrorist movements.[8]

ON DEFINING STATE TERROR

Although it is difficult to do so, it is essential to demarcate among the forms of state-directed political violence, especially oppression, repression, and terrorism. Our definitions of the first two forms follow the work of Richard Bissell and others who defined *oppression* as the situation where "social and economic privileges are denied to whole classes of people regardless of whether they oppose the authorities"[9] and *repression* as "the use of coercion or the threat of coercion against opponents or potential opponents in order to prevent or weaken their capability to oppose the authorities and their policies."[10]

In light of these differentiations, *terrorism* is the purposeful act or threat of violence to create fear and/or compliant behavior in a victim and/or audience of the act or threat. The ordinary language definition provided by the *American Heritage Dictionary* takes us even further as it incorporates the three distinct dimensions of terror this volume seeks to highlight:

"1. The use of terror, violence, and intimidation to achieve an end.

  2. Fear and subjugation produced by this.

  3. A system of government that uses terror to rule."[11]

Figure 1

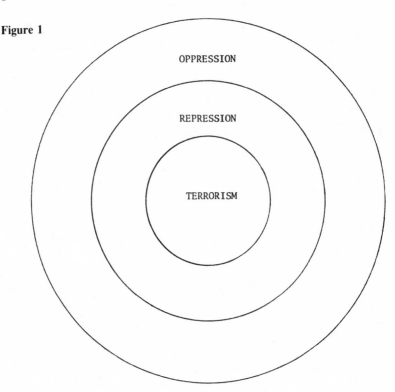

The third definition is one that, as we argued above, seems to have been ignored by most contemporary observers.

The definitional cut points are then twofold. First, we do not consider all coercive acts of the state to be terrorist. The scope of the chapters in this book do not aim to address the important but already widely discussed issue of violations of human rights. We maintain that terrorism is a very special form of state violence and behavior. Oppression, repression, and terrorism may be concurrent and coordinated policies and actions, but they are nonetheless different phenomena and should be distinguished. In the case of state activities, it might be useful to see terrorism as the most delimited of the phenomena, as suggested in Figure 1, where oppression defines the political arena within which repression and terrorism transpire.

Second, as is the case with insurgent terrorism, the audience to the act or the threatened act may be more important than the immediate victim. A government's actions have purposes wider than the simple destruction or harm that the brute force of violence creates. The goal includes carrying a message of intimidation and the creation of fear in an audience whose behavior the perpetrator seeks to alter. The Chinese understood this well in the proverb, "Kill one, frighten ten thousand." Thus the immediate victim of "torture short of death" is clearly an audience target, but since he or she still walks about the body politic, the victim serves as a persuasive advertisement of the power of the state, and the message reaches more people than the government might elect to coerce through direct physical acts.

This is not to say that governments as terrorists do not often undertake to kill victims, for they clearly do. Nor should analysts, particularly those of state terror, presume that terrorists are always open about their activity. Campaigns of extermination, both overt and covert, are all too well known, from the victims of the Nazi Holocaust to *los desaparecidos* ("the disappeared") of the authoritarian regimes of Latin America.

THE SCOPE OF THIS BOOK

In the chapters that follow, scholars have made a concentrated effort to grope with the elusive and complex issue of state terror. The chapters represent philosophical, descriptive, and national examples of the dynamics of governmental violence called "state terror." In the first chapter John McCamant argues forcefully that there are serious problems confronting social scientists in their attempts to conceptualize repression (and, by implication, to distinguish among terrorism, oppression, and repression). McCamant's exploration of these difficulties inform the work of the authors of the remaining essays as they grope with the challenge of systematically examining this phenomena.

Following McCamant's discussion, Michael Stohl explores the manner in which the international political system serves as the arena in which state terror policies unfold. He concludes through classification and detailed examples that the state terror mechanism operates internationally as well as domestically and has even greater impact on international politics than insurgent terrorism. George Lopez, making a strong case for tying the study of state terror to the literature available on insurgent terror, outlines a classificatory scheme for the analysis and comparison of government as terrorist.

In the geographic specific studies that encompass the remainder of the volume, a variety of descriptive and explanatory approaches unfold. John Sloan argues that in considering the dynamics of governmental violence in Latin America, we must separate repressive acts from those called "enforcement terrorism." Furthermore, explanations for governments of the region acting in a state of siege against their citizenry can often be found in the Latin political culture. In another study of Latin America, David Pion-Berlin employs a political economy mode of analysis to explain conditions of repressive rule in Argentina. Specifically, he examines the extent of the linkage between orthodox economic doctrine and repression.

That outside nations combine with internal trends and political actors to provide the climate, if not the stimulation, to systems of repression and/or state terror has become a popular assumption. In his study of the link between militarism and repression, Jim Zwick analyzes a variety of trends and questions related to this for the recent history of the Philippines. In their study of South Africa, Robert Denemark and Howard Lehman explore two related issues about the character of state terror and rule under an apartheid system. First, they detail the dimensions of state terror and its costs. Second, they review the possibility of South Africa being able to maintain its repressive systems against the background of its needs in the international economic order.

In the final case study, Frederick Homer provides a stimulating analysis of the political and cultural uniqueness of the United States environment. Homer discusses both the subtleties and implications of the containment system that operates internally in the United States. The final chapter of the book addresses the substantive and methodological issues that scholars interested in the study of state terror in the future must explore.

NOTES

1. See Edward Mickolus, *The Literature of Terrorism* (Westport, Connecticut: Greenwood Press, 1980), pp. 241-247, for an indication of how inadequate previous work on the topic has been in both scope and depth of coverage.

2. MacBride's comments are from a speech at the 12th International Council Meeting of Amnesty International, 1979. They are cited in Leo Kuper, *Genocide: Its Political Use in the Twentieth Century* (New Haven, Conn.: Yale University Press, 1981), p. 186.

3. W. T. Mallison, Jr., and S. V. Mallison, "The Concept of Public Purpose Terror," *Howard Law Journal*, 18:1 (1973), p. 18.

4. *The Christian Science Monitor*, 14 September 1972, p. 20.

5. E. V. Walter, *Terror and Resistance* (New York: Oxford University Press, 1969).

6. Alexander Dallin and George Breslauer, *Political Terror in Communist Systems* (Stanford, California: Stanford University Press, 1970).

7. Brian M. Jenkins, *A Strategy for Combatting Terrorism* (Santa Monica, California: RAND Paper Series, p. 6624, May, 1981), pp. 6-7. Emphasis added.

8. Paul Wilkinson, "Can a State Be 'Terrorist'?" *International Affairs*, 57:3 (Summer, 1981), p. 467. Emphasis added.

9. Richard Bissell, Clara Haignere, John McCamant, and Mark Piklo, "Varieties of Political Repression" (Unpublished manuscript, 1978), pp. 9-10.

10. Ibid., p. 6.

11. *The American Heritage Dictionary of the English Language* (Boston: Houghton Mifflin, 1969), p. 1330.

1

Governance without Blood: Social Science's Antiseptic View of Rule; or, The Neglect of Political Repression

John F. McCamant

Every government in the world uses at least some political repression; many use a great deal of repression, for it has proved to be an effective tool to shape the media, interest groups, political parties, and through them the ideas and attitudes of citizens. The human consequences of the application of repression have been amply documented by Amnesty International, which has described how all around the world people are imprisoned for their beliefs—or worse: they are hacked to pieces; shot; given electric shocks; forced to watch their children or spouses tortured, raped; and so on, all for political reasons. Although human rights advocates have awakened those who would listen to the human tragedy of violations of civil and political liberties, social scientists have, by and large, continued to ignore political repression.

One searches in vain through the thousands of articles and books written by political scientists, political sociologists, economists, and anthropologists for references to the awful and bloody deeds of governments and for explanations of how and why these deeds are done. For most writers on social affairs, governments hardly exist; for the rest, government is an antiseptic process where all is clean and fair. The only exception to this generalization is in the writing on totalitarianism, where it is clearly recognized that governments do use terror.[1] However, this writing makes totalitarianism into an aberration, and by implication, it presumes that governmental terror does not exist in other polities.

It may not be surprising that those who study only democracies should overlook political repression, but those who study authoritarian regimes likewise neglect it. The collection of studies included in S. P. Huntington and C. H. Moore's *Authoritarian Politics in Modern Society* looked at single parties, but not at

I thank David H. Bayley, James Caporaso, Alan Gilbert, and David Pion-Berlin for their valuable comments on an earlier draft of this chapter.

repressive apparatus or the acts of repression.[2] Guillermo O'Donnell dealt with all the political repression in Latin America with the euphemism "exclusion," without indicating how exclusion was accomplished.[3] Amos Perlmutter's new book, *Modern Authoritarianism*, makes a start with the statement: "The major purpose of modern authoritarian regimes is to establish the political elite's domination over society by arresting, subverting or destroying autonomous individual, collective, and institutional behavior and thus to enhance the power of the authorities at the expense of autonomy."[4] But it never delivers on the promise. Although the book discusses political police and the military and makes a few references to government terror, it never puts the two together. Instead, repressive organizations are discussed as if they were the same as any other institution of society, and politics of authoritarian regimes were primarily a matter of influence.

How far the antiseptic view of government permeates the U.S. culture was demonstrated by reports on the 1982 elections in El Salvador. Newspaper editorials waxed enthusiastic about the huge turnout of voters and exclaimed what a wonderful example of democracy the elections were. President Ronald Reagan said that we in the United States should be inspired by the Salvadoran example. It had been public knowledge for some time that some 30,000 civilians had been killed for political reasons over the previous two years, mostly by government troops, and that six leaders of the opposition Revolutionary Democratic Front were dragged by government troops from their last meeting in San Salvador in November, 1980, and brutally murdered. Yet the 200 observers brought in for the occasion still reported that the elections were free and fair. The public imagination seemed incapable of putting human rights violations together with political processes.

If generations of social scientists, as well as historians, have ignored political repression, the reason could be because political repression is not of any real significance. The dominant philosophy of social science and epistemology provides no argument for how or why important aspects of society could be overlooked.[5] Following this conventional wisdom, those few of us who have turned to the study of governmental violence and political repression would have to accept that we were studying a minor phenomenon of marginal importance. On the other hand, if we continue to insist that political repression is important, even critical in many cases, we are confronted not only with the task of arguing about its importance but also with the task of showing how the process of studying societies and polities is capable of overlooking important processes and variables. Convinced that political repression is significant on both empirical and value grounds, I argue that the absence of scholarly attention presents us with an anomaly that should make us question the methodologies of the social sciences, the major portrayals of how politics works, and the social relationships between scholars and rulers.

What follows is only a brief and preliminary sketch of an alternative view of how we know social phenomena.[6] The argument will point out the importance of cognitive maps in perception and of iconic models in science and then demonstrate that cognitive maps and iconic models of large-scale social phenomena present epistemological problems not found with physical or biological phenomena. With this alternative view, it is not surprising that the social sciences have overlooked a politically sensitive object. This discussion of philosophy of social science provides a background for the presentation of the major iconic models used in political science to show how, on the basis of their assumptions and emphases, political repression is not salient. The construction of a new iconic model, one that would highlight the importance of political repression, is no easy matter and poses a task beyond the scope of the present chapter, but is is possible to point out some core ideas that might fit in such an iconic model.

PHILOSOPHY OF SOCIAL SCIENCE AND POLITICAL REPRESSION

The conventional philosophy of social science, which stems from logical positivism, points to law-like statements as the core of scientific theory. The logical properties of these statements are no different in the social sciences than in the physical sciences.[7] This philosophy of social science is not concerned with the "psychological properties" of the creative process but only with the nature and validation of the law-like statements. I refer to the law-like statements part of theory as "variable models." This philosophy has provided no methodology or understanding for a major part of what social scientists do—namely, the creation and application of another kind of model for explaining society, for example, class conflict, interest group, and structural-functional models, which I refer to as "iconic models."[8] It is in the methodological problems of iconic models, rather than variable models, that social science differs dramatically from the physical and biological sciences. I argue that iconic models, which provide a holistic understanding of the overall social and political processes, are the source of variables and indicate their relevance. We need to examine iconic models of polities to understand why political repression has not been studied.

Before discussing iconic models, it is necessary to introduce a new model of perception and cognition of physical objects. Ulric Neisser rejected the conventional internal processing model where perception begins with a retinal image that is then processed with material from the memory storage until it appears in consciousness.[9] That view cannot explain how it is that some people notice different things, how units are formed, how successive glances and different senses are integrated, and how perception improves with experience. Instead of the internal processing model, Neisser proposed a dynamic model of continuous perception, which is illustrated in Figure 1.1. *Perception*, instead of being a linear and discrete process, is a continuous process whereby the observer anticipates what will be seen in a schema, directs his/her exploration, samples objects from the world, and with the information gained modifies the schema. Perception involves many cycles and, usually, several senses, not just sight. The immediate

Figure 1.1 The Perceptual Cycle

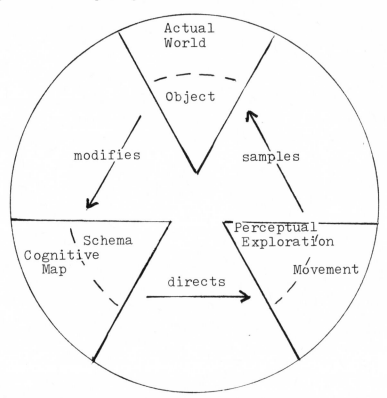

process is embedded in a larger and more extended process that involves a cognitive map that directs movement.

Neisser's model makes the perceiver and his/her anticipations critical in the process of perception and cognition; instead of being a passive recipient of information, he/she is an active pursuer of information. People can perceive so well because, for the most part, they know what to look for and are prepared to see what they see. Nevertheless, flexibility and self-correction are an important part of the process. The process, as Neisser noted, works remarkably well: "In real life, perceptual illusion is as rare as political illusion is common; people usually see the sizes, shapes, colors, positions, and potential manipulability of objects quite accurately."[10]

For our interests the schema and cognitive map are the parts of the process that are of greatest interest. Neisser defined the *schema* "as that portion of the perceptual cycle that is inside the observer, modifiable by experience, and somehow specific to what is being observed."[11] In some respects, the schema resembles a format in a computer programming language that specifies that information must be of a certain sort if it is to be interpreted coherently. It is also like a plan for finding out more about the world. The cognitive map is essentially a larger kind of schema in which the smaller schema are embedded and which directs the larger processes of learning that require movement. In the prolonged periods of traveling and having active but still ''unfulfilled'' expectations of what one will encounter, one is in a state of ''mental imagery.''

The use of Neisser's cognitive map in perception has much in common with Rom Harré's iconic model in the scientific process. Both emphasized the spatial configuration of the world and the identification of units. The thrust of Harré's work in philosophy of science emphasizes the key role played by the structure of things.[12] The iconic model can be interpreted as an articulated and formalized version of the cognitive map.

Harré broke with the tradition of philosophy of science since David Hume that has emphasized logic and deduction, an emphasis that arises from its exclusive attention to sentences. He suggested that pictures, models, and diagrams are also vehicles for thought. ''Certainly to draw a diagram, to make a model, is often to think.''[13] This kind of thinking he found essential to science:

Scientific knowledge consists of knowledge of the structures of which the world consists, and knowledge of how these structures can change, that is how they can behave....Characteristically, structure is presented diagrammatically (by pictures and models), and the possibilities of change sententially as conditional statements. By considering only conditional statements, and forgetting the structural ''picture'' from which they have been abstracted, one gets the characteristic ''event'' view of the world since it is just the successive states of things, but not the things themselves, that conditions describe. But the idea that event-series are the only true objects of knowledge can be maintained only by considering the statement part of knowledge. The picture represents the structures, the things, within whose relative permanence the events are changes, or short, internally organized, sequences of changes.[14]

Although both events and things form parts of knowledge, things take the central position in a theory:

The Copernican Revolution in the philosophy of science...consists simply in coming to see that the picture of the inner structure and constitution of things, and of the structure of the world, is what is essential to a theory, and that the existence of a deductive system among the conditional propositions which describe the possibilities of change for that structure is not essential, *but that its achievement is of great heuristic value.*[15]

Harré has reversed what is essential and what is heuristic from that of the Humean tradition, the tradition that still dominates social science methodology.

The structure of things that cannot be directly observed, such as the very small or the very large, or extended processes such as evolution, becomes known through the imagining of iconic models. The important iconic model for science is the *paramorph*, where a known structure or process is applied by analogy to an unknown structure or process. In the analogy some aspects are similar and some dissimilar, but the unlike does not invalidate the analogy. Rather, the success of the analogy depends on the positive aspects and their ability to highlight what is going on in ways that can be checked directly through new instrumentation or indirectly through the effects of the process. Harré pointed out, "the only possible connection that would allow both intelligibility and novelty is that of analogy."[16]

The structure, mechanisms, and processes of things form the critical part of theory, rather than the variable relationships, because they contain the "powers and liabilities" that make events happen. In philosophy of science, Harré distinguished between *succession theory*, where "a cause is just what usually comes before an event or state" and a *generative theory*, where "the cause is supposed to have the power to generate the effect and is connected to it."[17] The generative theory requires knowledge of the structures and processes that are portrayed in the iconic model. Science uses the generative theory. The goal of science is to understand the structure of a thing so well that the effects of a change in the condition of that thing will follow by "natural necessity."[18]

In recent years, Harré has turned his attention from philosophy of science and epistemology to social psychology, where he has applied methodological and substantive insights from philosophy to understand groups of individuals in face-to-face relations.[19] However, he is doubtful that present methodology can be applied to the study of complex social entities: "it has become clear that no method is available for the empirical study of the properties of very large aggregates of people in interaction. It seems unlikely that in the foreseeable future any such studies could be made. If we cannot have knowledge of global properties, then it follows that we have no direct knowledge of any changes that may occur in these properties."[20] He is not saying that scientific procedures are not appropriate for the study of human behavior, which has been the prevailing critique of social science methodology.[21] Rather, he doubts the reality of large-scale social structures:

But when we create icons in the pursuit of the social sciences, we cannot take it for granted that there is a real structure, some independent world, of which that icon, however imperfectly, is a representation. Indeed, both the existential status of society and the significance of societal concepts is highly problematic and cannot be taken for granted. We speak of the nation, the army, the middle class, as we were speaking of the island, the Thames valley, and so on. Our power to create societal concepts is, as we shall see, a creativity of another kind.[22]

He considers the explanations that we have in history and the social sciences to be nothing more than rationalizations after the fact, or retrospective commentaries, made to suit the purposes of the writers and other interests in society. These rationalizations or myths serve a social function but have no status as knowledge. As he said: "But that larger structure has its being only in the imagination of those who share the theory, a theory, of course, which any member can hardly fail to share."[23] Social scientists, then, are potent myth makers, and people do live their lives within the frameworks created by social scientists, "hardly ever suspecting that the framework is no more than a theory for making the messy, unordered flurry of day-to-day life intelligible, and so meaningful and bearable."[24]

Neisser's comment on the prevalence of political illusion and Harré's doubts about the possibility of knowing complex social processes suggest that we should not be surprised that political repression has been ignored even though it may be important. However, we must not stop with this overly skeptical view, for social scientists have studied large-scale social processes and will continue to do so. Furthermore, we must study them if we are to understand how political repression is used, or not used, with what consequences for a polity. Therefore, we must examine in more detail why it is so difficult to apply iconic models to societies and polities and seek solutions to overcome, at least partially, some of these difficulties.

Our understanding of physical and biological phenomena depends on a clear distinction between a structure and process that remains invariant—which is known as the iconic model—and changes, events, or behavior that vary—which is known as the variable model. Theory, as conceived in this alternative view, is the combination of the two kinds of models. Social and political empirical theory has failed to achieve the success of physical and biological theory, because iconic models of societies and polities cannot represent reality in the same way as do iconic models of physical and biological phenomena, and as a result, it is far more difficult to establish connections between the two kinds of models.[25]

One of the difficulties with social and political iconic models arises because societies and polities are not only invisible, a trait they share with much important physical and biological phenomena, but they are not literally spatial. What this means is that the remarkable ability of the mind to manipulate spatial phenomena nonverbally cannot be used to know societies and polities. The elaborate mental experiments used by Albert Einstein to develop the theory of relativity cannot occur in the same way.[26] People do use their social imagination in a way that seems to parallel imagination of spatial things, but this ability develops later in life after a person has been exposed to social life and presupposes language facility. Furthermore, individuals with both a strong imaginative and language ability are rare, because the talents seem to be competitive in cognitive development.

Large-scale social entities are also more complex and more fluid than anything known in the physical and biological world. The physical study that comes closest to the study of societies is the study of fluid dynamics, as in weather, and amorphous materials, but these things are simple subjects by comparison. The inconstancy of societies begins with the inconstancy of their basic parts, individual human beings—none of whom are like any other and each of which is always learning and adjusting. The possible combinations and permutations of these unlike and changing elements are infinite. It is still possible to make a clear distinction between structures and processes and events and behavior, but the structures and processes are never the same in any two places or at any two times. Compare that with the neat repeatability of copper atoms or mammal organisms.

The language available to apply to these infinitely complex structures and processes is extremely limited and inflexible.[27] The result is that iconic models of societies and polities, which can only be developed through language, cannot possibly capture anything but a small part of complex social reality. Although all models are simplifications and extract only a limited number of features out of the complex whole, the degree of simplification in the social sciences is qualitatively different. The Zen saying, "The instant you speak about a thing, you miss the mark," and the Indian story of the six blind men from Indostan who describe the elephant according to the part each feels seem especially appropriate to the elaboration of iconic models of complex social entities.

Another reason why iconic models of societies and polities rely so heavily on language is that their construction inevitably relies on a great deal of communication. Isolated individuals can neither study nor know societies. One finds out about them through communication with others, and in mass society, a large part of that communication takes place through the mass media. How each person in the communication network presents and discusses the social and political world depends on her/his implicit iconic model or cognitive map. Anthropologists, more than other social scientists, have been aware of the problem of translating from the portrayal of society by a member of a community to the portrayal by a visiting researcher.[28] Similar problems exist within a society when those communicating do not share iconic models. In any case, developing these iconic models is doubly a social process, for it involves not only communication between scholars or scientists but also communication between scholars, reporters of the mass media, and participants. Each communication can be viewed as a negotiation about an iconic model, and the language chosen forms part of the negotiating process.

Iconic models of societies and polities are built out of language through communication, but the meaning of language depends on its role in an implicit or explicit iconic model of how the world works. Language, as well as the prevailing iconic models, is a product of social interaction, but for any individual the language that he/she uses is given by society. Peter Berger and Thomas Luckmann remarked: "I encounter language as a facticity external to myself and it is coercive in its effect on me. Language forces me into its patterns."[29] Heidegger went further and questioned whether one should view persons as having language, or whether it was the other way around, that language is something that "has human beings."[30] Stephen Toulmin put it in a more balanced way and began his work *Human Understanding* by pointing out that "*Each of us thinks his own thoughts: our concepts we share with our fellowmen*,"[31] and "Intellectually, also, Man is born with the power of original thought, and everywhere this originality is constrained within a particular conceptual inheritance;

yet, on closer inspection, these concepts too turn out to be the necessary instruments of effective thought."[32] Toulmin discussed the importance of conceptual change in the development of science. The point here is that conceptual change becomes more difficult when the entire process of thinking must rely so heavily on language itself. Freedom to create can become possible only by becoming conscious of the power of language and learning to use it in a self-conscious way.

The power of language can be illustrated by considering that we talk about the events that one could conceive of as political repression all of the time, but we use language that gives it a different character. The events can be conceived as "maintenance of political order," and the source of disorder may be "bandits," or worse, "terrorists." More antiseptically, those who do not "conform" can be branded as "insane" and dismissed from employment, ostracized, or committed to asylums, and the activity is simply a matter of "controlling deviancy." Or the events may be a matter of "national security," and those that must be dealt with are "subversives," or "guerrillas," and the act of putting them down is "maintenance of national security" and "counterinsurgency." Each of these views reflects an iconic model of how the world works. It is harder to think about language that does not exist, but reflect for a moment what one could call the victims of political repression who were attempting to uphold the inherited freedom and constitutional rights of a country against government violation of these rights and were doing so nonviolently. These people are certainly not bandits or terrorists; they are not insane; they are not subversives or insurgents; they are not even dissidents, because they are attempting to uphold what has existed. Our language has no general term for these people that is not already loaded against their cause, because our society has no iconic model that makes political repression relevant.

The nature of social iconic models leads to some fundamental epistemological problems. Since no single model can begin to capture the full nature of this complex reality, multiple models are needed. Each of the major political iconic models that are discussed in the next section represent some part or aspects of political reality, and it is imposible to consider any of them true or not true. Each is true in some ways. The problem is similar to that of the theory of light, where both a wave model and a particle model are needed to explain different aspects of the same phenomenon. The proliferation of iconic models in the social sciences in recent decades suggests the need for many models. Robert K. Merton in a foreword to a book that discusses a variety of sociological models came to a similar conclusion, without considering the properties of iconic models. He wrote: "For the plain fact is that no single all-embracing and tight-knit theoretical orientation has proved adequate to identify and the deal with the wide range of problems requiring investigation in detail. It seems to be the case rather, that diverse theoretical orientations are variously effective for dealing with diverse kinds, and aspects, of sociological and social problems."[33] The recognition of the need for multiple models must *not* be interpreted as suggesting that all models are equally valid or invalid, but rather that each must be evaluated in terms of its adequacy to deal with certain problems and not in terms of its adequacy as a complete and total picture of society.

Most of the existing iconic models of societies and polities demonstrate considerable ambiguity and fuzziness, since each tries to cover more of social reality than it is possible to cover with one model. If we gave up the pursuit of a single view, we could create models that were more clearly articulated, and this greater precision would strengthen the implications for variable relationships that would be capable of rigorous testing. In the present state of social science, the implications of iconic models for variable models is at best extremely loose and for the most part nonexistent.

Iconic models can be evaluated without recourse to variable models, and we engage in these evaluations continuously. Geoffrey Vickers, who has analyzed the two ways of thinking in a way complementary to that of Harré, has pointed out that the aesthetic, intuitive, and creative processes that recognize form use standards different from those found in logical relationships of variable models: "This recognition of form is an exercise of judgement made by reference to criteria which are not fully describable because of the subtle combinations of relationships in which they reside and equally because of their dependence on *context*."[34] He referred to these criteria as "tacit norms." However, the intuition is less reliable for models of complex social processes than for the physical forms that Vickers was referring to, because our nonverbal ability to evaluate spatial things is not applicable, and social processes interfere so much more strongly.

Because iconic models provide a vision of the whole, they play a double role: They provide a vehicle for understanding that serves as a guide for finding one's way around the world, and at the same time they condition one's emotional response to and evaluation of the world represented in the model. Variable models, on the other hand, contain much more of a guide to action and hardly any of the emotional loading and value implication—except insofar as they serve as tests for iconic models. As Copernicus and Darwin could attest, physical and biological, as well as social and political, models can arouse intense reactions. The difference between physical and biological models and social and political models lies less in the emotional and value content than in the epistemological problems discussed above. The difficulty in relating evidence to iconic models in the social field makes the process of knowing much more susceptible to social influence from forces outside the science community. Furthermore, since the process of knowing is more intertwined with the structures of power, the social scientists have greater difficulty in detaching themselves from the distribution of power.

Iconic models, built by intellectuals, about societies and polities provide the only view or representation that exists of the whole society or polity. Others living in a society may have some unarticulated ideas and feelings about the society in which they live that are not represented in any iconic model, but at the same time, articulated iconic models greatly shape their ideas and feelings. Each of these models will tend to either legitimate or delegitimate the status quo. It is impossible to be neutral. As Sheldon Wolin pointed out, those intellectuals who retreat into methodology are simply accepting the conventional iconic models of society and reinforcing the status quo.[35]

Those with economic, social, and political power recognize the political significance of these ideas, and much of the political struggle in societies is about the appropriate interpretation of that society—that is, about which iconic model should prevail. Every press release, public speech, and media interview, usually prepared with the help of public relations experts, provides an interpretation that fits into and reinforces the iconic model that puts the originating person or institution in the best light. Dictators understand the importance of this process and censor all media, allowing only news that comes directly from the government itself, and often eliminate social science from universities. Powerful people in democratic societies resort less to coercive measures and more to manipulation. Funds are provided for certain kinds of research but not for others. Tenure and promotions are given more readily to those who do not disturb the rich who contribute to the university. Not too much overt manipulation is required where the distribution of power is highly unequal, because most people are trained to be obsequious and to gratify the powerful.

This philosophical sketch suggests that it might be easy for social scientists to overlook important phenomena. A concept like political repression, which is potentially subversive to existing power relations, would certainly be discouraged by powerful people and institutions. The powerful can have greater influence in the development of iconic models of societies and polities than in models of physical and biological phenomena, because it is so much more difficult to apply evidence to the testing of these models and because they are involved in the whole process of dissemination of information from which social scientists, as well as everyone else, find out about societies and polities.

The sociology of knowledge suggested in this sketch poses a real dilemma to socially sensitive social scientists. The viscious circle of language and iconic models, both of which are continuously influenced by social processes controlled by the powerful, makes it extremely difficult for any social scientist to break loose to understand the social world in a new way. There are no easy or complete solutions, because only by living in society and communicating in its language can we get to know society. The first step to greater freedom is to become self-conscious of the language, the iconic models, and the social processes that influence thinking.[36] The second step is to form and work within smaller communities of people who share a desire to find and articulate an alternative view. The extraordinary proliferation of human rights and peace groups has provided alternative sources of information, concerns, and views of the world, and communicating with people in these groups can make it possible to develop an understanding of the problems we are concerned with.

ICONIC MODELS WITH NO ROOM FOR POLITICAL
REPRESSION

None of the iconic models that have dominated the thinking of social scientists has a place in their scheme of things for political repression. Each leads us away from political repression instead of toward it; each makes political repression irrelevant. An iconic model is a statement that describes a "picture" of the important structures in the world and their powers to act or respond. What is left out or deemphasized is as important as what is put in, and of necessity, much more must be left out than put in. That which would be most useful for understanding political repression has been left out of all of the major iconic models in the social sciences.

Political repression refers to those coercive activities carried out by rulers against opposition, real or imagined, for the purpose of weakening its ability to oppose or take control. The meaning of political repression depends on the elaboration of an iconic model that would demonstrate how it fits into a wider scheme of things. Different models would give somewhat different meanings to political repression. As each of us differs in our implicit and explicit views of how the world works, we also differ in what we think is essential to the meaning of political repression.

Iconic models in the social sciences are numerous and varied. The disciplines have placed a premium on originality, with few writers building on others and many creating new schemes. Often iconic models remain implicit, with writers concentrating on events and variables. Thus although everyone who thinks about social affairs has at least an implicit iconic model, that model is often not acknowledged. Nevertheless, those who have made their schemes explicit in more formalized statements probably have expressed the ideas and images current in the culture. Within the United States, most people think in terms of some kind of interest-group model. In the 1950s, this model was nearly a consensus view, and since then many of the formalized models, for example, structural-functionalism and bureaucratic politics, have been outgrowths of the interest-group approach. The major rival to the interest-group view has been the class-struggle view, and since the mid-1960s it has been expressed in a variety of forms and adapted to the international world in the writing on *dependencia*. At a more popular level, some variant of elite theory has been common. The geopolitical iconic model articulates one of the oldest views of international relations.

Interest-Group Models

G. David Garson has described how interest-group theories developed from the pluralist critique of sovereignty, with its emphasis on formal institutions and jurisprudence.[37] He pointed out that group theory is hardly a theory at all, "Rather it is an eclectic set of images of a decentralized but consensual democratic polity.''[38] Nevertheless, Harry Eckstein has attempted a formal statement of the essential ideas:

Boldly stated, the group theory of politics may therefore be summarized as follows: Politics is the process by which social values are authoritatively allocated; this is done by decisions; the decisions are produced by activities; each activity is not something separate from every other, but masses of activity have common tendencies in regard to decisions; these masses of activity are groups: so the struggle between groups (or interests) determines what decisions are taken.[39]

As Eckstein recognized, groups in this elaboration are not collections of individuals but congeries of activities, and as entities they become difficult to pin down in the real world. Eckstein pointed out that for the scheme to take on any definite meaning, one must misinterpret it to suggest that decisions resulted from the activities of real pressure groups. Although the writers took pains not to say this, they did give primary attention to organized pressure groups.

The actors of importance in these models, then, are organized pressure groups who are motivated by the pursuit of their interests. These groups emerge from the normal activities of buying and selling within a cooperative and competing society. Although interest could refer to any goal, the implication is that selfish material gain is of most importance. However, the writers insisted that these competing interests operated within a broader consensus that limits their actions, which is represented by "potential groups" or "latent groups."

None of the principal actors laid down in the group model has any coercive means at its disposal and could not, then, repress anyone else, and they all face each other more or less equally in a symmetrical relationship. Nor does this view even see any deep conflicts developing, given the underlying consensus. Government hardly comes into the picture at all, being left behind with the concept of sovereignty. However, authoritative decisions are made, or emerge out of the process, but government has little individual force and is primarily a balance of other interests.

System Theory; Structural-Functionalism

David Easton and Gabriel Almond applied systems theory and structural-functionalism to political science, but their work should also be seen as an extension of interest-group theory.[40] The static notion of balance in interest-group theory was replaced with the system notion of equilibrium. Both still gave precedence to the expression of interests, called "demands" by Easton and "interest articulation" by Almond. Thus the moving force for both was the desires of an unarmed populace, and nothing they wrote suggested the existence of any force with strong coercive powers.

Easton's book-length depiction of the political system devoted exactly three paragraphs to the topic of coercion—but nothing to political repression. He considered coercion to be effective in achieving compliance to the law only in the short run as an expedient to gain time, during which support could be increased and make coercion unnecessary. Even so, Easton seemed to think that he was making an innovation as reflected in his opening statement on coercion: "Although it may not be customary to do so, we may view coercion as another possible kind of response to a decline in support."[41] It apparently did not occur to him that the same coercive power could be used to shape the pattern of demands in the system.

Gabriel Almond considered coercion at only one place—in the definition of the political system: "We agree with Max Weber that legitimate force is the thread that runs through the action of the political system, giving it its special quality and importance, and its coherence as a system."[42] In the phrase, "legitimate force," all of the emphasis was on *legitimate*; all political systems seemed to be completely legitimate. In his list of functions, Almond considered "system maintenance and adaptation," but he only mentioned communication and socialization as processes to achieve this function. Not even a little arm twisting now and then would be necessary.

Political scientists Easton and Almond were both influenced by the writings of Talcott Parsons, the father and leading spokesman for structural-functionalism in sociology. Parsons was enormously uninterested in political processes, but he did acknowledge that in the process of differentiation, specialized governmental structures would come into being. For Parsons, society was a normative order where consensus reigned. Nevertheless, he did concede, "the maintenance of a normative order cannot be dissociated from control over activities within territorial areas," and "The *ultimate preventative* of disruptive action is the use of physical force. The use of force takes many forms, notably defense vis-à-vis outside territory and deprivation of liberty (imprisonment) within."[43] We also owe to Parsons one of the most curious and obscure treatments of political power ever written, where political power, instead of belonging to an institution or some segment of society, was considered a free-floating force of society, akin to money, and subject to inflation and deflation.[44] In Parsons's scheme of things, there are no rulers, only people filling their roles. Nor could there be any opposition; misfits would be deviants. The analogy behind Parsons's treatment is the organic body: could one conceive of certain cells of the body being repressed? Only if they were cancerous.

One could dismiss the emphasis in interest-group theory and structural-functionalism on consensus, legitimacy, and equilibrium as being due to an inherent American parochialism. The writers of these ideas were not acquainted with less smoothly functioning political systems. But was the U.S. polity really like this? All of these writers lived through and wrote during the virulent anti-Communist period of the late 1940s and early 1950s, during the time when Communist professors were being purged from universities. The authors denied facts that were all around them as well as historical conflicts surrounding the development of political parties and labor groups. They overlooked all of the history brought out in Robert J. Goldstein's excellent *Political Repression in Modern America.* Goldstein documented the following thesis:

The holders of *certain* ideas in the United States have been systematically and gravely discriminated against and subjected to extraordinary treatment by governmental authorities, such as physical assaults, denials of freedom of speech and assembly, political deportations and firings, dubious and discriminatory arrests, intense police surveillance, and illegal burglaries, wiretaps and interception of mail. Such political repression has had a number of important effects upon American life. This book demonstrates that political repression has contributed significantly to the following:

—The failure of American labor to achieve major power until the 1930's.

—The destruction of radical labor movements.

—The self-censorship which Americans have imposed upon their own exercise of basic political freedoms.[45]

He went on to point out, "American social scientists have not seriously considered political repression as one important factor which helps explain the narrowness of the American political spectrum, but there is certainly no reason to exclude the possibility that it has helped to shape this narrow 'range of vision.' "[46] In particular, he accused those who explain the absence of radical labor movements to consensus or the availability of free land as neglecting a long history of intense labor conflict and repression.

One is forced to the conclusion that the consensus writers of the 1950s were exhibiting this very "narrow range of vision" themselves, which had resulted from the repression of radical labor movements and political parties and especially from the self-censorship that prevailed in intellectual circles during the harassment and firings of radicals in the 1950s. Even a parochial attention to the United States should have shown them that political repression existed, and if they had bothered to look at most of the rest of the world with "open eyes," they could have "seen" even greater amounts of political repression.

Marxism

Unlike the consensus theories that developed in the United States, in large part as a countertheory to Marxism, the Marxists have acknowledged the existence of political repression and have written about it. Nevertheless, Marxism is primarily a theory about *oppression*—the keeping of workers in a state of misery—not a theory about *repression*—keeping political opposition in a state of powerlessness. Nearly all of Marx's writing was devoted to elaborating the mechanisms whereby the owners of the means of production are able to keep the proletariat in an oppressed state. Political repression was discussed in relation to the "theory" of the state, but it was not developed or analyzed to any great extent. The first point to make, then, is that Marx's views are incomplete, and in general, writers who have followed in the Marxist tradition have shown little

Figure 1.2 Marx's Theory of the State and Repression

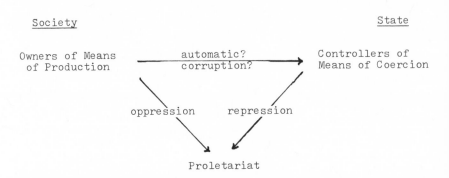

concern for political repression. Those who have addressed the issue, such as Ralph Miliband and Nicos Poulantzas, have not been able to overcome certain basic conceptual difficulties that prevent Marx's scheme from treating political repression adequately.[47]

The major theme of Marx's view of the state was summarized in a brief remark in the Communist Manifesto: "the bourgeoisie has at last, since the establishment of Modern Industry and of the world-market, conquered for itself, in the modern representative State, exclusive political sway. The executive of the modern State is but a committee for managing the common affairs of the whole bourgeoisie."[48] Thus the state is allocated to the super-structure and becomes entirely the product of class relationships. Since the bourgeoisie is the dominant class, the state is simply the instrument of the "whole bourgeoisie." However, as noted by Alan Gilbert, there is a minor theme in Marx's writing that comes from the *Eighteenth Brumaire of Louis Bonaparte* is which the parasite state is something of an independent force and crushes individual bourgeois and "plundered the bourgeoisie's collective wealth through increased taxes."[49] Marx wrote, "the individual bourgeois can continue to exploit the other classes... only on condition that their class be condemned along with the other classes to like political nullity." Gilbert raised the question, "Mightn't one view this Napoleonic apparatus as a new, wholly independent social force that contradicted Marx's theory and required either a fundamental change in the meaning of the term state or some new designation?"[50] Gilbert answered no. I would suggest that Marx contained a valuable insight here that needed to have been followed up if he were to have an adequate explanation for political repression.

To get at the conceptual difficulties, we can lay out the major actors and their interactions in Marx's model in Figure 1.2. The major theme in Marx's writing postulates that there was no need to make a clear distinction between those who own the means of production and those who control the means of coercion; the actors are one and the same. Yet the *Eighteenth Brumaire of Louis Bonaparte* demonstrated that the relationship is not automatic. If the relationship is not automatic, the way in which the bourgeoisie are able to obtain the appropriate actions from those who control the means of coercion needs to be specified. Aside from Marx's brief suggestion of corruption, he did not deal with the question.

Marx and Engels were contradictory in their treatment of the state. The state somehow comes out as being above society but below the dominant class—a spatial impossibility. In the *Origin of the Family, Private Property, and the State*, Engels wrote:

The state is therefore by no means a power imposed on society from the outside; just as little is it "the reality of the moral idea," "the image and reality of reason," as Hegel asserted. Rather it is a product of society at a certain stage of development; it is the admission that this society has become entangled in an insoluble contradiction with itself, that it is cleft into irreconcilable antagonisms which it is powerless to dispel. But in order that these antagonisms, classes with conflicting economic interests, may not consume themselves and society in a sterile struggle, a power apparently standing above society becomes necessary, whose purpose is to moderate the conflict and keep it within the bounds of "order"; and this power arising out of society, *but placing itself above it*, and increasingly separating itself from it, is the state.[51]

In his introduction to Marx's *The Civil War in France*, Engels wrote in a similar vein: "What had been the characteristic attribute of the former (before the setting up of the Commune) state? Society had created its own organs to look after its common interests, originally through simple division of labour. But these organs, at whose head was the state power, had in the course of time, in pursuance of their own special interests, transformed themselves from the servants of society into *the masters of society*."[52] Yet on the very next page he wrote: "In reality, however, the state is nothing but a machine for the oppression of one class by another, and indeed in the democratic republic no less than in the monarchy."[53] Neither Marx nor Engels wanted to see this as a contradiction and never worked it out.

Marx and Engels also predicted wrongly what would happen after the means of production were taken out of private hands. Their prediction was clear and consistent with the major theme of the state being no more than the executive committee of the whole bourgeoisie. Engels wrote in *Anti-Duhring*:

As soon as there is no longer any class of society to be held in subjection; as soon as, along with class domination and the struggle for individual existence based on the former anarchy of production, the collisions and excesses arising from these have also been abolished, there is nothing more to be repressed, and a special repressive force, a state, is no longer necessary. The first act in which the state really comes forward as the representative of society as a whole—the seizure of the means of production in the name of society—is at the same time its last independent act as a state. The interference of a state power in social relations becomes superfluous in one sphere after another, and then becomes dormant of itself. Government over persons is replaced by the administration

of things and the direction of the processes of production. The state is not "abolished,"
it withers away.[54]

Instead of the state withering away after the means of production were nation-
alized in the Soviet Union and other Communist countries, however, the state
increased in unprecedented proportions and carried out political repression of a
magnitude as great as ever before in history. A falsified prediction of such
importance should have led Marxist writers to modify the theory, but they have
not. However, Marx's insight in the *Eighteenth Brumaire of Louis Bonaparte*
and the general notion that the state is master of society suggests the direction
of the way the theory should be modified to allow for consideration of political
repression. The state must be seen as potentially autonomous and the means of
coercion should be seen to be equal in importance, if not superior, to the means
of production.

We have no trouble seeing the consensus theorists as responding to a sociological situation in which those who legitimize society are amply rewarded in
prestige and promotion, but the sociology of knowledge does not deal as obviously with the counterestablishment views of the Marxists. Yet Lenin was
engaged in a polemic with a large number of other Marxist and non-Marxist
writers and chose to emphasize the interpretation of Marx that best suited his
purposes—namely, the irreconcilability of class conflict and the total domination
of the bourgeoisie, which to correct required a violent revolution and the dictatorship of the proletariat. Lenin's interpretation was institutionalized into that
of the Communist International. Furthermore, Lenin imposed a rigid authoritarian
structure on the Communist party that prevented dissident views from being
discussed, an authoritarian pattern congenial to Russian culture and appropriate
for a secret organization engaged in armed struggle. After the Bolsheviks took
power and created the Soviet Union, Marxists everywhere were generally predisposed to overlook political repression in that country. Thus both before taking
power and afterwards, Marxist-Leninist writers were under some social pressure
to pay little attention to political repression.

Dependencia

Latin American intellectuals developed the various *dependencia* models to
explain the way in which their economies were tied into the world economy.
The view has both Marxist and non-Marxist intellectual roots. What unites the
various writing of this school is the idea that the poorer or peripheral countries
of the world must not be seen as autonomous, self-contained entities but as
entities that depend in nearly all that they do on the industrial or core countries
of the world. An enormous amount of misunderstanding in the United States
has come about by treating this body of literature as specifying variable models
in some direct way. Social scientists, who gave no thought to testing interest-
group theory, structural-functionalism, or the neo-classical economic model,

rushed out to test the *dependencia* model. Fernando Henrique Cardoso, among others, responded that that was not what they meant.[55] What is primary in this body of writing is a picture of the world.

In the *dependencia* scheme of things, the world can be divided into core countries, peripheral countries, and a few others that are neither here nor there but are semiperipheral. The peripheral countries are dependent on the core countries. The dependency does not arise from the same direct control found in colonialism but from a variety of indirect mechanisms that are related to the position of the peripheral nations in the world economy. Cardoso stressed the way the economic specializations allotted to the periphery shaped its social structure, producing dominant classes that had more interests in common with the interests of the industrial bourgeoisie of the center than with their fellow nationals.[56] The peripheral capitalists are "comprador bourgeoisie," who socially speaking are really part of the core.

However, there are so many varieties of *dependencia* thought that one must be careful not to ascribe even this view to all of the writers. Where there is agreement is that the poverty of the periphery has come about in large part because of its position in the world economy. Underdevelopment is not a primordial state that results from isolation from the world economy but the opposite; it is produced by the development of the center or industrial countries. In Andre Gunder Frank's provocative phrase, we have "the development of underdevelopment."[57]

As will be pointed out in the next section, this *dependencia* model has some important insights for the consideration of political repression, but as it stands, it suffers from the same inadequacies of the principal theme of Marx. It views the economy and not the polity as being important. Market and productive relations are more important than coercive relations. Now and then, as in Ronald H. Chilcote and Joel C. Edelstein's summary of *dependencia*, some coercive mechanisms, such as subversive activities of the core governments, are mentioned, but they are not worked into the theory.[58] Despite the fact that many of the writers came from countries that were ruled by military dictatorships, none of them has discussed the way the military fits into a *dependencia* picture.

Elite Theory

Elite theory retains the asymmetrical relations of Marxism and gives a more central position to political power. Curiously, however, it makes less mention of political repression than does Marxism. Whether in the variety of elite theory that served as intellectual precursors to fascism found in the writings of Gaetano Mosca, Vilfredo Pareto, and Robert Michels or in the variety of the later-day critiques of pluralism in the United States found in the writings of C. Wright Mills and G. William Domhoff, the relationship between the elite and the masses is not seen to contain an important element of coercion.[59] Pareto was the only one to suggest that the elite must be ready to use force from time to time, and the elite's downfall might arise from a failure of will. The inherent inadequacy of elite theory to consider political repression arises from what one might call the "best and the brightest" syndrome. Rulers rule because they have superior ability, although this prejudice was much stronger in classical elite theory than in the contemporary view. In some ways, elite theory is closer to structural-functionalism than to Marxist thought. The usually unstated other side to the superiority of the elite is the inferiority of the masses, who are by inference the "worst and the dumbest." None of the writers of elite theory find it necessary or useful to discuss the characteristics of the masses at any length, and this is as true of Mills and Domhoff as it is of the older theorists.

With this notion of the inferiority of the masses, it is not even necessary to specify how it is that the elite maintain control. However, in his most recent book G. William Domhoff took up the challenge of his pluralist critics, who had accused him of not specifying the mechanisms of control. *The Powers That Be* was devoted to specifying the processes of ruling class domination in America.[60] He showed how it is done in the special-interest process, the policy-formation process, the candidate-selection process, and the ideology process, but he never mentioned a coercive process. He did not consider, any more than the pluralists did, the repressive actions that have been so prominent in certain periods of U.S. history.

Elite theory became a very popular view in the United States in the late 1960s and early 1970s. Whatever was wrong with the country was blamed on the establishment. Both the Far Right with their conspiracy theories and most radicals accepted that an elite few dominated the institutions of the United States, but few considered how demeaning this view was to the majority of people in the country, whether workers or others. I would suggest that the "masses" are neither so inferior nor so compliant.

Geopolitics

While the *dependencia* writers ignored the military, geopolitical writers have exalted it. Their iconic model pictures the world as states struggling with each other to control territory and exert their will through military power. It is hard to characterize this model as antiseptic like the others, but curiously, these struggles come out more glorious than bloody. The term *geopolitical* applies most directly to the tradition that stems from Sir Halford Mackinder and Rudolf Kjellan and proceeds to the contemporary Latin American military writers, who make the occupation of certain territory or ocean the key to national power.[61] However, the essential aspects of their iconic model is shared by the "realists" school of international politics and national security studies.[62] Both take their lead from Karl von Clausewitz's classic work *On War*.[63] The difference between the moderates and extremists in international politics lies less in differences in the model and more in consideration of the partiality of the model. The moderates see other aspects of international reality and are less inclined to reify the state.

Anatol Rapoport summarized the key elements of Clausewitz's classic study *On War*:

"1. There exists a community of *sovereign states*—sovereign meaning that their heads or ruling bodies are responsible to no one for their actions.

2. Each state has *interests*. There is no need to inquire into the nature or genesis of such interests; they are self-evident: Each state strives to expand its domain and its influence. . . .

3. The interests of every state are normally in conflict with those of every other state. . . .

4. Politics (formulation of policy, statesmanship, diplomacy) is the art of bringing about situations that facilitate the pursuit of a state's interests.

5. War is a *normal* phase in the relations between states. . . .

6. At times the interests of two or more states may coincide, particularly when it is to the advantage of each to curtail or to resist the power of a third state or a combination of states. . . .

7. The power of a state is embodied in its armed might, that is, in military technology, in the strategic and tactical skills of its commanders, and in the morale of its troops. . . ."[64]

The 150 years since Clausewitz wrote have brought two modifications to this model, changes that have not altered its basic form. The first is that wars have become total and thus require a mobilization of the whole society and economy to prepare for the struggle, but Clausewitz had already fully appreciated the importance of nationalism and the involvement of the whole population in a People's War. The other change had to do with the nature of nationalism, as Rapoport wrote: "In the aftermath of World War I it looked for a while as if nationalism, the prime mover of wars as depicted (and glorified) by Clausewitz, collapsed. It made a comeback as fascism, but now with strong admixtures of eschatological ideology, something not found in the classical Clausewitzian nationalism."[65] Rapoport noted strong strains of eschatological ideology in both the Soviet Union and the United States. Both sides seem to imagine, at times, that the defeat of the other would take care of all of the world's problems. The stability of the model is remarkable considering the changes in the world: enormous technological change, including the development of nuclear weapons; the expansion of democratization and the decline of colonialism; the development of international and transnational institutions; and an increase in interdependence (and dependence) through the integration of the world economic system.

The geopolitical iconic model found few proponents in the United States until World War II. Then Hans Morgenthau, George Kennan, Reinhold Niebuhr, and others shaped a new discipline of "realist" international politics.[66] In later years, the discipline diversified into behavioral studies, interest in transnational institutions, and concern with interdependence and deemphasized this iconic model. However, the model became appropriated by the new field of national security studies. Within this new field, power became conceived almost exclusively in military terms with emphasis on the physical and quantifiable aspects of military power.[67] The morale of the population and the strength of the economy, aspects of national power emphasized by the earlier "realists," became downplayed.

Meanwhile, Latin American military writers revived the more extremist geopolitical view of European writers of the early twentieth century, ideas that were compatible with the counterinsurgency doctrines being promoted by U.S. military assistance.[68] Alfred Stepan called the resulting doctrine the "new professionalism" to distinguish it from the "old professionalism," which emphasized the control of the military by civilian authority.[69] The "new professionalism" expanded its view of national security to include all aspects of social and economic affairs, and if these affairs were not well managed, the military had an obligation to intervene. These writers placed their domestic struggles in the context of the larger struggle between the United States and the Soviet Union. Since the United States had contained the direct expansion of the Soviet Union, the Soviet Union, they concluded, has turned to subversion and the fomenting of revolutionary war in the Third World.[70]

Both the U.S. and Latin American versions of the geopolitical iconic model view the state as an organic unit, "the fusion of millions of wills into a single will pitted against other wills."[71] The U.S. version emphasizes external enemies, but the Latin American version concentrates on internal enemies who would weaken the national security system. These subversives and traitors must be dealt with in a manner appropriate to war. The geopolitical iconic model, thus, is the exception that does make political repression relevant; it makes repression natural and necessary for the preservation of national security. The geopolitical model rationalizes and legitimizes political repression, but the model never refers to these acts as "political repression."

The social processes that intervene in the development of ideas about iconic models of societies and polities is nowhere so obvious as in the development and propagation of the geopolitical iconic model. Clausewitz developed the model to aid the Prussians in defeating Napoleon and expanding their power in Europe. Ever since, it has been promoted by those who wished to further the interests of the military. When Cold War ideologues became concerned that the United States was moving away from this geopolitical image in the mid-1970s, they formed the Committee on the Present Danger to spread the doctrine and exert political pressure. Research institutes, such as the Hoover Institute and the Heritage Foundation, devoted their resources to elaborating and applying the model. The American Security Council, a private organization made up primarily of arms manufacturers, sponsored the making and distribution of films that gave visual representation to the model. It seems, although we know much less about the processes, that similar forces in the Soviet Union are promoting the model there; the two sides encourage each other, and together they make the model more plausible.

NOTES FOR THE CONSTRUCTION OF AN ICONIC MODEL FOR POLITICAL REPRESSION

The principal point of this chapter is that political repression has not been considered because the iconic models of society and polity that have prevailed in both academia and outside it did not focus on structures in a way that would make political repression relevant. It follows, then, that the major task for the study of political repression is to develop an iconic model that will make political repression as prominent in our theory as it is in the world. For the study of political repression, we must lay aside our interest-group models, structural functionalism, class struggle models, *dependencia*, elite "theory," and geopolitics in their present forms and begin afresh. However, the pieces for a new model will, for the most part, come from the collection of ideas that have been elaborated in earlier models. "Our concepts we share with our fellowmen."[72]

In working on a new iconic model, it will be most useful to keep in mind the patterns of political repression in the world and the association between political repression and other variables. Harré pointed out that the achievement of a deductive system among conditional statements that describe the possibilities of change for the structures is of great heuristic value. Whether we do statistical studies, as I did in finding that 85 percent of the political repression in the 1960s in Latin America was "explained" inversely by variation in societal institutionalization and educational expenditure, or proceed by other methods, we must always keep in mind the overall patterns of variation in political repression that exist and have existed in the world.[73] It will not do to claim that political repression has always existed everywhere and let it go at that. The differences between places and times have been large and are our best clue for identifying the interactions and structures that produce political repression.

Knowing the patterns of variation will keep us from going in false directions. For instance, putting the blame or credit on communism or capitalism will not serve as an explanation since both economic systems have had equally severe cases of political repression. Stalin's Soviet Union pairs with Hitler's Germany; Pinochet's Chile pairs with Castro's Cuba.[74] The massacre in Indonesia following the military's overthrow of Sukarno compares with the killings in China following the ouster of Chiang Kai-Shek.[75] The 1980s have brought wide-scale governmental terrorism in both Central America and Afghanistan. True, some capitalist systems have enjoyed more freedom than any Communist system, but given the deplorable conditions in other capitalist countries, it seems best to look to some other structures of society for an explanation.

Likewise, the pattern of variation in the world makes it difficult to sustain the thesis that the structures described as modernization can help us explain political repression. Hitler's Germany should have been enough to explode that myth in any case. The most modernized country in Latin America, Argentina, has over the years been the most repressive. In addition, Latin America as a whole, after a decade of rapid economic growth—almost as much as was called for by the Alliance for Progress—collapsed into its deepest political repression in all of its history in the 1970s.

The patterns of association and variation serve a better critical function than creative function. We still must imagine an iconic model that makes sense and fits the data. I do not have an iconic model to offer at this time, but I do have some suggestions in rough outline of some of the things that should be included.

1. Understanding of political repression requires acknowledging the central position of government in society—that the state is master of society—and the essential part that coercion plays in ruling. None of the models surveyed above recognized the awesome power of government, a power that comes from its near monopoly over the coercive forces. Those models were focused too much on society. The focus must be on what is truly political, not social, on the struggle for power and on the processes of ruling.

Despite the existence of, at least, some political repression in all states, repression is not, overall, applied often or in large amounts. We must consider, however, that political repression has both a visible and invisible aspect, a manifest expression and a latent one, and the invisible and latent is by far the more important. We can "see," if we have the schema and go looking, the persons jailed for political reasons, the press censored, or the labor union funds confiscated, but the important impact is on the others, those who think it could happen to them if they should get out of line. Fear is what gives political repression its significance.[76]

Fear, induced by relatively mild and rare incidents of visible repression in the United States, has had a pervasive and profound influence on most U.S. citizens. For the most part this fear is so internalized and psychologically repressed that the person is unaware of it. Countries that have sustained greater repression, and especially those such as Kampuchea, Guatemala, and Argentina that have suffered systematic government terror, must know fear that we in the United States have difficulty imagining.

Thus we must not be fooled into thinking that coercion against opposition is unimportant just because it is seldom used. Even a little has wide effects.

2. Conflict pervades all societies. The level of consensus has been greatly exaggerated in models generated by U.S. academics.[77] Instead of taking some idealized version of post-World War II United States as a prototype, it might be better to take a place like Colombia, where *la violencia* has continued for 140 years. When people are not constrained and forced to act out their antagonisms through institutions, these conflicts easily lead to widespread killing. The differences between people and groups are deep and passionate.

Moreover, the rulers are not above this conflict but are party to it. Whatever the sources of conflict, the most important *locus* of conflict is the rulers against those who might oppose. Those who organize the government have at their disposal most of the guns in society and all of the prisons plus huge bureaucracies to keep information on citizens. How much easier it must seem to these rulers to use guns to enforce their particular views of the world and to enhance their interests than to argue and negotiate. Political repression should not seem exceptional. What is puzzling is why it is used so little in some places. It follows, too, that one should never take political freedom for granted.

Marx demonstrated the irreconcilable differences that exist between workers and owners of capital. Political repression has often been used to keep workers in line and occasionally even to restrain capitalists. However, Marx neglected to consider many other sources of conflict. Ethnic conflict tends to be bloodier than class conflict when it erupts. Questions of religion and language are more difficult to negotiate and compromise than material questions because of their all-or-nothing character. The managers of state-owned enterprises seem as jealous of their prerogatives as are owner-managers. Certainly, in both, status and power provoke passion. Likewise, belief systems can stimulate extraordinary hatreds.

If we combine the importance of coercion through official means and the pervasiveness and intensity of conflict, we can begin to see how bitter the struggle for power may be, for obtaining control of the means of coercion will spell victory for that side of the conflict.

3. I have used "government" and "rulers" interchangeably to mean those who control the official means of coercion, whether or not the control is legitimate. These rulers should not be automatically identified with the occupants of official positions in the central government. In the majority of Western countries today that is the case, but in other places or other times, it is or was definitely not the case. Control of the means of coercion may be in the hands of those who hold no official position, such as bosses in the cities of the United States, some dictators such as Rafael Trujillo of the Dominican Republic, and secretaries of the Communist party in Eastern European states. It may be in the hands of local leaders, whether in official positions or not, such as sheriffs in the South of the United States, owners of large haciendas in rural Latin America, managers of corporations in company towns, and leaders of guerrilla forces in liberated areas. These examples may be misleading in suggesting that individuals are often the rulers, which has seldom been the case. Rulership results from structured relationships, whether formal or informal, which tie together large numbers of people into patterns of authority, and these relationships distribute power among large numbers of people.

Control of the means of coercion may also be shared with forces from outside the country. Under colonialism, the imperial power had all of the control, of course. Today the relationships are more subtle. Means of coercion are employed at times in greater quantities between nation-states than within nation-states. War could be said to be a form of political repression and vice versa; the Salvadoran junta seems to have declared war on its own people. War usually is a more symmetrical relationship, and the coercive forces are more concentrated, but not always.

Coercion, we have said, is important when it is not used as long as there is fear that it might be used. U.S. foreign policy makers are aware of the need to maintain the credibility of military threat, which was somewhat undermined by the withdrawal from Vietnam. Judging from the incidents of use rather than the rhetoric, the threat is aimed more at the weaker countries of the world than at the Soviet Union.[78]

Dependencia writers made us aware of the permeability of state boundaries in the periphery. If the comprador bourgeoisie have sold out national interests to international capitalism, so could those in control of coercive organizations. Military officers, who have been bred and reared to respect authority, might well look up to those in the core countries who are the sources of weapons and sophisticated training, and who could destroy their forces in a minute if engaged in military conflict.

Afghani military officers during the last two decades certainly showed sufficient obeisance and respect to the militarily superior neighbors to the north. When opposition groups rebelled against their rule and threatened to overthrow them, the Soviet Union demonstrated how real the Soviet threat was. A similar relationship exists between the military in Central America and the United States, with one major difference, namely, the possibility for Central Americans to influence the political process in the United States. The oligarchies and militaries of Central America have long realized how important U.S. policy was and exerted considerable effort and funds to affect it. Now, opposition groups in Central America have established ties with citizens of the United States through human rights groups and church organizations and are trying to reverse the U.S. government's support for their masters. The civil-guerrilla organization of the opposition in El Salvador has openly admitted that the decisive battle is in the United States against the interventionist tendencies of the U.S. government, for they have little chance of winning against massive intervention by the U.S. military. The U.S. government is an international government from the point of view of the Latin Americans because of its overwhelmingly superior military force, as well as its disproportionate control of capital and technology. We have no trouble recognizing this same relation between the Soviet Union and its East European satellites. France maintains a similar relationship with its ex-colonies. However, the U.S. government's control through the threat of military intervention extends to more parts of the world than does that of any other country today.

CONCLUSION

The conventional philosophy of social science hindered our thinking about our implicit and assumed views about the way the world worked. It has been those partly hidden views that limited thinking about political repression and relating it to political processes. To obtain a greater consciousness about these views, we must accept a different philosophy of social science—a philosophy that recognized the importance of cognitive maps for perception, of iconic models in the development of knowledge, and of social pressures in the construction of social reality. Then we can understand why some variables seem relevant and others not. As long as we thought variables could be pulled from a hat at random, we could not attack the problem. The philosophical sketch presented in this chapter outlines a philosophy of social science that provided us with a cognitive map for looking for what was missing from the prevailing iconic models that made us ignore political repression.

When we looked at the most common iconic models of societies and polities, it was clear why we had misjudged the importance of political repression. All the models, with the exception of the geopolitical, depreciated political authority and the power of coercion and made social forces, rather than political forces, the driving mechanisms of society. On the other hand, the geopolitical model glorified coercive forces and legitimated political repression. Some also over-emphasized the amount of agreement in society and the degree of symmetry or equality between sectors of the population. It follows that if we want an iconic model that makes political repression as prevalent in our theory as in the world, we must emphasize different aspects of the social and political reality. We must focus on rulers who control the means of coercion and how they use coercion against the population to enforce their interests and belief systems. Rulers fit into a structure of power that goes from the local community to the great empires of the United States and the Soviet Union.

In recent decades, parts of the world have clearly become more repressive, and presently we have no adequate explanation of why this has happened. If we believe in political freedom, we must try to understand why repression has grown and do something about it. If the urbanized and educated populations of Chile and Uruguay, with long histories of democratic government, could fall to bloody dictatorships, in part from forces located in the United States, we should not assume that any part of the world is immune. As long as we do not understand the dynamics of political freedom and repression, we cannot know how and where freedom is being undermined nor what can be done to shore it up.

NOTES

1. The literature on totalitarianism assumes a dichotomous division of the world into a totalitarian part and a democratic part. Political repression and governmental terror exist only in the totalitarian part. To make things worse, both totalitarianism and democracy were portrayed as ideal types. Thus the view had no place for authoritarianism that was not totalitarian, distorted the other parts of the world, and did not allow the consideration of changing levels of repression anywhere. A good critical review of the totalitarian literature is Benjamin R. Barber, Michael Curtis, and Carl J. Friedrich, *Totalitarianism in Perspective* (New York: Praeger, 1969).

2. S. P. Huntington and C. H. Moore, *Authoritarian Politics in Modern Society* (New York: Basic Books, 1970).

3. Guillermo O'Donnell, *Modernization and Bureaucratic-Authoritarianism* (Berkeley, Calif.: Institute of International Studies, University of California Press, 1973). No more was made of political repression by the authors commenting on O'Donnell's scheme

in David Collier (ed.), *The New Authoritarianism in Latin America* (Princeton, N.J.: Princeton University Press, 1979).

4. Amos Perlmutter, *Modern Authoritarianism, A Comparative Institutional Analysis* (New Haven, Conn.: Yale University Press, 1981), p. 25.

5. The dominant philosophy of social science and epistomology comes out of the interpretations of E. Nagel, C. G. Hempel, and K. Popper. It is reflected in the methodological writing of almost all social science. The philosophy has been on the defensive for twenty years, but the various criticisms have not yet provided a coherent alternative. The criticisms have had hardly any influence in the practice of social science.

6. This sketch emerges out of ongoing work on philosophy of social science, which when completed will elaborate and, undoubtedly, modify the views expressed here.

7. E. Nagel, *The Structure of Science* (New York: Harcourt, 1961), contains one of the most complete arguments on the similarities.

8. The term *iconic model* comes from Rom Harré's *The Principles of Scientific Thinking* (Chicago: University of Chicago Press, 1970). More recently he referred simply to "icons." Iconic models seem to be the same as what Abraham Kaplan referred to as "pattern models." See Rom Harré, *The Conduct of Inquiry, Methodology for Behavioral Science* (New York: Chandler Publishing Company, 1964), Chapter 38. It also has some resemblance to Thomas Kuhn's "paradigms," which is a more all-encompassing and looser concept. See idem., *The Structure of Scientific Revolutions* (Chicago: University of Chicago Press, 1962, 1970).

9. Ulric Neisser, *Cognition and Reality, Principles and Implications of Cognitive Psychology* (San Francisco: W. H. Freeman & Co., 1976), and in a more summary essay, "Perceiving, Anticipating, and Imaging," in C. Wade Savage (ed.), *Perception and Cognition* (Minneapolis: University of Minnesota Press, 1978).

10. Neisser, "Perceiving," p. 91.

11. Ibid., p. 97.

12. In addition to Harré's *The Principles of Scientific Thinking*, see his *The Philosophies of Science* (London: Oxford University Press, 1972), and R. Harré and E. H. Madden, *Causal Powers, A Theory of Natural Necessity* (Totowa, N.J.: Rowman and Littlefield, 1975). A good short summary of several of his ideas appears in Harré's "Creativity in Science," in D. Dutton and M. Krausz (eds.), *The Concept of Creativity in Science and Art* (The Hague: Martinus Nijhoff Publishers, 1981).

13. Harré, *Principles*, p. 12.

14. Ibid., p. 15.

15. Ibid.

16. Harré, "Creativity in Science," p. 19.

17. Harré, *The Philosophies*, p. 116.

18. The whole of Harré and Madden's *Causal Powers* is devoted to developing the concept of natural necessity and contrasting that view with that of the Regularity Theory of Hume.

19. Rom Harré, *Social Being* (Totowa, N.J.: Littlefield, Adams & Co., 1980); and Harré and P. F. Secord, *The Explanation of Social Behavior* (Totowa, N.J.: Rowman and Littlefield, 1972).

20. Harré, *Social Being*, p. 347.

21. The critique stems from Peter Winch, *The Idea of a Social Science and Its Relation to Philosophy* (London: Routledge and Kegan Paul Ltd., 1958), and has been abundantly

refuted. Hannah Pitkin's *Wittgenstein and Justice* (Berkeley, Calif.: University of California Press, 1972) has an excellent chapter that criticizes Winch.

22. Harré, "Creativity in Science," p. 38.

23. Ibid., p. 41.

24. Ibid.

25. The connections between the two models can go in either direction. If one begins with the iconic model, the structures and processes should suggest how they would respond to certain conditions (changes in variables), if not out of "natural necessity," at least through implication. If one begins with the variable model, one can argue for its plausibility through a causal interpretation that uses the iconic model.

26. Gerald Holton, *Thematic Origins of Scientific Thought, Kepler to Einstein* (Cambridge: Harvard University Press, 1973), p. 369.

27. Pitkin, *Wittgenstein and Justice*, and Michael J. Shapiro, *Language and Political Understanding, the Politics of Discursive Practices* (New Haven, Conn.: Yale University Press, 1981), both provide excellent discussions of the importance of language in the interpretation of societies and polities.

28. A good discussion of the anthropological treatment of the problem is Marvin Harris, *Cultural Materialism* (New York: Random House, 1979), Chapter 2, "The Epistemology of Cultural Materialism."

29. Peter L. Berger and Thomas Luckmann, *The Social Construction of Reality, A Treatise on the Sociology of Knowledge* (Garden City, N.Y.: Doubleday & Co., 1966), pp. 38-39.

30. Quoted in Shapiro, *Language and Political Understanding*, p. 59.

31. Stephen Toulmin, *Human Understanding, The Collective Use and Evolution of Concepts* (Princeton, N.J.: Princeton University Press, 1972), p. 35. Italics in original.

32. Ibid.

33. Robert K. Merton, "Foreword, Remarks on Theoretical Pluralism," in Peter M. Blau and Robert K. Merton (eds.), *Continuities in Structural Inquiry* (Beverly Hills, Calif.: Sage Publications, 1981), p. i.

34. Geoffrey Vickers, "Rationality and Intuition," in Judith Wechsler (ed.), *On Aesthetics in Science* (Cambridge, Mass.: MIT Press, 1978), p. 149. Donald T. Campell, who unfortunately fails to make clear the two ways of knowing, illustrates the importance of context for pattern recognition with the example of identifying a spot of ink on a printed page. The more of the page that is visible, the easier it is to recognize any particular spot. See his "Pattern Matching as an Essential in Distal Knowing," in K. R. Hammond (ed.), *The Psychology of Egon Brunswik* (New York: Holt, Rinehart and Winston, 1966), and several of his more recent works.

35. Sheldon Wolin, "Political Theory as a Vocation," *American Political Science Review* (December 1969), 63:1062-1082.

36. Edward S. Herman demonstrated this consciousness in *The Real Terror Network, Terrorism in Fact and Propaganda* (Boston: South End Press, 1982).

37. G. David Garson, *Group Theories of Politics* (Beverly Hills, Calif.: Sage Publications, 1978), and "On the Origins of Interest Group Theory: A Critique of a Process," *American Political Science Review* (December 1974), 68:1505-1519.

38. Garson, *Group Theories*, p. 71.

39. Harry Eckstein, "Group Theory and the Comparative Study of Pressure Groups," in Eckstein and David E. Apter (eds.), *Comparative Politics, a Reader* (New York: Free Press, 1963), p. 391.

40. David Easton, *A Systems Analysis of Political Life* (New York: John Wiley and Sons, 1965), and Gabriel Almond and G. Bingham Powell, *Comparative Politics, A Developmental Approach* (Boston: Little, Brown & Co., 1966), provide the most complete development of these ideas.

41. Easton, *A Systems Analysis*, p. 276.

42. Almond and Powell, *Comparative Politics*, pp. 17-18.

43. Talcott Parsons, *Societies: Evolutionary and Contemporary Perspectives* (Englewood Cliffs, N.J.: Prentice-Hall, 1966), p. 14.

44. Parsons, "Some Reflections on the Place of Force in Social Process," in Harry Eckstein (ed.), *Internal War: Basic Problems and Approaches* (New York: Free Press, 1964).

45. Robert Justin Goldstein, *Political Repression in Modern America, from 1870 to the Present* (Cambridge, Mass.: Shenkman Publishing, 1978), p. ix.

46. Ibid., p. xx.

47. Ralph Milband, *The State in Capitalist Society: An Analysis of the Western System of Power* (New York: Basic Books, 1969); and Nicos Poulantzas, *Political Power and Social Classes* (London: New Left Books and Sheed and Ward, 1973). Alan Wolfe gave a semi-Marxist account of repression in the United States that contains the same problems. See his *The Seamy Side of Democracy* (New York, D. McKay, 1973).

48. Robert C. Tucker (ed.), *The Marx-Engels Reader* (New York: W. W. Norton, 1978), p. 475.

49. Alan Gilbert, *Marx's Politics, Communists and Citizens* (New Brunswick, N.J.: Rutgers University Press, 1981), p. 229.

50. Ibid., p. 233.

51. Quoted in V. I. Lenin, *State and Revolution* (New York: International Publishers, 1932), p. 8. Emphasis added.

52. Tucker, *The Marx-Engels Reader*, p. 535. Emphasis added.

53. Ibid., p. 536.

54. Quoted in Lenin, *State and Revolution*, pp. 15-16. Italics in original.

55. Fernando Henrique Cardoso, "The Consumption of Dependency Theory in the United States," *Latin American Research Review* (Fall 1977), 12:7-24.

56. Fernando Henrique Cardoso and Enzo Faletto, *Dependency and Development in Latin America* (Berkeley, Calif.: University of California Press, 1978).

57. Andre Gunder Frank, "The Development of Underdevelopment," *Monthly Review* (September 1966), 17-31.

58. Ronald H. Chilcote and Joel C. Edelstein (eds.), *Latin America: The Struggle for Dependency and Beyond* (Cambridge, Mass.: Schenkman Publishing, 1974).

59. Gaetano Mosca, *The Ruling Class* (New York: McGraw-Hill, 1939); Vilfredo Pareto, *The Mind and Society* (New York: Harcourt, Brace & Co., 1938); Robert Michel, *Political Parties* (Glencoe, Ill.: Free Press, 1949); C. Wright Mills, *The Power Elite* (New York: Oxford University Press, 1959); and G. William Domhoff, *Who Rules America?* (Englewood Cliffs, N.J.: Prentice-Hall, 1967).

60. G. William Domhoff, *The Powers That Be, Processes of Ruling Class Domination in America* (New York: Random House, 1978).

61. Sir Halford J. Mackinder's paper read before the Royal Geographic Society in London in 1904, "The Geographical Pivot of History," is credited as being the first

geopolitical thought. Rudolf Kjellen's *The State as an Organism*, first published in 1916, provides a more extreme statement. Alfred Mahan and Karl Haushofer follow in this tradition.

62. John Garnett provided a useful summary of "realism" in "Strategic Studies and Its Assumptions," in John Baylis et al., *Contemporary Strategy Theories and Policies* (New York: Holmes & Meier Publishers, 1975). The most influential statement of "realism" was made by Hans J. Morgenthau in *Politics Among Nations* (New York: Alfred A. Knopf, 1948).

63. Karl von Clausewitz, *On War* (reprinted London: Routledge, 1966).

64. Anatol Rapoport, *The Big Two, Soviet-American Perceptions of Foreign Policy* (New York: Pegasus, 1971), pp. 38-39.

65. Ibid., pp. 208-209.

66. In addition to Morgenthau, *Politics Among Nations*, other influential works were E. H. Carr, *The Twenty Years Crisis, 1919-1939* (London: Macmillan & Co., 1946); George Kennan, *American Diplomacy, 1900-1950* (Chicago: University of Chicago Press, 1951); and Reinhold Niebuhr, *Christian Realism and Political Problems* (New York: Charles Scribner's Sons, 1953).

67. A review of strategic thinking is found in Adelphi Papers, No. 54, *Problems of Modern Strategy* (London: Institute for Strategic Studies, 1969), as well as in Bayless et al., *Contemporary Strategy*. The promoters of U.S. military expansion that took up their pens in the mid-1970s assume this model. For example, see Paul H. Nitze, "Assuring Strategic Stability in an Era of Detente," *Foreign Affairs* (January 1976), 54:207-232.

68. General Golberry do Couto e Silva, the major ideological thinker of the Brazilian military, published *Geopolitics of Brazil* in 1964. The Chilean dictator General Augusto Pinochet published *Geopolitics* in 1974. A good example of this extremist geopolitical thinking from Argentina and found in English translation is Ricardo Zinn, *Argentina, A Nation at the Crossroads of Myth and Reality* (New York: Robert Speller & Sons, 1979). A summary of the Latin American national security doctrine is given by Roberto Calvo in "The Church and the Doctrine of National Security," *Journal of Inter-American Studies and World Affairs* (February 1979), 21-1:69-88.

69. Alfred Stepan, *The Military in Politics, Changing Patterns in Brazil* (Princeton, N.J.: Princeton University Press, 1971); and "The New Professionalism in Internal Warfare and Military Role Expansion," in Stepan (ed.), *Authoritarian Brazil* (New Haven, Conn.: Yale University Press, 1973).

70. This is a standard view of most of the contemporary military security writers. It was expounded by Andre Beaufre in *An Introduction to Strategy* (London: Faber, 1965).

71. Rapoport, *The Big Two*, p. 31.

72. Toulmin, *Human Understanding*, p. 35.

73. Ernest A. Duff and John F. McCamant, *Violence and Repression in Latin America* (New York: Free Press, 1976), p. 129.

74. Different ways of operationalizing political repression will give somewhat different results on the amount of repression. The difficulties of operationalization are discussed in John McCamant, "A Critique of Present Measures of 'Human Rights Development' and an Alternative," in Ved P. Nanda, James R. Scarritt, and George W. Shepherd, Jr. (eds.), *Global Human Rights: Public Policies, Comparative Measures, and NGO Strategies* (Boulder, Colo.: Westview Press, 1981). The comparison here is based primarily on the number of people killed and jailed.

75. Amnesty International's reports on the two countries give data that suggest that Indonesia's blood bath could have been greater than China's. *Indonesia* (London: Amnesty International Publishers, 1977); and *Political Imprisonment in the People's Republic of China* (London: Amnesty International Publishers, 1978).

76. The writing on terrorism, primarily of the oppositional sort, treats fear as being the primary goal of terrorism, but this notion is seldom considered as a governmental process. Peter R. Knauss and D. A. Strickland do suggest that the same process sometimes applies to governments in "Political Disintegration and Latent Terror," in Michael Stohl (ed.), *The Politics of Terrorism* (New York: Marcel Dekker, 1979).

77. T. Nardin critiques U.S. writing on this matter in *Violence and the State* (Beverly Hills, Calif.: Sage Publications, 1971).

78. Michael T. Klare, *Beyond the "Vietnam Syndrome," U.S. Interventionism in the 1980s* (Washington D.C.: Institute of Policy Studies, 1981), and Noam Chomsky, *Towards a New Cold War* (New York: Pantheon, 1982).

2

International Dimensions of State Terrorism

Michael Stohl ⎯⎯⎯⎯⎯⎯⎯⎯⎯⎯⎯⎯⎯⎯

Students of international relations are well aware of the role of force and the threat of the use of force as a major component of international relations. Nonetheless, this awareness has not interfered with the conventions of scholarship on international relations that prescribe and proscribe the use of descriptors for such activity. For most activities undertaken by the national state in the conduct of its international relations and foreign policy, the employment of the descriptor *coercive diplomacy* is acceptable, but the term *terrorism* is not normally condoned. Exceptions are of course made for propaganda purposes and to condemn particular tactics, terror bombing of innocent civilians, for example, but for the most part it is clear that international relations scholars have steered clear of the use of the term *terrorism* to describe state behaviors in international affairs.

In this chapter I argue that the concept of terrorism will describe many of the uses and threats of the use of force within the international system, and thus I do employ the term. I argue that the use of terror tactics is common in international relations and that the state has been and remains a more likely employer of terrorism within the international system than insurgents and with much greater effect. The state then is as much a user of terror in its international affairs as in its domestic activities.[1]

I do not employ the term *terror* to describe state behavior merely for affect. I am in fact challenging an unspoken covention within the international relations scholarly community, but I do so by presenting a definition of *terrorism* that is consistent with that employed to examine both insurgent and state terrorism in domestic situations. By *terrorism* I mean "the purposeful act or threat of violence to create fear and/or compliant behavior in a victim and/or audience of the act or threat." The legitimacy of the national state is itself normally conceived as providing legitimacy to actions that would be condemned as terrorism if such behaviors were executed by nonstate actors. Rather than preempting the issue by providing this analytically indefensible legitimacy, I prefer to examine the behavior of states and describe behaviors that have as their intent the purposeful creation of fear for coercive purposes. I leave the problem of justifying such behaviors in national interest or other "higher" moral terms to the actors themselves.[2]

Three broad categories of state terrorism in international relations are described in this chapter. Terror as *coercive diplomacy* constitutes the first. Here the aim is to make noncompliance with a particular political demand, in the words of Schelling, "terrible beyond endurance." Although the threat is openly communicated by the actions of the state, the threat may be implicit and often is nonverbal. Coercive diplomacy is overt behavior. The parties to the conflict are fully aware of the nature of the threat.

Covert behavior categorizes the second form of state terrorism. The clandestine services of the national state are responsible for these actions. Government agents operating across national boundaries may choose either national elites or the foreign society itself as the target. In this type of state terrorism, states may thus attempt to intimidate government officials directly through campaigns of bombing, attacks, assassinations, and the sponsoring and participation in attempted coups d'état. Alternatively, national states participate in the destabilization of other societies with the purpose of creating chaos and the conditions for the collapse of governments, the weakening of the national state, and changes in leadership. The threats to the regime and the society are obvious, and often the actual perpetrator may be obvious, but there is an attempt at deniability nonetheless. It is the pattern of such behavior and the threat of such a pattern being initiated that constitutes the terroristic aspect of this type of action.

The third form of state terrorism involves assistance to another state or insurgent organization that makes it possible or "improves" the capability of that actor to practice terrorism. This form I label *surrogate terrorism*, since the obvious effect and intent of the assistance provided is the improvement of the assisted actor's ability to either carry out terrorist actions to maintain regimes rule or to create chaos and/or the eventual overthrow of an identified enemy state regime.

I. COERCIVE DIPLOMACY AS STATE TERRORISM: THE DIPLOMACY OF VIOLENCE

The reliance on the doctrine of reason of state and the pervasiveness of realism in foreign policy analysis has clouded the analysis of state terrorism in international affairs. Realists prefer to exclude "legitimate" state pursuit of what statesmen are willing to declare as the national interest from the discussion of terrorism. *Terrorism*, a term of opprobrium, must, they argue, be reserved for actors without legitimacy. Nonetheless, in the subsequent analysis, the definition of *terror* stipulated above is employed to explore state activities.

Perhaps the most notorious recent use of terrorism as coercive diplomacy by the United States was the Nixon-Kissinger Christmas bombings of Hanoi in

1972. These bombings involved massive saturation runs over Hanoi and the rest of North Vietnam and were code named Operation Linebacker II. They were ordered by Nixon after negotiations with the North Vietnamese had stalled because of South Vietnamese objections to the Kissinger-Tho proposed treaty. For twelve days American B-52s flew sortie after sortie "at levels of intensity and sustainment never before achieved in the history of warfare."[3] About 100 B-52s and 500 fighter bombers flew round-the-clock raids with each B-52 carrying about two dozen 500-pound bombs. As John Stoessinger has argued: "Nixon's logic was that he was bombing for peace. He was trying to bomb Hanoi back to the negotiating table and trying to convince Saigon by this show of force, that he was loyal to his ally. Both parts of Vietnam, Nixon reasoned, would be ready to sign with the United States once the shock treatment was over. By this reasoning, much of Hanoi and Haiphong was reduced to rubble."[4] As a result of the bombings, both "Vietnams" came to the negotiating table, and Nixon was able to achieve what he termed "peace with honor." This behavior occurred during a war situation (even if officially undeclared) and thus is by convention often placed in a special category of international behavior concerned with the conduct of war. Although there are formal and informal limits through international law and historical practice placed on a nation's conduct in war situations, exceeding these limits is not often labeled "terroristic."

The case of Israel's behavior in its relations with neighboring Arab states and the Palestine Liberation Organization demonstrate that it is not only great powers and superpowers that have the wherewithal to resort to the use of terror tactics in international relations. It is only necessary to be *relatively* more powerful to undertake coercive diplomacy in general and terrorist applications in particular. Israeli behavior vis-à-vis both its Arab state neighbors and the Palestinians within those states is probably the most conspicuous example of Third World state terrorism in international affairs. Israeli reprisals and bombing raids are designed as much to instill fear as they are to produce damage. The Israelis perceive that they must constantly remind their adversaries how costly another war or assistance to the Palestinians is and will continue to be. The key elements of such a tactic are available to any Third World nation that is in a position of clear superiority vis-à-vis a nearby adversary. It is not necessary to be able to project a nation's power on a global scale to employ coercive diplomacy. Furthermore, we may expect that as Third World nations acquire nuclear weapons, they too will consider entering the diplomacy of the balance of terror. Israel's destruction of the Iraqi nuclear reactor in 1981 sent a message to both the Iraqis and Israel's other Arab neighbors about the Israeli position on their development of nuclear capability. The bombing raid had, in other words, a wider audience than the immediate victim of the raid. The Arab nations were placed on notice about the likely impact of a decision to go ahead with a nuclear weapons program: They would face the likely prospect of an Israeli attack.

In June 1982 Israel invaded Lebanon for the avowed purpose of ending the ability of the Palestine Liberation Organization (PLO) to attack Israeli settlements near the Lebanese border. Prime Minister Begin charged that "the scourge of terrorism must be stamped out." To accomplish this task the Israeli army swept across Lebanon and into the outskirts of the capital, Beirut. From there the war was clearly transformed into a series of coercive diplomatic actions that may easily be designated as terrorism. With the Israeli army clearly outnumbering the outmaneuvered Palestinians and the Israeli air force controlling the air, the Israelis commenced a series of mock air raids of Beirut. Israeli jets dropped smoke bombs and flares and sent the civilian population rushing to shelters. The Associated Press reported an Israeli official as saying: "Time is running short. . . . We are very rapidly reaching the limit of our patience."[5] The Israelis demanded that the PLO surrender its weapons and leave Lebanon or face a full-scale assault. The target of these mock air raids and the intimidation and threat of physical harm was the population of Beirut as much as the PLO itself. The widening of the target was obviously designed to increase the pressure on the PLO to surrender by convincing the people of Beirut, through the threat of destruction, that expelling the PLO was in their best interest. Whether one argues that this may have eventually saved lives by reducing the actual fighting, one must also recognize that the people of Beirut were held hostage to the coercive bargaining that was thereby developed.

Major powers and other relatively stronger powers have often employed terror tactics in their relations with less powerful nations in *nonwar* situations as well. In May 1975 the merchant freighter *Mayaguez* was seized by Cambodia. The Ford-Kissinger team responded with a dramatic show of force.

Air attacks were initiated against Cambodia, and marines were landed on Koh Tang Island in the Gulf of Siam where, incorrectly, it was assumed the American crew was being held. In contrast with the regular resort to diplomatic means when American fishing vessels have been seized, their crews beaten and even shot at off Ecuador, no diplomatic channels were used until after the show of force was completed. It mattered little, however, for the entire incident seemed a useful pretext to demonstrate that the United States would, in Henry Kissinger's words, maintain its reputation for fierceness.[6]

By some interpretations this response could be explained as thereby the result of a communications breakdown or perhaps a mere lashing out. This I would argue would be an overly generous and misleading position. As Walter LaFeber suggested, "The seizure occurred just after Vietnam fell, OPEC had quadrupled oil prices without an American response and Kissinger had been unable to stop the MPLA [Popular Movement for the Liberation of Angola] in Angola. In this political climate, Ford with Kissinger's strong encouragement. . . used military force to show that he was decisive and not afraid to get tough with communists."[7] In other words, lest any small nation believe that the United States in the post-Vietnam era was not going to maintain its interests by force, and terror, where necessary, the Mayaguez incident was an opportunity to communicate the Ford administration's willingness to uphold American power. The Cambodians were

Table 2.1 Coercive Political-Military Operations, by Subject of Soviet Concern, June 1944-August 1979

Subject of Soviet concern	Coercive[a]
Expansion of territory or political authority	26
Maintenance of fraternal Communist regime	43
Security Relations	45
Third world influence	41
Other	3
Total incidents	158

[a]Source: Stephen Kaplan The Diplomacy of Power

the immediate victims of the bombing raid and the rescue attempt (which took place after the merchant crew had already been released), but the world was the target audience for the acting out of the terror game.

Stephen Kaplan has examined the Soviet Union's use of coercive diplomacy since World War II.[8] His analysis illustrates a number of different purposes and tactics for coercive diplomacy available to strong nations. There were 158 incidents is which the use of USSR armed forces or the threat of armed forces use were employed.

Important patterns regarding each of these types of Soviet activities are summarized in Table 2.1. Kaplan argued that the USSR pursued coercive diplomacy for expansionary purposes only once after 1951, when it employed a "show of force" in 1975 in the form of a missile test in the Barents Sea that was aimed at Norway.[9] On the other hand, the use of armed force to maintain fraternal Communist regimes remains an important instrument of Soviet diplomacy. The USSR has threatened intervention, placed ground forces in nearby positions, activated units, repositioned military units, and participated in the active suppression of outbreaks against Eastern European regimes throughout the past three decades, and it has intervened with military force in East Germany, 1953; Hungary, 1956; and Czechoslovakia, 1968, to protect "orthodoxy" in Eastern Europe.

The USSR also used coercive diplomacy to "intimidate neighbors or react to perceived threats presented by neighbors."[10] This pattern shifted from the early postwar period when the concern was more clearly the intimidation of neighbors for USSR-perceived security needs to the more recent past when the issue has been the manipulation of threats to gain diplomatic advantage or reduce possible threats to the USSR. This use of the threat of armed force within the Eastern European sphere of influence is, of course, a conventional behavior pattern for a great power. Nonetheless, this "convention" involves the threat of the use of force for coercive bargaining purposes. It is meant to intimidate not simply the government whose behavior is being challenged at any time but also the other fraternal governments. It should therefore properly be labeled "terrorism."

Soviet Union use of coercive diplomacy in the Third World appears very different from American usage. Kaplan recorded only one small action in the Third World after the autumn of 1962 in which the USSR threatened military force, the deployment of two warships near the coast of Ghana in 1967 after two Soviet trawlers had been seized.[11] This is not to say that the Soviet Union has not been active politically in the Third World. Rather, it is simply to state that the Soviets appear to employ an approach different from the United States. On the other hand, both the United States and the Soviet Union have developed straightforward and similar justifications for their use of force in what they define as their legitimate spheres of influence. In 1968 Lyndon Johnson had provided the explicit rationale for such a policy. In justifying the American intervention in the Dominican Republic, Johnson announced: "The American nations cannot, must not, and will not permit the establishment of another communist government in the Western Hemisphere."[12] The United States openly justified its coercive behavior in the pursuit of foreign policy objectives. This message of coercive diplomacy is not generally lost on Third World elites and those that would challenge them within their nations. The United States will protect its interests, as it defines them, by the threat and use of force.

The development of U.S. doctrine on the use of force within its sphere of influence has been mirrored by the Soviet Union. As Thomas Franck and Edward Weisband[13] have shown, the development of the Brezhnev Doctrine in the wake of the invasion of Czechoslovakia in August 1968 is a faithful reproduction of American justifications of U.S. interventionary behavior. In essence one simply substitutes worldwide imperialism for world communism and socialist community for the free world, and the doctrines are essentially equivalent. The Soviet Union does have, however, given its smaller "legitimate" sphere of influence, a smaller zone in which to operate.

II. A SPECIAL FORM OF COERCIVE DIPLOMACY: NUCLEAR DETERRENCE, THE BALANCE OF TERROR

By convention, the threat of nuclear deterrence is not normally labeled "terrorism" by international relations scholars despite the fact that it meets the two denotative criteria that the commonly used dictionary definition of the term sets forth.[14] But the terrorist threat is central to the current military doctrine of the superpowers and other nuclear nations. Modern deterrence theory, which underlies American (and NATO) strategic relations with the Soviet Union is based on the threat of nuclear holocaust. In its earliest incarnation this strategy was clearly labeled as "the Balance of Terror," and it was understood that what was threatened was the loss of life of the entire population of the societies engaged in the deterrent relationship. Thomas Schelling was straightforward in pointing out that this remains the essence of the deterrent concept. After noting the common usage or dictionary definition of *terrorism*, a definition consistent with that introduced above, he posited that "there is a 30 year tradition that the appropriate targets for nuclear forces are cities or populations, and that strategic nuclear forces induce caution and moderation in an adversary by threatening the destruction of the enemy society. I imply nothing derogatory or demeaning about strategic nuclear force by emphasizing the traditional expectation that their primary use is to deter or to intimidate, and thereby to influence behavior, through the threat of enormous civilian damage."[15] The populations of both superpowers are held hostage to the threat of destruction by the logic of deterrence. Although one may argue that this is a different form of hostage-taking than that practiced by insurgent terrorists, it is nonetheless hostage-taking. Michael Walzer pointed out that as in the case of seizing innocents to bargain for a "higher goal," the threat presented by recourse to nuclear deterrence is also not justifiable: "the enterprise is immoral. The immorality lies in the threat itself, not in its present or even its likely consequences."[16] Schelling referred to deterrence or the passive form of "massive retaliation."[17] We should recognize that the passive form is not the only use of the threat of nuclear terrorism that has occurred since the invention of nuclear weapons. "It is worth remembering that on the only occasion of the hostile use of nuclear weapons, they were used in a fashion that has to be considered 'terrorist.' . . . Hiroshima represented intimidation: the object was not to eliminate that city; the true target was the emperor's palace in Tokyo."[18] Furthermore, as Table 2.2 from the study of United States use of force in the post-war period by Barry Blechman and Stephen Kaplan illustrates, the United States has employed the mobilization of its nuclear forces as an instrument of threat within the context of international crises.[19]

The current debate concerning a pledge of "no first use" regarding nuclear weapons may in this context be understood not merely as part of the deterrent that underlies U.S.-Soviet nuclear strategic interactions but also as part of American reliance on the threat of nuclear weapons in "crisis management" interactions as well. A no-first-use pronouncement would deprive the United States of a tactic that has been employed at least nineteen times in the post-war period with explicit understanding of the implication of the threat of nuclear use.

It should be clearly understood that U.S. nuclear forces are not used merely in a "passive" deterrent manner but are employed as threats during crisis periods when the possibility of terror is activated. Recalling Schelling once again, "The proper question is not whether an organization of the kind that we think of as 'terrorist' will get nuclear weapons in pursuit of their goals. It is whether any organization that acquires nuclear weapons *can be anything but* terrorist in the use of such weapons."[20]

In contrast, it is interesting to note Kaplan on the USSR and the use of strategic nuclear forces. In the parallel study to that of Blechman and Kaplan previously noted, Kaplan concluded: "No information was discovered that would indicate that the USSR has ever deployed strategic bomber units during a crisis. To be

Table 2.2 Incidents in Which Strategic Nuclear Forces Were Involved

Incident	Date
U.S. aircraft shot down by Yugoslavia	November 1946
Inauguration of president in Uruguay	February 1947
Security of Berlin	January 1948
Security of Berlin	April 1948
Security of Berlin	June 1948
Korean War: Security of Europe	July 1950
Security of Japan/South Korea	August 1953
Guatemala accepts Soviet bloc support	May 1954
China-Taiwan conflict: Tachen Islands	August 1954
Suez crisis	October 1956
Political crisis in Lebanon	July 1958
Political crisis in Jordan	July 1958
China-Taiwan conflict: Quemoy and Matsu	July 1958
Security of Berlin	May 1959
Security of Berlin	June 1961
Soviet emplacement of missiles in Cuba	October 1962
Withdrawal of U.S. missiles from Turkey	April 1963
Pueblo seized by North Korea	January 1968
Arab-Israeli War	October 1973

Source: Blechman and Kaplan   Force Without War

sure about these matters is impossible, however."[21] As far as scholars have thus far been able to determine, nuclear threats appear to be the particular preserve of the United States government through the first thirty-seven years of the nuclear age.

III. CLANDESTINE TERROR

Whereas the terror of coercive diplomacy is obvious to all observers, even if many shrink from labeling the behavior as such, the terror of the clandestine apparatus of the state in international relations is often difficult to discern. Knowledge of these instances of international governmental terrorism is dependent on investigators bringing them to light and often long after the fact. This type of terror in international relations is not directly aimed at producing compliance but rather fear and chaos. It is hoped that as a result of increased fear and chaos, governments at some later point will be in a weaker bargaining position or have a different composition induced by the terror. It is the threat of this type of behavior *in general* that serves to keep elites fearful of outside interference and produces public statements by Third World leaders regarding American interference that to the American public often (particularly before the Pike Committee Report was made public in 1975) are dismissed as the ravings of unstable, paranoid, or ideological opponents who seek merely to embarrass or blame their internal difficulties on the United States.

The reaction by the U.S. media and public to the claims of Fidel Castro and Mu'ammar Qadhafi that the CIA had attempted to assassinate them are excellent cases in point. We have, at present, no direct knowledge in the case of Qadhafi, but by now the attempts on Castro throughout the past two decades are well known.[22]

The clandestine services of the United States have had much experience in the past few decades in this type of behavior. The organization most often responsible for such behavior is the Central Intelligence Agency. Victor Marchetti and John Marks suggest that "the crudest and most direct form of covert action is called 'special operation'...by definition, special operations are violent and brutal."[23] A partial listing of well-known CIA special operations indicates the range of such activities. In Guatemala, 1954; Indonesia, 1958; Iran, 1953; the Bay of Pigs, Cuba, 1961, the United States trained, equipped, and provided tactical assistance to groups attempting to overthrow established governments. In the 1950s the United States also assisted the forces of Chiang Kai Shek against the People's Republic of China. "National Chinese troops in Burma (when not engaged in their principal posture of trafficking in opium) were induced to conduct occasional raids into the hinterland of Communist China."[24] Similar raids were made with United States support by followers of the Dalai Lama into Tibet. Are these attacks terrorist? Their purpose was disruption and the attempted overthrow of established regimes through violence. U.S. involvement was presumed, and the message to other Third World governments was clear—the United States would not sit idly by during and after the establishment of Left governments.

More recently, in the period 1970–1973, the United States worked on a number of levels to overthrow the elected government of Salvador Allende in Chile. In addition to nonterroristic strategies such as bribery after the election campaign, the United States embarked on a program to create economic and political chaos in Chile. The CIA was implicated in the assassination of René Schneider, the commander-in-chief of the Chilean army, who was selected as a target because he refused to prevent Allende from taking office. "The United States government attempted to foment a coup, it discussed coup plans with the Chileans later convicted of Schneider's abduction, it advocated his removal as a step toward overturning the results of a free election, it offered a payment of $50,000 for Schneider's kidnapping and it supplied the weapons for this strategy."[25] After the failure to prevent Allende from taking office, efforts shifted to obtaining his removal. At least $7 million was authorized by the United States for CIA use in the destabilizing of Chilean society. This included financing and assisting opposition groups and right-wing terrorist paramilitary groups such as *Patria y Libertad* ("Fatherland and Liberty"). Finally, in September 1973 the Allende government was overthrown in a brutal and violent military coup in which the United States was intimately involved. The message for the populations of Latin American nations and particularly the Left opposition was clear: the United States would not permit the continuation of a Socialist government, even if it came to power in a democratic election and continued to uphold the basic democratic structure of that society.[26]

The Soviet Union has been far less able or perhaps willing to intervene in the Third World on the scale that the United States has achieved in the past few decades. This is apparently the case for both overt and covert interventions. Although much is made in Western society of the strength of the Soviet KGB and the threat that the Soviet Union poses in the Third World, in much of the Third World the Soviet presence appears to be relatively benign. It has far less leverage than the Western powers and far less infrastructure within which to conduct covert operations. Alvin Rubinstein argued that in Third World policy in general the Soviet Union appears opportunistic and responsive to local initiatives and conditions.[27] Unlike the United States, "the Soviets have not been well placed to meddle effectively in leadership quarrels and have wisely concentrated on maintaining good government-to-government relations, reinforcing convergent policy goals and providing such assistance as is necessary to keep a client in power."[28] This is not to argue that the Soviet Union does not involve itself in "liberation struggles." It often has assisted groups (for example, the MPLA in Angola) it believed would be predisposed to it after achieving power.

In the past few years there has been growing suspicion and charges that the Soviet Union is responsible "for training, funding and equipping international terrorists."[29] Thus far the Reagan administration has been unable to convince any of its own intelligence agencies (at least in public documents) to support its view of the Soviet role, nor has it been able to produce any hard evidence for the existence of a Soviet terror network.[30] There is no doubt that the Soviet Union has provided assistance in the past to various Palestinian groups and that it provides and sells military hardware to a number of Arab states that in turn have made equipment available to Palestinian organizations. The Saudi connection to the PLO is also well known by area specialists and the media, but the Saudi role in bankrolling the PLO is conveniently forgotten by the media and the Reagan administration. Although it is unclear as to the "media's" motive of forgetting the Saudi role, the Reagan administration (as others before it) ignores the Saudis because their role does not fit the ideological purposes it is pursuing. This task should prove harder in the wake of Israeli revelations, after their assault on Beirut, of large numbers of M-16 rifles found in the hands of the PLO. These rifles had been sold to Saudi Arabia by the United States.

The Libyan connection to Palestinian terrorist organizations is well known.

What was not known until recently was that former CIA officials were also selling sophisticated equipment to Libya. This equipment and the Soviet equipment may obviously be transferred to the Palestinians. Thus the Soviet Union (and the United States) is willing to help political groups when they appear to serve some larger Soviet (or American) purpose. Terrorist opportunity and capability is often the result. This is different from suggesting, however, that the Soviet Union (or the United States) creates, directs, or controls a worldwide terrorist network.

It is not simply First and Second World superpowers that have evidenced the ability to operate beyond their borders in a clandestine manner. The attempt to eliminate opposition and instill fear in both domestic and external enemies is within the power of many Third World nations. Before the overthrow of the Shah, SAVAK agents were known to be employed within the United States to monitor Iranian students. Colonel Qadhafi's Libyan regime has been responsible for the murder of Qadhafi opposition in Rome, Athens, and London and has "been accused of 'masterminding' the attempted assassination of a Libyan student hanged in Colorado."[31]

Israeli and Arab agents have engaged in a campaign of assassination and terrorism on foreign soil. The Israeli MOSSAD (the Hebrew acronym for Central Institute for Intelligence and Security) has assassinated Palestinian agents in Cyprus, Algeria, Norway, Athens, Beirut, and Paris. Palestinians have in turn used letter bombs and more direct means of assassination to kill Israelis in London, Washington, New York, Madrid, and Rome.[32] This is a relatively low-cost, low-risk, but highly effective technique of political terrorism.

Third World nations have also been active in attempting to eliminate threats to their policies and interests by striking or attempting to strike at the heart of opposing nations by sponsoring and assisting in assassination attempts. Under Nkrumah, Ghana established a Special African Service to conduct covert operations and assist in the assassination of neighboring foreign leaders.[33] Although these events are not necessarily instances of terrorism in that they may have "simply" been designed to eliminate the foreign leader directly, knowledge of such attempts does influence the security preparations and foreign policies of neighboring states. Likewise, Colonel Qadhafi of Libya has been linked to numerous attempts of assassination and coup plots vis-à-vis his neighbors to the East, Egypt and Sudan.

IV. SURROGATE TERRORISM

Within the structures of dominance that exist within the international system, powerful states do not simply exert military force and threats to control all aspects of both the internal and external relations of subordinate states. Above I discussed the intervention of relatively powerful states in the affairs of the less powerful. Powerful states also assist the less powerful states in their domestic and international affairs. When a government sells, grants, and in other procedures provides favorable terms by which a coalition partner, ally, friend, or client state (and at times neutrals and even adversaries) obtain equipment that a "reasonable person" should perceive would likely be used to *continue* practices of repression and terrorism, that government is practicing a form of surrogate terrorism. When governments train the personnel that conduct the terror operations, consult with and advise (for "reasons of state") the security services of a "friendly" state in its use of terrorism, this tool is a form of surrogate terrorism. When a seemingly reasonable idea, such as an International Police Academy, which has as its stated purpose to "professionalize" the security services of less developed states but eventuates in the consistent "production" of experts and professionals who are found to torture, how long do we wait before we conclude that the curriculum at the academy leads to this behavior? If the academy's graduates are not condemned and future students of offending nations are not barred from the academy, do students not gain an understanding of what expected and acceptable behaviors are taken to be? These questions are not merely abstract and rhetorical.[34]

The professionalization of Latin American police forces was the object of the International Police Academy and the International Police Services, Inc., the latter a CIA-sponsored organization that also had students from Asia and Africa.[35] Graduates of the academy often returned home to practice their trade with exemplary zeal. Arthur John Langguth reported that students at the International Police Academy (IPA) were shown Pontecorvo's *Battle of Algiers*. "The film portrayed policemen loyal to France regrouping at night into secret squads that wreaked reprisals on Algerian nationalists, bombing their homes and killing their families."[36] The message was clear even if the advice was indirect. If politicals were evading the police and security services because the judicial process was not equal to the task, the security services could take it upon themselves to administer justice. Thus although official IPA policy was against torture and so on, students seem to have become proficient at interrogation while enrolled. Knowledge of the establishment of the *Esquadrao da Morte* ("Death Squad") in Brazil did not reduce American assistance to Brazilian security efforts. Similar efforts in other nations were accepted for long periods without sanction by the United States. Communism and instability were considered more important enemies than "due process" violations and state-sponsored and supported terror practices. Death squads have appeared in ten Latin American states whose military and police were supported and trained by the United States.

States also have been willing in the past decade to help provide other states with the tools of the terror trade. Steve Wright, Michael Klare, and Cynthia Arnson made clear that the new technologies of repression are widely available and easily distributed.[37] The United States has been an active provider of the instruments of terrorism and repression to Third World client states to employ on their populations and also in a number of cases to train the security services of these societies in the proper employment of these instruments.[38] It is a lucrative trade, and the U.S. government has been an active assistant to U.S. corporations in the purveyance of their wares.

Other Western governments similarly assisted their national corporations in this regard, and the Soviet Union has sought needed hard currency by supplying small (and large) arms to willing purchasers. When in November 1979 the Carter administration informed the Shah of Iran that his administration would continue to back the Peacock Throne and sent tear gas, police batons, protective vests, and other riot control equipment, it was clear that even a president reviled by his conservative critics for being ''soft'' and placing human rights above security was not going to deny the instruments of repression (which were used for terror purposes as well) to an ally in need. This followed, of course, upon the heels of Carter's post–Black Friday (September 8, 1979) phone call to the Shah in which he reiterated U.S. support and hopes for continued liberalization following the imposition of martial law and the gunning down of somewhere between 700 and 2,000 people.[39] In the end, the Shah's use of terror fell short. Once the population, en masse, had indicated they were not afraid to continue to die in order to rid themselves of the Shah, the threat of death that the security forces could present no longer was politically meaningful. On the other hand, the reaction of many American policy makers and particularly those of the new administration is important in this regard. The presumption appears to be that the Shah's regime fell in the end because the Carter administration was unwilling to provide *enough* military hardware and possibly the actual employment of American troops to prevent the overthrow. The U.S. use of surrogate terror thus apparently also fell short of providing the ''proper ending.'' But it was not for lack of trying and most importantly not because policy makers assumed that such strategies were illegitimate.

CONCLUSION

The preceding pages thus argue that strategies and tactics of terrorism have become integral components of the foreign policy instruments of the modern state. As in the domestic realm, the practice of terror, when identified as such, brings almost universal condemnation. But as in the domestic realm, when it is the state that is the perpetrator of the terrorist act, few even pause to label the action as such. States and proponents of their actions shrink from labeling what they themselves do as terror, preferring more ''neutral'' designations such as coercive diplomacy, nuclear deterrence, and assistance to a friendly state in its pursuit of internal security.

This chapter has reviewed three dimensions of state terror in international relations. As we have seen, there is much evidence of the regular use of terror in international affairs. But as long as scholars are unwilling to consider these behaviors as constituting the practice of terror, they will continue to fail to understand these processes and their implications for international relations. Scholars have invested great energy in the past two decades in the study of terror; it is now time to study the actors that have been the most persistent and successful users of the strategy.

NOTES

1. For certain types of states, such as First World states that do not widely practice terrorist policies at home, this is perhaps more so. For a fuller explanation, see Raymond D. Duvall and Michael Stohl, "Governance by Terror," in Michael Stohl (ed.), *The Politics of Terrorism* 2nd Edition, Rev. (New York: Marcel Dekker, 1983). For a discussion of the conditions of state terrorism in domestic and international affairs, see Raymond Duvall, Michael Stohl, and James Austin, "Terrorism as Foreign Policy" (Paper presented to the Annual Meeting of the International Studies Association, Mexico City, April 1983).

2. For a discussion of the development of national interest and its relation to the use of force and terrorism by states in international affairs, see Michael Stohl, "National Interests and State Terrorism" (Paper presented to the Annual Meeting of the Southwest Social Science Association, San Antonio, March 1982).

3. Alexander Kendrick, *The Wound Within* (Boston: Little, Brown, 1974), p. 383.

4. John Stoessinger, *Henry Kissinger: The Anguish of Power* (New York: Norton, 1976), p. 73.

5. Begin's statement and that of the unidentified official were reported on radio news broadcasts.

6. James Nathan and James Oliver, *United States Foreign Policy and World Order* (Boston: Little, Brown, 1981), p. 378.

7. Walter LaFeber, *America, Russia, and the Cold War, 1945-1980*, 4th Edition (New York: John Wiley and Sons, 1980), p. 287.

8. Stephen Kaplan, *Diplomacy of Power* (Washington, D.C.: The Brookings Institution, 1981).

9. Kaplan, *Diplomacy of Power*, p. 34.

10. Ibid., p. 39.

11. Ibid.

12. Johnson's statement is reprinted by Cecil Crabb, *American Foreign Policy in the Nuclear Age*, 3rd Edition (New York: Harper and Row, 1972), p. 31.

13. Thomas M. Franck and Edward Weisband, *World Politics* (New York: Oxford University Press, 1972), pp. 96-113.

14. A fuller discussion of the conventional distinctions is provided by Duvall and Stohl, "Governance by Terror."

15. Thomas Schelling, "Thinking About Nuclear Terrorism," *International Security*, Vol. 6, No. 4 (Spring 1982), pp. 61-77. This quotation is from page 67.

16. Michael Walzer, *Just and Unjust Wars* (New York: Basic Books, 1978), p. 272.

17. Schelling, "Thinking About Nuclear Terrorism," p. 66.

18. Ibid., pp. 67, 70.

19. Barry Blechman and Stephen Kaplan, *Force Without War* (Washington, D.C.: The Brookings Institution, 1976), p. 48. Milton Leitenberg, "Threats of the Use of Nuclear Weapons Since World War II," in Asbjorn Eide and Marek Thee (eds.), *Problems of Contemporary Militarism* (New York: St. Martin's, 1980), p. 389, argued that this list should be considered only partial.

20. Schelling, "Thinking About Nuclear Terrorism," p. 66.

21. Kaplan, *Diplomacy of Power*, p. 54.

22. Warren Hinkle and William Turner documented the U.S. alliance with anti-Castro terrorists and the ramifications of this policy without and within the United States in *The*

Fish Is Red (New York: Harper and Row, 1981). This Cuban connection played a significant part in the assassination of Orlando Letelier by the Chilean DINA and is discussed in Saul Landau and John Dinges, *Assassination on Embassy Row* (New York: Pantheon, 1980); Donald Freed, with Fred Landis, *Death in Washington* (Westport, Connecticut: Lawrence Hill and Co., 1980); and Taylor Branch and Eugene Propper, *Labyrinth* (New York: Viking, 1982).

23. Victor Marchetti and John Marks, *The CIA and the Cult of Intelligence* (New York: Dell, 1974), p. 108.

24. Ibid., p. 114.

25. Robert C. Johansen, *The National Interest and the Human Interest* (Princeton, N.J.: Princeton University Press, 1980), p. 210.

26. James Petras and Morris Morley, *The United States and Chile: Imperialism and the Overthrow of the Allende Government* (New York: Monthly Review Press, 1975), and Tad Szulc, *The Illusion of Peace* (New York: Viking, 1978), provide much detail on the overthrow of Allende and the policy-making process in the United States in regard to the overthrow.

27. Alvin Z. Rubinstein, *Soviet Foreign Policy Since World War II: Imperial and Global* (Cambridge, Massachusetts: Winthrop, 1981), pp. 214-235.

28. Ibid., p. 254.

29. Alexander Haig, "News Conference," *Current Policy No. 258* (Washington, D.C.: United States Department of State, January 28, 1981), p. 5.

30. The *New York Times* has had a series of news analyses following this story. See Philip Taubman, "U.S. Tries to Backup Haig on Terrorism," *New York Times*, May 3, 1981, p. 1; Robert Pear "F.B.I. Chief Sees No Evidence Soviet Aids Terrorism in U.S.," *New York Times*, April 27, 1981, p. 8; Judith Miller "Soviet Aid Disputed in Terrorism Studies," *New York Times*, March 29, 1981, p. 4.

31. *Time* (June 8, 1981), p. 30.

32. Terence Smith, "Israeli and Arab Agents Go On Killing—Each Other," *New York Times*, January 16, 1977, IV, p. 4.

33. W. Scott Thompson, *Ghana's Foreign Policy, 1957-66* (Princeton, N.J.: Princeton University Press, 1969), pp. 388-389.

34. Nor should they be considered as outside the scope of the policy-makers' concern, as Henry Kissinger apparently thought. When the U.S. ambassador protested the torture methods of the newly installed Pinochet government, Secretary of State Kissinger is reported to have ordered him "to cut out the political science lectures." Roger Morris, *Uncertain Greatness* (New York: Harper and Row, 1965), pp. 239-244; *New York Times*, March 6, 1975, p. 37. The citations are taken from LaFeber, *America, Russia, and the Cold War*, p. 278.

35. Arthur John Langguth, *Hidden Terrors* (New York: Pantheon, 1978), p. 124.

36. Ibid., p. 120.

37. Steve Wright, "An Assessment of the New Technologies of Repression," in M. Hoefnagels (ed.), *Repression and Repressive Violence* (Amsterdam: Swets and Zeitlinger, 1977), pp. 133-165; Steve Wright, "New Police Technologies," *Journal of Peace Research*, Vol. XV, No. 4 (1978), pp. 3035-3322; Michael Klare and Cynthia Arnson, *Supplying Repression* (Washington, D.C.: Institute for Policy Studies, 1981).

38. For a discussion of U.S. operations in Latin America, see Langguth, *Hidden Terrors*. For the U.S. role in Iran, see Barry Rubin, *Paved with Good Intentions* (New

York: Penguin, 1981): For a discussion of the phenomenon in general, see Noam Chomsky and Edward Herman, *The Washington Connection and Third World Fascism* (Boston: South End Press, 1979).

39. Rubin, *Paved with Good Intentions*, p. 214.

3

A Scheme for the Analysis of Government as Terrorist

George A. Lopez

This chapter constructs a framework by which detailed study and systematic comparison of governments that consistently rely on the use of terror to control their citizenry might proceed. In keeping with the general distinction postulated in the introduction, among oppression, repression, and terrorism, I focus specifically here on the political climate and circumstances surrounding the initiation of terror practices and policies; the variety of ideologies that serve to legitimize government terror; the particular array of terror tactics employed by rulers; the mechanisms that support purposeful acts of violence and threats of violence by government against its people; and the outcomes of the dynamic of state terror.

In many respects this chapter commences where John McCamant's argument concludes. I employ the most basic tool of social science investigation, the development of a taxonomy with citation of appropriate empirical referents, to begin to delineate what for so long has evaded our inquiry: styles of rule in which the attachment of electronic devices to human sexual organs during questioning; detention without statement of charges or promise of trial; and the rape, murder, and mutilation of "undesirable" citizens have become standard political practice. In so doing, I examine a complex array of factors descriptive of and associated with the dynamic of state terror. At this early stage of investigation, I have chosen not to develop a logically related and mutually exclusive set of categories, and I have consciously rejected the positing of a causal model. There is no question that these tasks are essential to thorough scholarship in this area. But such approaches must emerge from analyses such as this essay in order for researchers to further delimit the parameters of state terror, its development, and its sustenance.

THE POLITICAL CLIMATE SURROUNDING THE INITIATION OF STATE TERROR

The first major factor to scrutinize involves the political climate surrounding the initiation of terrorism as a government practice. Scholars of anti-state group terror have gone to great pains to sketch the complex mix of socio-political ingredients that gave rise to this brand of revolutionary violence in the past fifteen years. Group terror emerged against the background of the failure of the revolution of rising expectations of the late 1960s in the developing world[1] and in light of the increased bureaucratization of government structures in the advanced industrial world.[2] Although there certainly were national and cultural circumstances that made the character of anti-state terrorism by the Tupamaros in Uruguay distinct from that of the Liberation Front of Quebec (FLQ) in Quebec, most scholars agreed on the explanatory power of the contours of the political environments in which each terror group operated.[3]

No less useful for the analysis of government as terrorist becomes the character and condition of the political atmosphere as official violence begins. In an examination of the state as terrorist, an investigation of background political circumstances operative at the time permits us to assess how, and possibly why, government availed itself of this form of social control and political power. Two dimensions of the political climate will be explored: the "state" of the state and the manner in which the government develops and executes terror policy.

By the "state" of the state, I mean those historical events that precede terror action by goverment with a focus specifically on those changes in government structure and/or leadership that make rule by harsh and arbitrary force more viable, defensible, and advisable than under prior conditions. In terms of the literature of comparative political violence, the most interesting cases on which to dwell in the analysis of the "state" of the state fall under the rubric of regime change.[4]

First, we examine the development of terror following the deposition of a dictatorial ruler. Under such circumstances, whether it ascended to power via coup d'état or through more widespread revolt, and particularly after a long-term rule by force of its predecessor, pressures operate on the new regime in two directions. On the one hand, the new rulers want to build processes and institutions distinct from the autocratic style of the past. In the place of harsh, arbitrary, and particularistic policies and actions, they would like to erect more standardized, open, and universalistic modes of government and societal operation and change.

On the other hand, however, the toppling of the central political power may have unleashed a host of factions that despite their union against the common enemy of the past, now desire either to garner the spoils of political victory or to vie for full governmental power with the ruling faction. In the latter case, sometimes compounded by concerns about external threats, the new government feels extreme pressure to consolidate power. In such a situation, short of full-scale purges or campaigns of extermination, a government may resort to terror tactics such as detention legislation, press censorship, travel restrictions, and even the economic coercion of certain groups.

An analysis of political environments such as this permits a comparison of policies pursued by ruling groups reacting to perceived and real challenges to their ability to conduct affairs of state. The factional and ethnic violence that continues to permeate government policy in Uganda can be compared with the large-scale executions that occurred during the first two years of the Khomeni regime in Iran. Similarly, both of these polities can be juxtaposed against the government-initiated political changes unfolding in Ethiopia after the demise of the Selassie dynasty and in Nicaragua since the fall of Somoza.

A second regime change with implications for the study of government terror occurs when ruling elites in societies undergoing increased pressure for social, economic, and political reform appear to find no way (or consciously choose to find no way) of translating these forces into the development of more effective rule. Rather, the government, whether democratic or autocratic, capitalist or socialist, civilian or military, begins to respond to the changing national environment with a curtailment of civil and human rights, with increased militant policies of coercive control of collective and individual behavior. In its final stages of development this ruling style stimulates a general system of repressive practices and policies designed to maintain the power of the incumbents and the benefits accruing to their allies.

Of all types of dynamic changes in the "state" of the state, this pattern is the most pervasive in the recent political history of Second and Third World states. It leads to questions concerning the particular political, legal, or extra-legal mechanisms that actualize these alterations in governance and of the ideologies or symbolic constructs that spark and legitimize them. This form of rule has clearly emerged as a reaction to pressure for internal change of either government policies and/or social structure. The government response has been to withstand such pressure via new methods of persuasion, enforcement, and coercive rule called "state terror."

The course of events that developed in Brazil after the military coup of 1964 and in the Philippines under the reign of Marcos clearly fits this pattern. The scenario developed more quickly in Uruguay in the early 1970s, beginning as the counterterrorist policy of a democratic government and ending in the dissolution of that democracy under authoritarian military rule. The terror response, with large-scale social consequences, came even more rapidly to Chile with the overthrow of Allende by the armed forces in September 1973 and to Poland in late 1981 with the crushing of the Solidarity trade union movement and the imposition of martial law on the nation as a whole.

The third and most distinct variety of regime change that may give rise to the dynamic of state terrorism occurs in the aftermath of a major civil war.[5] Here the pressures toward centralization of control mentioned above in connection with the disposition of an autocratic ruler are pushed to their extreme. Murder, torture, and kidnapping as state policy can bring the victory gained in the formal military struggle to its "logical" conclusion via the elimination of groups and persons hostile to the perspective of the victors. Such acts of extermination seem to have unfolded in the final phases of the Russian revolution and in Vietnam and Cambodia in the late 1970s. Beyond this, terror presents itself as a powerful and persuasive mode of accomplishing post-revolutionary goals such as changes in the distribution of wealth, land holdings, and the structure of the educational system. In varying degrees this occurred after the Mexican revolution of 1917 and the Chinese civil war in the late 1940s. Although some detention and special security measures still exist "on the books," it appears that only Zimbabwe serves as a modern case where post-revolutionary goals and practice involved the loosening rather than the tightening of coercive control of the state.[6]

Another consideration under the rubric of political climate relates to the manner of institutionalizing state terrorism. By the "institutionalizing of state terror," I mean how a governmental elite develops and implements a program of terror in the context of the political climate and political system in which they find themselves. The aim of this categorization is to permit us to distinguish between those regimes that clearly invoke terror as a cautious, temporary, and limited policy approach and those who opt for state terror as a full-scale and legitimate government policy. Underlying this approach then are a number of alternatives and tensions that are explored in some detail below.

Of primary concern to students of government terror is whether acts of government terror emerge in a spontaneous and uncoordinated fashion or whether they develop out of a conscious and a priori decision to conduct politics in this fashion. In terms of the former, terror acts may be expressions of revenge or an "in-the-field" reaction to the changing conditions of factional conflict. Such appeared to be the situation in the Garissa section of Kenya (hardly a repressive country) in 1980. In response to the murder of a number of government officials, the security forces, according to Amnesty International:

engaged in reprisals against ethnic Somalis in Garissa. They reportedly burned down a section of the town, committed numerous assaults, and killed an unknown number of people. Virtually the whole ethnic Somalis population of Garissa was rounded up and detained for several hours; some were held under these conditions for two days without food or water. Many ethnic Somalis living in other parts of Kenya were also arrested for short periods and interrogated. By April 1981 no one had been charged in connection with the murders in Garissa.[7]

Further along the continuum that begins with sporadic and unpremeditated terror and ends with systematic repression and government involvement in all atrocities, we have those actions considered counterterrorist policies. Most notably, critics and analysts concerned about the overreaction of the state have pointed to Italy, where detention legislation was adopted that permits the government to hold those suspected of involvement with terrorist activity for forty-eight hours without notification of any outside contacts. Similarly, when Canada witnessed a wave of FLQ kidnappings, some observers wondered about the implicit power and potential of the state in counterterror as Prime Minister Trudeau responded to a reporter's question about possible government "overreaction'' in invoking martial law measures: "How far will we go? Just watch me."[8]

Charges of government security force atrocities in El Salvador and South Africa in recent years clearly fit into the cases of spontaneous and local terror but with an important twist: these acts are tolerated or encouraged based on the official, but unarticulated, policy that more general "toughness" is necessary in dealing with civil strife attacks on the government or those loyal to it. At the end point of the scale, those cases of premeditated torture, arrest, and extermination are well documented. They begin with Robespierre and end with contemporary practices of Chile and Argentina.

Another area of examination is whether there appears de facto reasons for the government to invoke extraordinarily harsh and repressive measures, or whether the government appears to be engaging in unilateral and unprovoked actions. In the former case, we might examine the problems of the Uruguayan government in the late 1960s as it attempted to respond to the pervasive action, philosophy, and numbers of citizens involved in the Tupamaro movement. Basically, President Bordaberry yielded to military and some civilian pressure for state-of-siege legislation and in doing so began the process of the demise of civilian democracy in Uruguay. The combination of economic instability, internal attacks from the terrorist group, and increasing control of the military proved too much to bear.

On the other end of the scale are the worst and classic cases of state repressors. Hitler, Stalin, and Amin all perceived enemies that had to be squelched. But their individual acts and the policies they developed clearly cast a much larger net and can be seen as unprovoked and actions beyond reasonable reasons of state. In the middle point on this dimension might be the government of Colombia, which has been in a perennial state of siege for the past twenty years as it attempts to quell political violence, banditry, and other "uprisings."

In Eugene Walter's classic anthropological analysis, he devoted some substantial attention to the practice of the ruling-group recruitment of "the king's knives" as the artisans of state terror.[9] This raises a central question for the contemporary and cross-national study of such repression: what is the level of involvement of governmental leaders and how do they ensure that the policy and process of terror is expedited?

The options we need to investigate and for which we already have some anecdotal evidence in the affairs of states include:

The "toleration" by government of the terror actions of "popular" or vigilante groups against segments of the population that the government would rather be rid of under most circumstances. This, of course, is the case of the early phases of the Argentine Anti-Communist Alliance and in the operation of Escuadrao Da Morte of Brazil.

The use of secret police or special paramilitary units for internal security purposes. These groups have a high level of technology backing them and often a high degree of independence. Hitler's SS and Gestapo constitute a classic case with the Shah's SAVAK a more current example. This form ties in directly with training and technology as discussed later in this essay.

The use of government armed forces in an organized and direct way to terrorize individuals or groups. This often develops as a response by government to what it claims was illegal or intolerable behavior on the part of the group. Salvadoran and South African troop raids on neighborhoods and villages constitute cases in point in their respective contexts.

Governmental decree or some form of legislative action that legitimizes any of the tactics previously listed or empowers the state to engage more freely and openly in any of the above. South African racial registration and settlement laws fit well here. This style of government involvement has become sufficiently complex so that it warrants further discussion below.

The final theme for consideration under the mechanisms that governments use to institutionalize their rule of terror poses the tension between opting for extra-constitutional or extra-systematic acts and policies and the adoption (legitimation) of certain policies that yield for the state a legal basis of repressive rule. This may be one of the more sophisticated mechanisms and complex phenomena to analyze in the cross-national study of state terror in the near future.

The traditional pattern of government terror is well known: the ruling group suspends the constitution, invokes a state of emergency, and rules by the guarantee and ''legality'' of force. Not until the government issues a number of decrees do the average citizens come to know what types of political action or behavior on their part will be considered a threat to the state and hence illegal. What is curious abut the current development or more appropriately the maturation of such rule by force and decree is that in a number of political systems we witness the institutionalization of such measures via approval of or promise of a parliamentary or semi-democratic system.

Although the ability of Hitler to architect the 1935 Nuremburg laws or the various rulers of South Africa to pass discriminatory legislation ought not to surprise students of political science, the contemporary wave of legislative approval of repressive laws is more intriguing. In a nation such as Uruguay, for example, where most estimates claim that one in every fifty persons has at some time been interrogated by the government about his or her activities, contacts, or relatives, we have a situation where all viable political opposition has been killed, imprisoned, or so thoroughly intimidated that virtually no questioning of the constitutional plebiscite of November 1980 occurs. The result: the population at large ratifies a document that not only ''legally'' ends the democratic constitution of 1967, but also legitimates the systematic violations of human rights by actions of the armed forces and absence of judiciary procedures after arrest that have characterized the political system since 1971.[10]

In Brazil and Chile a more subtle pattern has developed. President Figueirdo has been able to appease both internal and external, Left and Right, critics of his regime. On the one hand, via his evolutionary program of liberalization called *abertura*, he has promised an easing of the system of government repression that is concluding its second decade of existence. On the other hand, both to protect the order and stability that have assured Brazil economic progress in recent years, *and* to guarantee that no radical group or faction will abuse the coming of more democratic possibilities, the government has had the national assembly legitimize the state national security law, which is similar to the Uruguayan legislation noted above.

In Chile a referendum in March 1981 put in place a new constitution and formally replaced the 1925 democratic constitution, which had been politically nonexistent since the 1973 Pinochet coup. The "liberal" and promising part of the document is that the character of rule initiated in 1973 will end—in 1997! Until that time, or in exchange for such a guarantee, the new constitution virtually guarantees the legality of techniques of arrest and torture for particular patterns of thought, expression, or association.[11]

The curious irony of these measures in Uruguay, Brazil, and Chile is that the governing elite appears to go to great pains to constitutionalize its ruling style. Furthermore, after establishing coercive control over the population and its assembled "representatives," they attempt the semblance or promise of a less repressive order. They then obtain the mandate that legitimizes their claim that the best way to ensure democracy and human rights for future generations is to ban them for the time being.

IDEOLOGY

A second general factor of significant import to the study of state terror is the ideology of the ruling group of the state. As Roy Macridis has defined it, "an ideology consists of a set of ideas and beliefs through which we perceive our outside world and act upon our information. It is a medium through which we try to learn and comprehend the world: but it also generates emotions which hold people together. Finally, ideologies are action-oriented. That is, they consist of ideas shared by many people who act in unison or who are influenced to act in unison in order to accomplish posited ends."[12]

In the classification and comparison of group terrorism, ideology has proved to be a very powerful discriminator among groups. We can clearly illustrate the differences in a host of other group characteristics and group tactics by knowing that the ideology of minority nationalism guides actors like the South Molloccans, Basques, and Croatians, and a revolutionary Marxist ideology undergirds the activities of M-19 in Colombia or the history of the Tupamaros of Uruguay.[13] Thus a similar approach to government terror may prove fruitful.

Here I focus on four distinct ideologies, including *authoritarianism, militarism, national security consciousness*, and *patriarchy*. In a description and explanation of state terrorism, ideology, in its discrete types as discussed below and especially in its interlocking nature, serves as a *sine qua non*. It stimulates, rationalizes, and blesses as patriotic political behavior government actions that deny others their basic human dignity and their universal political rights. It reifies the state, making it the highest institutional value to which the ruling elite must maintain their highest commitment. Although other factors noted in this chapter are important components of the puzzle of state terror, they would not fit so neatly together or be mobilized so dynamically were it not for the perspective and prescription provided by ideology.[14]

More than any other ideological factor, scholars have focused at length on increases in *authoritarianism* as directly linked to increases in government terror and repression. A significant refinement of the focus of authoritarianism in its traditional sense in political science comes from the work of David Collier, which synthesized the work of Guillermo O'Donnell and Fernando Cardoso into a full bureaucratic-authoritarian model with three components: "(1) The central role in the dominant coalition of a highly internationalized and oligopolized bourgeoisie; (2) Rule by the military as an institution—as opposed to rule by one or a few military leaders; and (3) The relationship with the agricultural sector."[15]

Although this contribution is important for identifying the structural dynamics of and the organizing mind set that undergirds repression, the model is generated by and verified from the Latin American experience only. Thus scholars interested in the role of the authoritarian ideology as a component of the development of state terror might be better advised to examine the recent work of Richard Falk.[16] Although Falk's vision of authoritarianism is broad and would subsume as indicators of it some form of those ideas and trends discussed below as ideologies distinct from authoritarianism, his perspective permits comparison across diverse polities and political cultures.

In approaching the general worldwide tendency toward an authoritarian style of rule, Falk suggested that this becomes operationalized differently in different political systems. In the First World sector, for example, capitalist systems opt for trilateralization and socialist for Stalinization. The authoritarian mode of the southern (developing)-area capitalist systems is Brazilianization, with Leninization being the corresponding trend in socialist nations. For those southern-area states without a significant industrial sector, authoritarianism takes the form of Praetorianization.[17]

The contribution of Falk's thesis to our understanding of state terror across diverse political cultures and ideologies is clear: imbued with the firm sense that the development and nurturing of the centralized state and its functions in the political, economic, military, and social order is the highest good, governing elites impose a harsh discipline on the polity as a whole. In some political systems this will take the form of technocracy controlling phases of life from information to economic livelihood; in others it will demand a network of secret police, "emergency" policies for the suspension of political and human rights; and in others to a history of a thoroughly intimidated population that knows well (and therefore acts accordingly) the repressive potential of the state.

One of the advantages of the Falk approach to authoritarian rule is that it permits a distinct analysis of militarism, which serves as a component of Collier's analysis of the Latin American authoritarian pattern. As a distinct ideology, *militarism* involves changes in the values, psychology, economy, and politics of the nation.[18] In addition to visible manifestations of the militarization of the nation, via an increase in the political role of the military, increased armaments, and the development of military-tied industrialization, changing notions of the rule of law and the role of force in the polity are central. Values of loyalty and patterns of recruitment and socialization to organs of the state change. Questions of national honor take on heightened importance. Whereas authoritarianism provides the sense to rulers in government that they embody and personify the state, militarism produces for the rulers a social sense (and often the means) of the legitimacy of vigilance (that is, terror tactics) in acting for the state.

In the development of motivations and rationales for state terror, two other ideologies, each much less scrutinized than authoritarianism and militarism, warrant close attention. In many respects these latter two, national security consciousness and patriarchy, combine with the two more prominent modes of thought to form a logically related package for explaining and justifying continuous repression.

National security consciousness is a set of ideas about the tasks of geopolitical security and economic development in the post-World War II world and the crucial role that governing elites play in these distinct but highly related processes. As explained by John Child, with particular reference to the Latin American scene, geopolitical thought:

involves an intellectual approach to internal development and foreign policy in which power politics and the need to struggle to survive in a hostile world are major concerns. Geopolitics as an intellectual approach had declined in respectability in Western Europe and the United States after World War II, but retained its vitality in the military circles of the Southern Cone; because of the way United States strategic thinking dominated the Western Hemisphere until the late 1960's little attention was paid to this current of thought.[19]

Its importance to a consideration of the domestic dynamics of government terror is clear. Concerns about internal security in general, and about internal strife in particular, derive directly from the geopolitical bent that involves regional/international projection of power, a settlement of border problems through force rather than negotiation, and the assumption that one's neighbors stand perched at your borders, eager to take advantage of your imminent decline in power. Geopolitical thinking mobilizes the search for the conspiracies that lurk within to destabilize programs of national development and to assist external enemies.[20]

Another linkage between the geopolitical predisposition of leaders and the onset of state terror can be found in William Hazelton's analysis of small state foreign policy behavior in the inter-American system.[21] He claimed that, given the pressure placed on leaders because of the geopolitical imperative, governments will often engage in stringent internal security measures due to the real or imagined external threat. The presence of a real threat constitutes a particularly intriguing case, since national leaders play the role of repressor to "protect" their citizens from the wrath of the external aggressor. Alternatively, to ensure one's sovereignty vis-à-vis large patron states, small state leaders engage in harsh measures as a show of force for the external audience that "needs to" sense the government control and inherent stability of the client state.

Although developed with the Latin context in mind, the geopolitical assumption appears a useful and timely framework in light of the imposition of martial law in Poland at the end of 1981 under the assumed and imminent invasion of the Soviet Union or Warsaw Pact states. The argument that the willingness of the Afghan armed forces to engage in continued hostilities against their own people to reach the goal of removal of Soviet troops fits this pattern well. The extent to which the ideology permits the interface of internal security with external crisis also begs for a thorough investigation of the connection between external militant policies of the Galtieri regime in Argentina during the Falklands War and the politics of internal terror for which Argentina has become noteworthy.

The second component of national security consciousness focuses on economic development. As first articulated as a pattern of thinking in international affairs and national political economy[22] and later as a doctrine of substantial force in the mind sets of Latin leaders, the doctrine of national economic development in security consciousness calls on leaders to exercise the same uncompromising resolve in approaching the political and economic problems of development as they do in the pursuit of military goals during war. In doing so, the ideology's problématique, in the words of Genaro Arriagada Herrera, unfolds:

The nature of war only allows a single relationship, friend or enemy. It does not tolerate intermediaries or shades of gray. In politics, on the other hand, nothing is more dangerous than adventurous generalizations. Not to recognize the disparity of interests that exist in society, to deny the enormous plurality of conflicts which in society crisscross vertically and horizontally, is simply to deny the possibility of legitimacy and consensus, and to begin to move toward dictatorship and terror as a form of government. The world of the relationship of war is extremely simple; that of politics is disturbingly complex.[23]

Child added a further note that provides the final underscoring of the link between this espoused pattern of thought and rule by terror: "The Doctrine argues that it is dangerous for developing nations under threat of subversion to permit full and free democratic processes because this tends to give the subversives a free hand; furthermore, these open democratic processes are usually accompanied by a tendency towards populism and demagoguery which leads to a welfare state which in turn limits the nation's ability to modernize and preserve its military strength."[24]

The final distinct ideology to discuss may well raise the rancor of some social scientists, but it appears too pervasive to exclude. Whereas authoritarianism, militarism, and national security consciousness are directly observable in the individual behaviors and actions of leaders and can be dissected from government documents and speeches, the ideology of *patriarchy* is much more elusive. Just as John Sloan argues strongly elsewhere in this volume that repression by government emanates historically from Latin political culture and thus constitutes an almost unconscious but constraining environment in which to forge a participatory and democratic political system, so too patriarchy operates but at the individual and group level of political behavior.

As Sheila Ruth has astutely synthesized, the dynamic of patriarchy operates on two interlocking levels in the socialization of boys and in their subsequent behavior as cultural males. First, the emphasis on masculinity demands the assumption of warrior-hero characteristics: a proclivity for violence, an aura of the fighter, and an explicit rejection of those characteristics associated with the frail and womanly aspects of human beings: sensitivity, pity, emotionality, tenderness toward others, and so on.[25]

The second dimension, the machismo element of masculinity, appears crucial for an understanding of the impact of this ideology, however unconscious, on national leaders who rule by terror. It develops the image of

the bad boy, of mischief that can and sometimes does slip into downright evil. The configuration is not an aberration, peripheral to masculinity. It is essential. Encouraged by parents (Trouble, trouble, trouble; isn't he all boy?), tolerated in school, and enhanced by sports, military traditions, and many rites of passage—the bachelor dinner, for example, Friday night with the boys, or "sowing wild oats"—machismo is real and present. Although its expression may vary with class, race, or location, it forms an important part of the male world view, for its alternative is the sissy/goody-two-shoes, an object of ridicule and rejection.[26]

Patriarchy, then, in its dual image of the warrior-hero and the machismo syndrome of masculinity predisposes leaders in Latin and Arab cultures in particular, but not exclusively, to behaviors that hold them above the boring convention of international law and morality. Furthermore, it permits them to distance themselves from and fully technocracize torture, brutal means of interrogation, and the rape and murder of innocent people for the purposes of the state. Its most common manifestation in the political jargon of governance lies in the traditional and sarcastic Latin American assessment of the limits that constitutions place on national leaders: "I comply but I do not obey."

THE CHARACTER OF STATE TERROR

The character of state terror constitutes our third general factor for examination. Within this category we investigate the types of atrocities that may be perpetrated by government, the targets/message complex, and the technologies available to the state terror apparatus.

Relatively little scholarly work has been done in the area of terror tactics available to governments since such analyses are left to documentation agencies like Amnesty International and "survivor" or journalistic accounts. This presents a challenge to those interested in the systematic analysis of state terror because writers on nongovernmental terror housed in the RAND Corporation and the Central Intelligence Agency, in particular, have engaged in sophisticated data-collection analysis of various types of group-terrorist acts.[27]

Organized in the following list are the alternatives that a state may operationalize against its population according to tactics designed to terrorize through information control, economic coercion, control of legal and law enforcement mechanisms, and those that appear directly life threatening.

Alternative Techniques Available to the State as Terrorist

Information Control
Surveillance of personal activity via wiretapping, "bodyguarding," and so on
Attachments/falsification of personal documents and records
Press censorship
"Thought reform"

Law Enforcement/Legal
Legislation of a discriminatory bent
Expulsions/exile
No protection against the crimes and terrors of other citizens
Direct and arbitrary arrest

Economic Coercion
Economic discrimination
Extortion/bribery
"Guilt" due to one's economic associations or activities

Life Threatening
Direct attacks-beating/bombing of home or business/letter bomb
Kidnapping/disappearance
Threats on one's family
Torture and interrogation when under government control

For purposes of both careful social science investigation and citizen understanding of policy, an important qualifying point must be made as we examine these techniques. The modern state and its ruling government are by definition coercive. In the culture of the United States, citizens are coerced under penalty of law to file income tax reports by April 15 annually. In even the most egalitarian of societies, some groups at some time are going to feel that a given piece of legislation is aimed discriminatorily at them. The issue then is not that all techniques, particularly those housed within the information control and economic rubrics, are inherently repressive or terrorist. Rather, for all multiple tactics available to the state, we must examine closely the context and circumstances surrounding their development and implementation.

A few criteria apply here. First, the tactics should be considered in light of prior attempts of government to deal with the problem or issue it claims the new tactic is designed to handle. Here the role of groups external to the state, like Amnesty International, play an important role as they seek to decipher if new and extraordinary means aimed at violence or threat to violence are arbitrarily being applied. Under consideration as well comes an analysis of the sequencing and array of actions. For example, it has often been considered a relatively minor and acceptable act of state, in time of war, to control the flow of information, as the British seem to have done in the Falklands War. But to follow this action, under the auspices of national security, with arrests of those who opposed the war effort would have overstepped the bounds that most British would grant to the legitimate coercive control of the state even in crisis circumstances.

Second, we would certainly examine the "state" of the state based on the considerations sketched earlier. Third, if the ruling group has gone to great pains to justify the techniques within a much larger vision of the state, it might indicate direct linkage between some of the ideological dimensions discussed previously and the modus operandi being outlined. Finally, analysts would want to be particularly concerned about the relationship between perpetrators of certain acts and targets. In fact, the interrelationship between targets and the messages that government terror means to send comprises a second area for study in the character of government terror.

In the comparative analysis of nonstate terror, the dynamic of the terror act intertwines directly with the selection of targets and the determination of the type of message the atrocity is to send to the target and wider social audience. Whereas the nonstate terrorist group may simply want to force a bargaining situation, achieve publicity, or provoke government repression,[28] the terror act of the state may not be designed to be as interactive. But what are the messages? Which targets are selected and why? Is this a "rational" process explained in large part by the dominant ideology of the rulers?

Although there may be some indications of how to respond to these queries, full-scale answers are not yet available. Some patterns do warrant attention since we are able to distinguish among governments that engage in terror against only political opponents and those ruling elites that cast their net extremely broadly. The latter operated in the first days of the Pinochet regime, when some 30,000 were detained, and with the Argentinian government, which has been held responsible for the disappearance of more than that number since 1976. Also, especially harsh and premeditated types of acts that indicate the depth of repressive action can be analyzed.

Of particular concern has been the recent pattern of governments that conduct extensive search campaigns beyond their own borders. Although Stohl has noted in a prior chapter the activities of DINA and other state organs in celebrated assassinations, it is important to point out that the national surveys of Amnesty International are reporting a dramatic increase in both kidnapping of those labeled former dissidents and the harassment, assassination, and kidnapping of family members of political undesirables, some of whom were already "executed" by the government.

A second target group whose selection carries substantial message about the scope and direction of government resolve in a terror campaign are members of the legal system, particularly lawyers and judges. Bert Lockwood recounted some of the dynamics of this terror that have confronted students and colleagues from other nations. The stories have become typical:

> Juan Mendez was one of my students at American University. Juan was an Argentinian lawyer. He was one of eight lawyers in his community who were willing to handle "political" cases. Juan was lucky. He was the first of these lawyers to be arrested and tortured—after which he sought asylum in this country. His seven legal colleagues disappeared in the night never to be heard from again.... What is it like to be a civil rights attorney in South Africa? One of my friends, now in exile, had his office bombed. He would never talk with clients in his office or home because they were bugged. He left after many years of fighting the battle when his ten year old daughter received in the mail a tee-shirt treated with acid—sent presumably by the Secret Police.[29]

One of the more curious patterns of target and message occurs when government terror expands to encompass those who generally support a number of crucial national policies but who would advise the government against excesses of terror and repression. In such nations the target/message interaction is clear: the government will not tolerate reformist behavior, whatever the prior support of government the parties involved have manifested. Discipline, stability, and order under all conditions must operate. Such a "loyal" target situation operates in Richard Falk's analysis of actions of the Seoul government:

> In South Korea, this pattern of extended repression is especially clear, as the targets are often prominent religious or cultural figures boasting strong anti-communist, anti-North Korea credentials (e.g. Hon Suk Han). They pose a menace because they question the fairness of the economic arrangements—especially, squeezing the poor—and object to official claims that the denial of civil liberties is necessary for the sake of national security.[30]

Finally, in examining the target/message complex we must not lose sight of the important possibility that systems of terror become so institutionalized and permeate so many dimensions of government life that no identifiable pattern between the government goal, target, and message and the audience exists. In a scintillating analysis that focuses on both state and anti-state terror, William May has theorized that often the terrorists themselves fall victim to the process of indiscriminate murder and destruction of persons and values. Although some a priori strategy may determine which particular types of tactics are employed under certain conditions, this level of control and planning operates for only a short period. Soon terror as strategy gives way to terror as ecstasy, a fulfillment in the use of violence for its own sake.[31] This pattern is substantiated by Alexander

Dallin and George Breslauer's analysis of the highly planned campaigns of terror that operated in the power consolidation phases of post-revolutionary Russia and China. The policy of terror took on a dynamic of its own, sometimes in direct opposition to stated priorities of the government.[32]

The final category within the general discussion of the character of state terror involves the particular technologies available to the state for perpetrating the kind of acts noted earlier. Such a variable becomes important, because without mechanisms for the delivery of terror and training for the use and maintenance of such technology, even those regimes armed with powerful ideologies and the proper conditions would not be able to implement the all-pervasive and penetrating systems that operate in a number of nations.

The most comprehensive approach in this area to date comes from Steve Wright who has detailed seven major instruments that he labels "the new police technologies."[33] In linking this aspect to the character of state terror, researchers in the future must examine these terror tools in their own right. They also must chart the dynamic relation between the center of production, the pattern of training, and use rate. That an "arms race" of sorts has developed in these areas would also be a subject of inquiry.

In this volume Michael Stohl has discussed this issue in terms of the transnational training and contact mechanisms that permit states to operationalize such technology. Also in this book Jim Zwick has provided an in-depth analysis of the interlocked nature of available technology, an allied relationship with a surrogate, and increased internal repression in his case study of the Philippines.

SUPPORT MECHANISMS

A large number of considerations fall under the area of support mechanisms for government as terrorist. As one might easily surmise, support develops both internally for and externally to the national terror apparatus. Most analyses, as is the case with the chapters of Zwick, David Pion-Berlin, and Robert Denemark and Howard Lehmen in this compilation, have found it fairly easy to document, at least in aggregate form, which international actors benefit from and thus sustain the operation of repression and government terror. In fact, in some cases like the Philippines, the analyst wonders whether or not the system of state control could be maintained in its present form without such a high investment of support, technology, and monetary arrangements by a patron state. A number of analysts have demonstrated pervasive links among technocrats, industrialists, and military personnel and institutions.[34] This permits an in-depth investigation of the processes that bring together these powerful actors in the advanced industrial world with those designing a new order for their developing nation.

Beyond this, however, relatively little work has been done on an equally important dimension of government support for terror: the internal factions and forces that sustain and legitimize such rule. Given the nature of political economy, investigative strategies, and the problem of information acquisition in such circumstances, it obviously is not possible to generate a comprehensve answer to the question: Who in this society gains economically, politically, and socially from this system of terror? But we do know that each society has its oligarchy that forms the key support groups for regimes. The question is how to identify them precisely and their investment in the strategy of terror.

Beyond those who directly benefit, there are clusters of internal support groups that sustain the legitimacy of repression. As Stohl has noted in a discussion of the distinctions among First, Second, and Third World systems of terror, some states, particularly those that have a history of terror in their post-revolutionary experience, have simply made such a strong impression on the consciousness of the majority of the citizenry that only in the most extreme and rare cases does the state need to avail itself of its repressive power. Basically, the citizens self-censure themselves.[35] Furthermore, the pattern of anti-state terror, counterterror, and outright vigilantism in a number of nations illustrates that extremist groups, usually for ideological reasons, will provide demonstrated support for techniques of repression against "dissidents."

In examining internal support mechanisms, the changing nature of public support for actions of governments, especially in societies undergoing rapid change, and levels of violence becomes intriguing. Brian Jenkins's compilation of public attitudes in Western democracies regarding the actions citizens are willing to permit government to take, given a challenge from group terrorists, provides evidence that labeling dissidents as "terrorists" (by governments) and governments as "terrorists" (by dissidents) may be much more than a battle of semantics. It may begin a crucial contest of sorts for popular legitimacy:

Most people appear to support draconian punishment or military actions against terrorists. By 55 to 31 percent, Americans polled indicated they would favor a law providing that "all those caught committing acts of terror should be convicted and given the death penalty" and by 55 to 29 percent, respondents said they would support the organization of a "special world police force which would operate in any country of the world and which would investigate terrorist groups, arrest them, and put their members and leaders to death." Lest anyone think that this sort of rough frontier justice is uniquely American, it should be pointed out that the margin of support for this same measure was even wider in the United Kingdom. Ninety-three percent of the Israelis questioned in a 1980 survey support the assassination of terrorist leaders; 75 percent support reprisals even if innocent civilians are hit during the operations. Dutch respondents favored by 73 to 21 percent that especially stern and harsh actions should be taken against terrorists as opposed to dealing with them as ordinary criminals.[36]

The combination of internal and external support systems for the perpetration of terror by rulers against their people thus presents social scientists with ample room for further investigation across all political systems.

THE OUTCOMES OF STATE TERROR

The final factor to be considered here is the success or outcomes of state terror. One of the central themes espoused by the literature on group terrorism is that transnational group violence of this type is sustained because of its success.[37] Terrorists always get publicity, virtually always accomplish some of their goals, and a large percentage of the time escape to personal safety. But what of state terror? Here too can we say that nothing succeeds like success?

As we examine in detail the post-1945 world, it is difficult to suggest on the basis of the empirical realities that terror by government does other than accomplish the ends that government seeks in choosing such means. Only Rhodesia, in a peaceful transition to Zimbabwe, cast aside the repression of racism in its formal and legal dimensions. Nicaragua and Iran overthrew a system of state terror via revolution. Yet in the latter case, executions for different reasons than in prior eras still appear to be legitimate political methods. The rise of repression throughout Latin America, the spectre of tighter government controls in Eastern Europe, and terror regimes of Korea, the Philippines, Vietnam, Cambodia, and South Africa all still reign supreme. The data raise serious questions about traditional liberal thinking that such repressive societies implicitly carry the seeds of their own destruction.

William May supported this notion, in a discussion of the fate of Hitler's Nazi state:

the Nazis carried out a policy of genocide against the Jews—even in later stages of the war when both materials and personnel were in desperate short supply for prosecuting the war against the allies. The Nazi leaders, in effect, made decisions against their own best interests and against their own survival while carrying out the ghastly scenario of the final solution. Terroristic action seemed to become an end in itself—with a momentum of its own. It stood outside of the ordinary arena of political means and ends. This is but an extreme instance of what we might call an ecstatic, frenzied, terroristic overkill...it would be well to remember that this deterioration of Nazism from within was accompanied by a massive assault from without. It is unclear as to whether Hitler's regime of terror would have destroyed those social bonds upon which it depended—without external intervention.[38]

Thus it seems that governments are often successful in accomplishing their political and social control visions in opting for repressive policies and terror action against their populace, and that when these governments do not maintain their hold, however rarely, it is only through massive civil war or destruction from external enemies. But what of political and economic outcomes in those many "successful" terror states. As social science analysts we appear led to three distinct directions.

The first emerges from the thesis developed by Luigi Bonante in his analysis of the relationship between the emergence of coercive government policy and anti-state terror. He suggested that governments that have adopted systematic measures of repression often so institutionalize these modes of governance that they become "blocked." On the one hand, their room for maneuver in social policy is stifled lest they appear to be giving in to the radicals that challenged the regime. This carries over to their freedom to loosen political controls, even if they desire to move to a less constrained state of affairs. On the other hand, the development of the terror mechanisms required such political and bureaucratic effort that there exists no prospect that they will disintegrate on their own.[39] Bonante did not make the assertion himself, but the logical conclusion of his analysis is that gradual reform generated from within is virtually impossible.

The second thesis comes from the celebrated and controversial essay of Jeane Kirkpatrick, "Dictatorships and Double Standards," which maintains that there are in fact differences among repressive regimes. Traditional autocrats, most often being family-based authoritarian regimes friendly to the United States and Western capitalism, are simply less repressive overall than revolutionary autocracies that come to power as victors in civil strife against social or economic privilege. The latter, also referred to as "radical totalitarians," drastically alter society and create scores of refugees.

In a comparison of the two styles of rule and the outcome we might expect, Kirkpatrick's prediction is clear:

Moreover, the history of this century provides no grounds for expecting that radical totalitarian regimes will transform themselves. At the moment there is a far greater likelihood of progressive liberalization and democratization in the governments of Brazil, Argentina, and Chile than in the government of Cuba; in Taiwan than in the People's Republic of China; in South Korea than in North Korea; in Zaire than in Angola; and so forth.[40]

The third alternative route for discussing the outcome of state terror in continually repressive systems lies in the analysis of goals and outcomes of this pattern of rule. Such a study would demand a thorough use of techniques of political economy and focus on the issue: if the managers of the state claimed that economic development and prosperity require such tactics, what does the pattern of economic progress appear to be? Embodied in such an investigation would certainly be a host of controversies over appropriate indicators, as was the case in the assessments of the impact of Castro economic policy in Cuba during the late 1960s. Some analysts accurately noted that the Gross Domestic Product of the country had not changed. Others argued, just as accurately, that income distribution, as a more appropriate indicator of economic success, had changed drastically in the direction of improved quality of life. Only the Denemark and Lehman chapter in this volume begins to approach this style of analysis of the outcomes of state terror policy. But its use, as will be noted in the conclusion of the book, is imperative to both scholarship and policy regarding state terror.

Finally, state terror affects, more than any analysts to date have noted, the character of foreign, regional, and global political relations. On the one hand, governments like the United States have in their power, even under simple actions such as protocol changes in diplomatic policy, a large effect on the legitimacy of action that a repressive client state might take. Beyond the celebrated and well-known discussions of the positive reactions of Latin leaders to the election of Ronald Reagan, the fate of arms sales given human rights conditions in nations like El Salvador, or even the actions of the Pinochet government in the aftermath of the Kirkpatrick visit of 1981, we must consider the case of U.S. behavior vis-à-vis the Dung regime in Korea.

Traditional U.S. foreign relations has clung to the protocol that the first Asian leader to whom the president would accord a state visit after entering office would be from Japan. However, in the case of post-inaugural diplomacy under the Reagan administration, the first head of an Asian state received by the president was General Dung, the political-military dictator of Korea. That this reception occurred in this manner *and* followed immediately after the "trial" and death sentence of Kim Dae Jung, an opposition political leader who called for free elections in Korea after Park's assassination (and the subsequent arrest and torture of Jung's three nationally known lawyers), did not evade those who worry about American support for the regime.[41]

Impacts of state terror are also appearing in regional and global systems of organization. Given the concern with "national" control of economic development policy and the tendency for authoritarian regimes to opt more often for right of center economic philosophies than left-leaning ones, we are likely to witness more terror elites pulling back from traditional commitments and participation in regional economic trade agencies. Brazil shunned its own participation in the Latin American Free Trade Association (LAFTA) after the mid-1960s. One of the Pinochet government's first economic acts was to repudiate the agreements of Chile with other Andean countries made as part of a comprehensive business investment code in that region. As Denmark and Lehman have shown, there is no question but that South Africa's policies have restricted its economic relations with other African states in the region. In all three cases, the regional economic organizations of Second and Third World states, long considered ingredients to the overall economic development of the regions, have suffered.

Finally, Falk, although working within his own frame of reference of world-order values, made a number of observations about the long-term effect of increasing numbers of authoritarian regimes on global cooperation and decision making. At the most basic level, it will be difficult to sustain and impossible to build from international commitments to fundamental tenets of the international legal and humane order, like Genocide Conventions and Nuremberg principles, when leaders do not, as manifested in their behavior within their nations, hold these values and processes dear. Furthermore, the ideologies of authoritarianism and national security protect centralized power in the state. These pressures work against leaders imbued with such ideals as working cooperatively in the sharing

Figure 3.1 A Scheme for the Analysis of Government as Terrorist

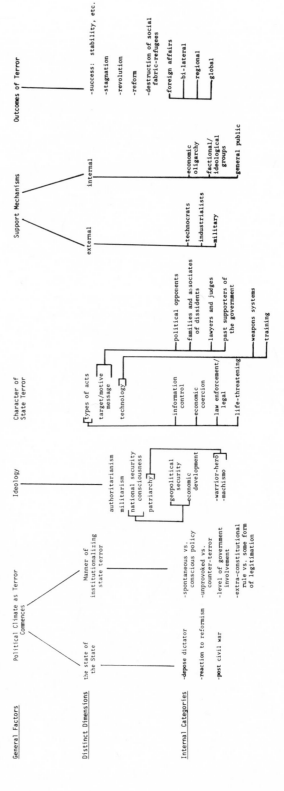

of resources like those found in the deep seabed or outer space. This may be especially true when jurisdiction over the issue in question is to be transferred from the nation-state to a supranational authoritative body.[42]

Thus the final element in our taxonomic approach for analyzing state terror provides not only discrete categories for analysis but also an agenda for future research. We are just beginning to recognize the outcomes of the terror ruling style and to subject it to critical review.

SUMMARY AND CONCLUSION

This chapter has demonstrated that by drawing from a variety of literatures on state rule and on anti-state terrorism we can develop a scheme (see Figure 3.1) for the analysis of government as terrorist that has yet been missing in the study of this phenomenon. The general factors we have isolated, their distinct dimensions, and further categorizations are outlined in this scheme.

It is important to note that I have taken care in this chapter to ground the categories in the behavior of states and that I have also raised some serious questions for future research. My approach has attempted to be consciously comparative, including civilian or military systems, Communist and non-Communist nations. Although due to my familiarity with Latin America there may be a greater emphasis on that geographic area, the thrust of the chapter aims for scholars to take some pain to analyze this phenomena without respect to classifications like right-wing and Communist. Such distinctions will only lead us away from the necessary task of a comprehensive theory of state terror. Scholars, in educating citizens and sharing their findings with policy makers, must move beyond convention and jargon to understand terror in its diverse manifestations, causes, and outcomes.

The words of Under Secretary of State for Management Affairs Richard Kennedy so aptly apply to our need to consider government terror. The bitter irony is that he casts them in the direction of group terror only: ''terrorism is an assault on civilization itself. In addition to the lives and freedom of the innocent, the rights of the individual, democratic institutions, and the rule of law are under attack. In a real sense, terrorism strikes at our vital national interests and those of our closest friends and allies.''[43]

NOTES

1. Bowyer Bell, *Transnational Terror* (Washington, D.C.: The American Enterprise Institute, 1975), pp. 76-77.

2. Paul Wilkinson, *Political Terrorism* (New York: John Wiley & Sons, 1975), pp. 130-131.

3. For a compilation of how scholars have analyzed the attributes of terror groups and the social conditions that give rise to them, see Timothy B. Garrigan and George A. Lopez, *Terrorism: A Problem of Political Violence* (New York: Learning Resources in International Studies, 1980), pp. 16-24.

4. Certainly, there are other categories to be added here, if not clarifications on the meaning and implications of some regime changes over others. The most infamous argument in this latter area has been made by Jeane Kirkpatrick, "Dictatorships and Double Standards," *Commentary* (November, 1969), pp. 34-45. More discussion of this is in the remaining parts of the chapter.

5. Although we consciously choose the category "aftermath of civil war," we do so cognizant of the atrocities and government terror that can be perpetrated during a conflict of such proportion whether it be formally labeled a "civil war," as the case of Nigeria versus Biafra or Pakistan versus Bangladesh, or not so termed, as the case of El Salvador more recently. The point is that both the state of war and the fact that the government is not undergoing regime change complicate this for the scheme presented and it is thus omitted.

6. Amnesty International, *Amnesty International Report 1981* (London: Amnesty International, 1981), pp. 102-104.

7. Ibid., p. 51.

8. As quoted from the BBC Documentary, "Terror: To Confront or Concede"(London: British Broadcasting Company, 1979).

9. Eugene V. Walter, *Terror and Resistance* (New York: Oxford University Press, 1969).

10. Amnesty International, *Amnesty International Report 1981*, pp. 184-185.

11. Ibid., pp. 122-123.

12. Roy C. Macridis, *Contemporary Political Ideologies* (New York: Winthrop Publishers, 1980), p. 4.

13. Garrigan and Lopez, *Terrorism: A Problem of Political Violence*, pp. 17-18.

14. It should also be noted that our approach here is not to give an exhaustive account of the internal dynamics of each ideology we mention. Rather, the essay highlights the important and distinct elements in each ideology and attempts to argue why each sustains the ethos and practice of state terror.

15. David Collier (ed.), *The New Authoritarianism in Latin America* (Princeton, N.J.: Princeton University Press, 1979), p. 368.

16. Richard A. Falk, *A World Order Perspective on Authoritarian Tendencies*, Working Paper Number 10, The World Order Models Project (New York: The Institute for World Order, 1980).

17. Ibid., pp. 5-7.

18. As cited elsewhere in this book by Zwick, the most comprehensive analysis of militarism is provided by Michael Randle, "Militarism and Repression," *Alternatives: A Journal of World Policy*, 7, 1 (Summer, 1981), pp. 61-144.

19. John Child, "Strategic Concepts of Latin America: An Update," *Inter-American Economic Affairs* (Summer, 1980), p. 76.

20. John Child, "Geopolitical Thinking in Latin America," *Latin American Research Review*, 14, 2 (Summer, 1979), pp. 89-111.

21. William Hazelton, "Will There Always Be a Uruguay: Interdependence and Independence in the Inter-American System," in Elizabeth Ferris and Jeannie Lincoln (eds.), *Latin American Foreign Policies* (Boulder, Colorado: Westview Press, 1980).

22. See the discussion of the emergence of the national security straight-jacket and its linkage to development thinking in Gerald Mische and Patricia Mische, *Toward a Human World Order: Beyond the National Security Straight-Jacket* (New York: Paulist Press, 1977).

23. Genaro Arriagada Herrera, "National Security Doctrine in Latin America" (translated by Howard Richards), *Peace and Change: A Journal of Peace Research*, 6, 1-2 (Winter, 1980), p. 56.

24. Child, "Strategic Concepts of Latin America: An Update," p. 77.

25. Sheila Ruth, "The Dynamics of Patriarchy," in Sheila Ruth (ed.), *Issues in Feminism* (Boston: Houghton-Mifflin, 1980), pp. 46-47.

26. Ibid., p. 98.

27. See especially David L. Milbank, *International and Transnational Terrorism: Diagnosis and Prognosis* (Washington, D.C.: Central Intelligence Agency, April, 1976); and Edward Mickolus, *Codebook: ITERATE (International Terrorism: Attributes of Terrorist Events)* (Ann Arbor, Michigan: The Inter-University Consortium for Political and Social Research, 1976).

28. Garrigan and Lopez, *Terrorism: A Problem of Political Violence*, pp. 13-14.

29. Bert B. Lockwood, "They Shoot Lawyers Don't They?" (A speech delivered in Denver, Colorado, May 6, 1982), pp. 8-10.

30. Falk, *A World Order Perspective*, p. 23.

31. William F. May, "Terrorism as Strategy and Ecstasy," *Social Research* (Summer, 1974), pp. 277-298.

32. Alexander Dallin and George A. Breslauer, *Political Terror in Communist Systems* (Stanford, California: Stanford University Press, 1970), pp. 103-131.

33. Steve Wright, "The New Police Technologies," *Journal of Peace Research*, 15, 4 (1978), pp. 305-322.

34. See Falk, *A World Order Perspective*; Collier, *The New Authoritarianism*; and Randle, "Militarism and Repression," respectively.

35. Michael Stohl, "The Three World of Terrorism" (A paper presented at the Inter-University Center for Post Graduate Studies, Dubrovnik and the UNESCO Symposium on Political Violence, June 29-July 3, 1981), pp. 11-12.

36. Brian M. Jenkins, *The Psychological Implications of Media-Covered Terrorism*, RAND Paper Series, p. 6627 (Santa Monica, California: The RAND Corporation, June, 1981), pp. 5-6.

37. Milbank, *International and Transnational Terrorism*, p. 22.

38. May, "Terrorism as Strategy and Ecstasy," p. 283.

39. Luigi Bonante, "Some Unanticipated Consequences of Terrorism," *Journal of Peace Research*, 16, 3 (1979), pp. 197-211.

40. Kirkpatrick, "Dictatorships and Double Standards," p. 44.

41. Lockwood, "They Shoot Lawyers Don't They?" pp. 4-5.

42. Falk, *A World Order Perspective*, pp. 54-55.

43. From testimony delivered before the Senate Foreign Relations Committee, June 10, 1981.

4

State Repression and Enforcement Terrorism in Latin America

John W. Sloan

As a nation modernizes, it is normally expected that it will provide greater protection and security for its citizens. In Latin America, however, there are authoritarian governments whose machinery is often employed to repress and sometimes even terrorize its population. Although there are some Latin American countries—Costa Rica and Venezuela, for example—that have combined democratic development with social modernization, there are still many nations that rely on governmental repression to resolve political problems. *Repression* can be defined as "the use of governmental coercion to control or eliminate actual or potential political opposition."[1] Repression is a coercive and frequently a secretive style of governing; it is essentially a substitute for a bargaining style of politics. The more repression a government employs, the more a government reveals how insecure and threatened it perceives itself to be. Repressive governments cannot induce voluntary compliance and support. *Enforcement terrorism* is the most extreme form of governmental repression. Whereas activities such as arbitrary arrests, press censorship, and the outlawing of demonstrations, unions, and strikes may be defined as some of the techniques or repression, assassinations and secret arrests followed by torture, mutilation, and perhaps death can be interpreted as enforcement terrorism. Acts of enforcement terrorism are more severe than acts of repression. The former are more likely to be deliberately lethal and cruel. Both are designed to force compliance through a climate of fear; both can be employed for reactive or preemptive purposes; and both are indicators of illegitimate authority. For the most part, authorities who possess legitimacy do not have to resort to repression and especially enforcement terrorism.

VARIETIES OF POLITICAL REPRESSION IN LATIN AMERICA

All Latin American nations are not politically repressive. Costa Rica is one of the most democratic nations in the world. Until the military coups of 1973 both Chile and Uruguay had democratic forms of government. Since 1958 Colombia and Venezuela have been relatively democratic. However, since 1950 every Latin American nation has utilized the state of siege as an emergency means to govern because of threats to internal security. Colombia and Paraguay have been ruled under nearly a constant state of siege. In Mexico repression is used subtly, selectively, and sparingly; it is sometimes said that the government will use two carrots before it applies the stick. But the stick can occasionally be the enforcement terrorism of the 1968 "massacre of Tlatelolco" in which an estimated 300 students were killed. In short, repression remains an optional technique that is employed in varying amounts by different Latin American governments. Freedom from repression certainly exists in Latin America, but it is more tenuous than the freedom that exists among the democratic nations of the North Atlantic region. Political leaders in Western democratic systems often resent political opposition, criticism, and autonomous political participation; they certainly try to control and orchestrate the kinds of demands and support they receive. But if they go beyond persuasion into the realm of coercion (for example, Watergate), they have violated the rules of the game and will frequently have to pay a price. In the more authoritarian political systems of Latin America, leaders are freer to use illegal methods. Greater levels of repression are possible because of the institutionalized styles of governing; the state of siege provisions in the constitution; and the usual lack of an independent press, judiciary, and legislature.

The history of Latin America is filled with examples of authoritarian regimes that depend upon repression, including selective assassination, as one of the principal means to stay in power. Such examples include Rosas (1835-1852) and Perón (1945-1955) in Argentina; Díaz (1930-1961) in Mexico; Trujillo in the Dominican Republic, and Batista (1952-1958) in Cuba. Today one encounters leftist repression in Cuba and Nicaragua, and rightist repression in Brazil, Argentina, Chile, Uruguay, Paraguay, and especially Guatemala and El Salvador. In the southern cone countries and in Guatemala and El Salvador, arbitrary arrests, disappearances, torture, and assassinations occur frequently and have been institutionalized as a regular characteristic of government policy in dealing with dissenting groups or individuals. These repressive policies are implemented by the military, police, and/or quasi-official vigilante groups. In their minds, the treachery of leftist guerrillas more than justifies their own employment of official repression and terror. Since governmental groups have the resources of the state at their disposal, they are usually capable of engaging in higher levels of terrorism than the guerrillas.

The repressive activities of many governments are often aimed at controlling the mass media and preventing the independent mobilization of peasants and workers. Radio and television can generally be controlled through their need for a government license to broadcast. The press can be manipulated through the government's control of imported newsprint, the newspapers' need for governmental advertising, and bribes, censorship, and intimidation. The media in Castro's Cuba are totally controlled, and in Nicaragua the Sandinistas have tried to censor and intimidate *La Prensa*. Most governments are particularly sensitive about the mobilization of peasants. The traditional rural economies have been based on docile, low-paid labor, and any social change or policy that threatens this situation is considered subversive by large landowners. Much of the repression in the countryside is not recorded, but we hear about numerous examples of assassinations, beatings, beheadings, disappearances, and so on, and recognize that repression is still severe. Enforcement terror of this nature is used in many rural parts of Latin America to intimidate anyone who might help organize the peasants—priests, nuns, teachers, lawyers, students, and peasants who display leadership qualities.

The repression of the working class has been less comprehensive and more subtle that the coercion of peasants. In twentieth-century Latin America the working class has been subject to labor codes that were eclectic combinations of corporatist, Catholic, liberal, positivist, International Labor Organization, and socialist influences. Howard Wiarda stressed that these

codes consist of a complete body of written law covering virtually all contingencies and issued by nonjudicial authorities. In this context the chief aims of workers' organizations, and the means they use, are ordinarily directed toward inducing the state, particularly the labor ministry, to expand the provisions in the code, effectively implement them, and enact new provisions that can be applied to specific cases at issue through the law and state machinery. This helps explain why collective bargaining is so weakly institutionalized, why the unions are so "political," and why they ultimately turn to government for satisfaction of demands and not to employers.[2]

The labor codes thus provided a framework through which the elites hoped the growing power of labor could be accommodated and controlled. That framework combined concessions and controls—carrots and sticks—to reward labor when it behaved and punish workers when they violated the rules.

For purposes of control, labor law has operated to divide the working class. First, the laws make it difficult to form a union, so only 15 to 20 percent of the work force is unionized. Thus a division exists between most of the workers who are not unionized and the minority who are. The second split separates blue-collar workers (*obreros*) from white-collar workers (*empleados*). In a situation that is analogous to the U.S. salary/wage distinction, white-collar workers are usually paid on a monthly basis (*sueldo*), and blue-collar workers are paid on an hourly or daily basis (*jornal*). The law reinforces the status divisions between these two types of workers and has contributed to the competition and lack of cooperation between them. The third means for dividing the labor force is the enforcement of laws that fragment the categories of white-collar and blue-collar workers. According to Louis Goodman, "In some countries this is achieved by prohibiting unions from national organization on industrial or craft lines and restricting them to single workplaces. In other countries further fragmentation can be achieved by enforcing geographic or type-of-industry divisions. Another device is the common prohibition against public and private employees joining the same union."[3] Fourth, labor is made insecure by the fact that new governments and/or new decree laws may change the rules and classifications at any time. Having obtained a favorable status, some unions are reluctant to jeopardize their benefits (which sometimes include special social security programs) for less powerful unions or unorganized workers. Most labor movements have experienced a roller coaster of state policies toward them, depending upon who was in power. For example, in Argentina there were periods of relative indifference (pre-1930), active repression (1939-1943), and paternalistic support (1943-1955). Edward Epstein reported that in Chile, labor's share of national income increased from 31 percent under President Alessandri (1958-1964), to 37 percent under President Frei (1964-1970), to 55 percent under President Allende (1970-1973), and then dropped drastically under the Pinochet dictatorship.[4]

The repressive policies of right-wing military regimes that replace civilian governments are particularly frightening. The military blame populist leaders, political parties, and union officials for the inflation, corruption, balance-of-payments problems, and subversion that triggered their coup. Hard-line factions in the military claim that the only solution to these problems is the end of politics and an increase in state repression. In Uruguay, to defeat the Tupamaros, the military arrested about 55,000 persons; since 1973 about 1 in every 50 persons has been subjected to arrest, interrogation, imprisonment, or torture. In Chile, an estimated 60,000 persons were arrested and detained for at least twenty-four hours between the September 1973 coup that ousted Allende and March 1974. The Pinochet dictatorship launched an unprecedented reign of enforcement terror to remove all of those of leftist leanings from positions of authority and to prevent leftist terrorism. The Amnesty International report summarizes the Chilean reign of terror in these words:

When people are arrested they are usually taken first to a military barrack or a police station or to one of the special interrogation centers established by the intelligence services. They may be held there for weeks or even months. "Pressure," often amounting to severe physical or psychological torture, is frequently applied during this period of interrogation.... Methods of torture employed have included electric shock, blows, beatings, burnings with acid or cigarettes, prolonged standing, prolonged hooding and isolation in solitary confinement, extraction of nails, crushing of testicles, sexual assaults, immersion in water, hanging, simulated executions... and compelling attendance at the torture of others. A number of people have died under torture and others have suffered mental and nervous disabilities.[5]

Argentina has been plagued by left-wing terrorism and governmental repression since 1969. After the ouster of Isabel Perón in 1976 by the military, General Jorge Rafael Videla's government asserted that left-wing terrorism could be effectively countered only by state violence. The military was clearly able to mobilize a greater level of terror than the guerrillas. Between 1976 and 1979 the guerrillas killed about 700 people, and the military eliminated somewhere between 6,000 and 20,000 people. Almost 1,000 expectant mothers and 100 children under the age of seven have "disappeared." Peter Smith wrote, "To wage its 'dirty war,' the junta decentralized power, creating many separate units within the military and the police. Analogous to the independent *focos* of the guerrillas, these units operated with nearly total autonomy, selecting victims according to their own criteria."[6] Each chief officer of a military district had his own prisoners, prisons, and style of justice. The decentralization, secretiveness, and competition among the military services meant that friends and relatives of the victims, no matter how influential they were, were usually not able to take advantage of their social contacts. The standard operating procedure of most of these repressive units was as follows: the intelligence unit would identify a "subversive"; an operational unit of five or six men in civilian clothes would kidnap the victim; the victim would be taken to secret detention camps where he/she would be interrogated and tortured; the victim would be heavily sedated and then dropped in the Atlantic Ocean. Such victims became known as the "disappeared" (*desaparecidos*). A 1979 decree reduced to a few months the time that had to pass before a missing person could be presumed to be dead. In Smith's words, "Observers everywhere drew the same chilling conclusion: all the disappeared have been killed—they are indeed, in the language of a general, *ausentes para siempre* (forever absent)."[7]

However, one of the many journalists (about sixty) arrested during this period "reappeared" and has written an insightful analysis of state terrorism in Argentina. On April 15, 1977, Jacobo Timerman, the editor and publisher of the newspaper *La Opinion* in Buenos Aires, was arrested by the First Army Corps counterinsurgency investigators. Timerman was tortured and interrogated by a hard-line, anti-Semitic faction within the military, who objected to his publishing accounts of the victims of enforcement terrorism and suspected that he might be connected with left-wing terrorists. Despite a ruling by Argentina's Supreme Court that there were no judicial grounds for his confinement, Timerman was imprisoned for thirty months, until September 1979, when he was stripped of his citizenship and exiled to Israel.

Timerman believes that "The Argentine military tapped their vast reservoir of hatred and fantasy so as to synthesize their action into one basic concept: World War III had begun; the enemy was left-wing terrorism; and Argentina was the initial battleground chosen by the enemy."[8] In such a conflict, the enemy had to be ruthlessly annihilated. The enemy was not only the leftist guerrillas but all who sympathized with or contributed in any way to their cause. In a conversation with an Argentine naval officer before he was arrested, Timerman was told that the treachery of the guerrillas justified the military's response of a "final solution." The naval officer explained that we must "exterminate them all" so "there'll be fear for several generations." By "all," the officer meant about 20,000 people. "And their relatives too—they must be eradicated—and also those who remember their names."[9]

In brief, Argentina has substituted enforcement terrorism for its political incapacity to resolve problems. Timerman sadly described Argentina's condition: "No one is immune to episodes of violence and terrorism; yet it should be possible at least to avoid a situation in which terrorism and violence are the sole creative potential, the sole imaginative, emotional, erotic expression of a nation."[10] The failure to develop political capabilities is particularly discouraging, because Argentina is one of the most socially modern nations in Latin America in terms of urbanization, literacy, education, health, and percentage of the work force that is unionized. One hopes that the less developed nations of the region are not seeing their future in the coercive conditions of Argentina.

According to Amnesty International, since the end of the 1970s acts of enforcement terrorism have decreased in Argentina, Brazil, Chile, and Uruguay but have increased in El Salvador and Guatemala. El Salvador is a small nation, a bit larger than New Jersey, with a population of almost 5 million. About 2 percent of the population own 60 percent of the land. For the past several years the 15,000-member Salvadoran army, which has traditionally been allied with the oligarchy, has been fighting about 6,000 guerrillas. Church and human rights groups estimate that somewhere between 20,000 and 30,000 people have died since the military junta took power in the October 1979 coup. The majority of those who have died have been killed by the military and right-wing vigilante forces. Politically, the government's cause has been damaged by the assassinations of agrarian reform officials, nuns, the archbishop, newsmen, labor officials, peasant leaders, and moderate leftist politicians. The government can hardly hope to obtain significant international support when its security forces are implicated in the rape and murder of nuns. Such sadistic behavior on the part of the Salvadoran security forces continues despite the fact that it is so obviously counterproductive. Part of the explanation for this phenomenon is that local commanders often have more loyalty to local traditional interests than to national headquarters. More importantly, the persistence of such behavior indicates how institutionalized political repression is within the El Salvadoran political system; it has enormous difficulty altering its "normal" conduct even when it is obviously in its rational self-interest to do so. This style of governing makes peaceful, political compromise almost impossible.

Similar problems exist in Guatemala, a larger nation, about the size of Tennessee, with over 7 million people. Again, you have a situation where 2 percent of the total number of landowners control 63 percent of the cultivated land. About half of the population is Indian, who have traditionally been subject to prejudice and economic exploitation. Daniel Permo wrote that "The majority of *minifundistas* (owners of tiny plots of land) are illiterate Indians, divorced from national life, who subsist on the production of corn. AID reported in 1979 that an estimated 60 percent of the rural population had a per capita income of less than $880 a year. As a result, some 200,000 landless peasants and an estimated 400,000 Indian *minifundistas* are forced by poverty and tenancy agreements to migrate to the southern coastal areas every year at harvest time to supplement their incomes by picking cotton or cutting cane on the rich *latifundia.*"[11] The wealth of the landed oligarchs and 75 percent of Guatemala's exports depend upon migratory labor remaining cheap and docile. Guatemalan landowners have amassed great wealth in recent decades based upon low-paid, labor-intensive agriculture (coffee, cotton, and sugar). They have viewed any policy (agrarian reform, rural cooperatives, and education) or group (moderate Christian Democrats and liberal members of the Catholic Church) that might increase the independent well-being of Indians and peasants as subversive and a threat to their economic existence. Such a threat is used to justify the most barbaric behavior. They have employed vigilante groups (the White Hand, the Purple Rose, the New Anti-Communist Organization, and the Secret Anti-Communist Army) and the military to repress, torture, and murder any persons or groups attempting to reform the system. Any Indian or peasant who displays leadership qualities is immediately identifying himself or herself as a target for enforcement terrorism.

In the past 15 years more than 25,000 people have died through political violence; almost 11,000 were killed in 1981. Most of these deaths can be attributed to the security forces (the military consists of 18,000 men) and not the four left-wing guerrilla forces that are composed of between 2,000 and 4,000 armed insurgents. Only the security forces have the organization and resources to engage in mass killings, move the bodies in vehicles over heavily policed highways, and then dump the mutilated bodies (to prevent identification) miles away from the home village. The pattern of enforcement terror in Guatemala is summarized by Amnesty International: "death threats, governmental denial of protection, abduction, torture, murder, and finally, neglect on the part of the government to investigate these violent incidents."[12] Elias Barahona y Barahona, the exiled former press secretary to the Guatemalan minister of interior, described, in a September 1980 press conference in Panama, how members of the presidential staff and Military Intelligence convened regularly with high officials of the Ministries of Defense and the Interior to decide on the lists of assassination victims. The targets of right-wing assassination groups include those who are in opposition to political leaders (76 Christian Democrats were killed in 1980), labor leaders, university professors and officials, university and high school leaders, journalists, peasant leaders, intellectuals and professionals, and priests who sympathize with the Indians.[13] The government's forsaking of the rule of law is exemplified by the fact that there are no cases of long-term political imprisonment in Guatemala; there are only political murders. The self-defeating nature of such enforcement terrorism is reflected in the fact that it has created a situation where young, socially responsible people, who before might have been recruited by the labor movement, moderate parties, and left-of-center groups, are now finding that their options are either isolated despair or joining left-wing guerrilla organizations. Permo concluded that, "The use of assassination as an instrument of repression is a recognition of failure to achieve a more benign politics of conciliation or cooperation. In the case of Guatemala, terror by assassination has become a deliberate policy alternative in recent decades for suppressing population demands to broaden political participation, and to avoid the implementation of structural reforms needed to alleviate long-standing social and economic antagonisms."[14]

REASONS FOR GOVERNMENTAL REPRESSION IN LATIN AMERICA

Confronted with the question of why there is so much governmental repression in Latin America, I believe the basic answer to be that the fragmented political culture in the hemisphere inhibits the creation of stable political systems that can adapt to change and successfully confront the problems of promoting development and reconciling group conflict. The combined and often interrelated failures to establish legitimate political systems and resolve the problems of promoting economic growth, social justice, and political participation mean that governments resort to repression to stay in power.

A major source of this problem lies in the colonial period. Latin America endured 300 years of Spanish and Portuguese colonialism, and this legacy still affects political behavior today. The Spanish colonies were considered the *personal* property of the monarch. In establishing and maintaining their rule over people thousands of miles away, the Iberian monarchies institutionalized a style of governing that was overcentralized, authoritarian, paternalistic, bureaucratic, only narrowly participatory, burdened by unrealistic legal controls, and often corrupt. This legacy has inclined the nations of Latin America toward a top-down approach to modernization, whose characteristics are variously described as bureaucratic-authoritarian, a corporative tradition, or a patrimonial state. Proponents of a bureaucratic, state-centered style of development do not have to overcome a major liberal heritage; there are no strong ideological or institutional (checks and balances, free press) obstacles to statism in Latin America. Instead, there is an inherited belief system that holds that most of the population—Indians, peasants, workers, and urban squatters—do not have the capacity either to care for themselves or to influence public policy. The possibilities of the peaceful evolution of increased political participation, which is associated with social modernization, have been inhibited by the colonial legacy that stressed the non-participation of Indians and peasants and their economic exploitation at the hands of large landowners. The impact of that repressive legacy is nicely summarized by Mario Vargas Llosa:

Although natives were officially excluded from economic, political, and social life when the colonial system was instituted, their "invisible" presence had a profound effect on the shape that the system assumed. The colonial governments not only deprived indigenous society of all standing and participation but also set about exploiting it in a methodical fashion; and to do so they had to create a means of overseeing it and keeping it in a state of total submission and servitude. This was the function of agrarian feudalism. It was repressive, isolationist, and hostile to any hint of modernization, not only because it was the only way of maintaining the continued helplessness of the enormous peasant masses (whom the republican as well as the colonial governments deliberately avoided integrating into the rest of society), but because. . .it also served the interests of the center [the state].[15]

In the twentieth century, as the elite structure has grown larger and more complex because of modernization, the elites have had to adapt to each other *and* to a more complex and less docile citizenry. There was political instability in Latin America when the elites were much smaller and simpler, and so it is not surprising that the pattern of instability has persisted. One historian wrote, "In so far as public affairs are concerned, perhaps the most important Latin American characteristic is the habit of not cooperating. This is the continent of 'personalism,' and since the early days of independence the various sectors of the population in most of the republics have had an aversion for cooperation: *caudillo* has been against *caudillo*, the capital city against the provinces, the inhabitants of the mountains against those of the lowlands."[16] In the nineteenth century the elites were split by the issues of who was to rule, church-state relations, and unitary versus federal governments. As the nations tried to develop and to industrialize, the limited consensus and mutually supportive role of the power elite toward the issues of the proper role of government and the scope of political participation was shattered. Today the elites struggle over who is to rule, how rulers are to be chosen, who is to be allowed to participate in politics, what levels of repression are justified, and how to deal with a whole host of developmental policies. As the elites are confronted with adapting to the complexities of modernization, they frequently defend their traditional privileges with cold war ideology. They contend that adapting to peasant and working-class rights is surrendering to subversion and that allowing unions to organize will break the dam that holds back communism.

The elites are insecure because they mistrust the lower classes, the future, one another. They feel vulnerable because they cannot agree on a formula to institutionalize their rule. Jack Hopkins captured this notion by writing that "there appears to be a weak consensus, if any, among Latin American elites about the desirable form of government. Various elite groups—the military, intellectuals, business and economic leaders, political party leaders, and bureaucrats—have seldom in the recent period reached any but the most tenuous agreement on the form of government and the proper nature and scope of participation in its politics."[17] Daniel Goldrich added that "While personalism is ordinarily treated as a prohibitive barrier to the development of democracy, a more general conclusion is probably that this mode retards the institutionalization of any rules of the political game, so that the society is continuously thrown back on coercion as the only workable means of social control."[18] Because the political culture is fragmented by the conflicting traditions of authoritarianism, Catholicism, corporatism, liberalism, and socialism, it is terribly difficult to establish any political systems that are compatible with the societies the elites are trying to govern. The result of this situation is often political instability and cycles of failed attempts to establish either democratic or authoritarian political systems. The dilemma for Latin America is that neither the democratic nor authoritarian form of government is compatible with the nature of the social forces that must now be dealt with. In Latin America, development does not necessarily produce democracy, as was believed during the 1950s; nor does development necessarily produce bureaucratic-authoritarianism, which was asserted by Guillermo O'Donnell during the 1960s reflecting the experiences of Brazil and Argentina.[19]

Trying to create a legitimate political system in Latin America is analogous to constructing a large dam over several fault lines. The shifting fault lines are personal, group, generational, sector, regional, ideological, and class cleavages. Despite their shared colonial heritage of language, religion, and culture, the nations of Latin America have evolved in a variety of directions. There are democracies and dictatorships; no party, one party, and multiparty systems; unitary and federal systems; corporatist and noncorporatist systems; military and civilian regimes; traditional caudillo, patrimonial, bureaucratic-authoritarianism, and socialist caudillo governments. This variety suggests that no regime is "natural" to Latin America. Within most of the nations multiple and incompatible political traditions compete with one another, sometimes peacefully, sometimes violently. No ideological blueprints seem adequate to construct the political system that would appear legitimate to most of the population. There have been political experiences that seemed compatible with national situations but that proved incapable of adapting to changing conditions: the Porfirio Díaz regime in Mexico in 1911, the *Estado Novo* in Brazil in 1945, Perón's government in Argentina in 1955, Goulart's populism in Brazil in 1964, Christian democracy in Chile in 1970, Allende's socialism in Chile in 1973, Ongania's military dictatorship in Argentina in 1970, and Peru's left-wing military dictatorship in 1975. Howard Wiarda suggested that "Patterns of fragmented political culture have been increasingly prevalent, contributing to non-consensual political styles and making for periodic crises and occasional breakdowns. Of course, the Latin American political culture has always been 'individualistic' and 'atomistic,' but in the present context the differences have become both more intense and they reach further down into the society. As politics has tended to become more class, interest, and issue oriented, the possibility for society-wide disintegration and collapse has also increased."[20] To forestall such a collapse, many of the elites have responded with repressive public policies. When severely threatened, some elites have responded with orchestrated acts of enforcement terrorism.

The increasingly insecure elites confront an increasingly assertive population. The citizens of Latin America have become more urbanized, more literate, more educated, more in contact with the mass media, and more conscious that the state makes decisions that affect their individual and group welfare. According to John Booth and Mitchell Seligson,

Social forces connected with economic modernization and a revolution in communications have helped transform the Latin American masses from a state of relatively low political awareness and activity into much more politically conscious and active...citizens....Among the processes described in the mobilization literature are the historical expansion of the politically active population from the tiny elite sectors of the colonial era to include the growing middle strata, the expansion of the electorate, the development of nationalism, the integration of increasing percentages of the population into the participant sector, the growth of the number and size of organizations making demands upon the political system and the increasing activism and political significance of the urban and rural lower classes.[21]

Under these conditions, and unlike the situation in the nineteenth century, regimes without significant support will be overthrown. The dilemma for most Latin American nations is that their political systems lack diffuse support, that is, they lack legitimacy; and they do not have the political will, resources, and administrative capability to play the politics of distributive justice efficiently enough to create a sufficient level of specific support. The low level of support accounts for the low level of compliance of so many groups in the region. Since the success of most policies requires the coordinated activities of numerous social sectors, this lack of compliance seriously weakens the impact of many strategies of development. The lack of compliance means that difficult developmental problems become insoluble problems.

This lack of compliance is partially caused by the inability or unwillingness of policy makers and interest-group representatives to institutionalize communication and bargaining networks. The colonial period established a style of governing that emphasized the nonparticipation of most of the population. Rulers were not expected to consult widely. Indeed, such behavior was a sign of weakness; the leader should know what to do. Traditional notions of the *caudillo muy macho*, who would not surrender to pressure because compromise was considered a feminine characteristic, have combined with fears of displaying weakness and thus inviting ouster, causing leaders to stress their independence from societal pressures. Latin American policy makers habitually underestimate their need for information and overestimate their ability to induce and/or command the behavior they seek from different social sectors. Hence systems of mistrust, uncertainty, and lack of cooperation are maintained, which increase the probability of irrational and repressive policy making.

The lack of institutionalized channels of political participation in many countries of Latin America increases the already high levels of insecurity due to the overcentralization of formal authority. Partially because of the weakness of interest groups and political parties, many problems are ignored until they reach a crisis, and violence is frequently used as a signaling device, which then encourages state repression. In overly centralized political systems it is almost impossible for the president or military dictator to appear nonpartisan, for the top executive must decide too many conflictual issues. Political conflict is not deflected and dispersed as it is in more participatory and decentralized political systems. Where only members of the ruling coalition are allowed to influence public policy, the intensity of political conflict between the "ins" and "outs" is likely to be overly intense. The few "ins" have automatic access to the great wealth generated by governmental decision making; the many "outs" either receive nothing or can actually be victimized by policy making. The crucial point is that the stakes of winning or losing power in Latin America are generally much higher than in the Western democracies, which explains why there is often electoral fraud and violence accompanying elections.

The elites, understanding that the desire for modernization is irresistible (it can also be profitable), want to guide transformation of their nations with a hard, visible, bureaucratic hand while maintaining their political and economic privileges. To paraphrase Barrington Moore, they want to rule and make money.[22] But they are terrified of the autonomous mobilization of the working class, urban squatters, and peasants. The elites believe that group autonomy leads to diversity, and diversity easily becomes anarchy. Indeed, Glenn Dealy claimed that for both the Batistas and Castros in Latin America, "the idea that the existence of a plurality of competing interests could lead anywhere except to anarchy is almost beyond comprehension."[23] The elites' fear that loss of control would lead to anarchy is exemplified by the Mexican Revolution in 1911, *la violencia* in Colombia in 1948, and the Bolivian Revolution in 1952. To prevent such anarchy, the elites feel justified in practicing state repression.

Latin American military governments can be particularly repressive. When the military takes over a government, it claims to be the sole, legitimate expression of the national will in much the same mythical way that the Communist party claims to represent the interests of the proletariat. The socialization process within the military convinces it that in promoting its corporate interests, it is simultaneously defending the national interest; conversely, anyone opposing the military is opposing the national interest and can legitimately be repressed. The military view Marxism as a rival alien army, a social disease that must be eliminated by radical surgery in which the patient (society) must be confined and controlled during a long convalescence under the tutelage of military doctors.

Whereas before the 1964 Brazilian military coup the military used to be content as a moderator or arbiter in politics, today there are more likely to be powerful factions within the armed forces who are exasperated with corrupt political parties, fearful of the internal security threat posed by rural and urban guerrillas, and confident that they possess the wisdom to play a permanent political role in producing more rapid development than regimes directed by political parties. After coming to power, the military's major dilemma is that it is more clear and united in what it opposes than in what it supports. In attempting to create a new legitimizing formula to justify its new developmental role, the military is hindered by its belief that "politics" has retarded national development, and, therefore, it should rule without succumbing to the morally eroding game of politics. Since the military represents the national interest, there is no need to engage in elections, consult with interest-group representatives, negotiate with dissenting groups, or provide incentives to ensure compliance. This style of governing requires the military government to isolate itself from society; to formulate the most rational decisions on the basis of technocratic criteria; and to substitute administration, and eventually repression, for politics. In brief, the military wants to decree development. But the military cannot decree economic growth, higher farm production, honesty in administration, higher labor productivity, an end to capital flight abroad, and higher rates of private investment. Nor can order be simply decreed or maintained by high levels of repression.

Since the 1964 military coup in Brazil, many of the military governments have assumed the characteristics of bureaucratic-authoritarian (B-A) regimes that are different from the traditional dictatorships of Duvalier (in Haiti), Trujillo (in the Dominican Republic), and Stroessner (in Paraguay). Because most Latin American societies are now more structurally differentiated than before and old forms of domination will no longer suffice in a situation where there are higher levels of participation and greater commitments to modernization, bureaucratic-authoritarianism appeals to governing elites in Argentina, Brazil, Chile, and Uruguay as a means of promoting and controlling change from above. The traditional dictatorships governed far less modernized societies, used repression to terrorize the opposition and to extract wealth for their personal benefit, and penetrated less directly and extensively into lower class life. B-A regimes, composed of an alliance between the military and the bureaucracy, try to combine political repression and developmental rationality. Robert Kaufman stressed that B-A regimes "display a rhetoric and intent which is modernizing and impersonal. Their 'arbitrary' rule over workers, politicians, students, and intellectuals is accompanied by attempts to establish pragmatic and predictable relations with the private entrepreneurial sector, particularly international business, and to rationalize and advance the economy as a whole."[24] O'Donnell suggested that B-A regimes use their "conspicuous capacity for coercion" to try to depoliticize societies that have been agitated by populist politicians (Goulart, Perón, Allende), labor union leaders, peasant league officials, and demands for the redistribution of income.[25] Through corporative controls and fear, B-A policy makers hope to hold down the consumption of most of the population, thus producing the surplus capital necessary to promote economic growth that will eventually legitimize the regime. However, few B-A regimes have produced such growth; and even the one that did, Brazil, found that the benefits of this growth overwhelmingly accrued to a small portion of the population and some foreign capitalists, which meant that most of the citizenry were in no way induced to provide allegiance toward the government.

Brian Loveman and Thomas Davies suggested that the military assumptions of anti-politics allow for a great diversity of policy choices:

Antipolitics is committed neither to capitalism nor to socialism. It is anti-liberal and anti-Marxist. It assumes repression of opposition, silencing or censoring of the media, and subordinating the labor movement to the objectives of the regime. . . . It seeks order and progress; the latter assumed contingent upon the former. It places higher priority on economic growth and is usually little concerned with income distribution except insofar as workers or white-collar discontent leads to protest and disorder. It can pragmatically emphasize either concessions or repression in obtaining its objectives. . . . [But] above all, military antipolitics produces a regime of. . . rulers and the ruled. Sometimes the masters use torture and other forms of repression to enforce their will and maintain their power; sometimes prosperity permits the use of more pleasant instruments of persuasion.[26]

The military style of governing is not compatible with running a society and promoting development. What the military desires is often a political silence that can be achieved only temporarily and at the expense of a great deal of repression. Its autocratic style inevitably alienates many of its original supporters and engenders pressures for liberalization. Even if outside pressures are decreased by outlawing parties, strikes, and demonstrations, it is likely that similar pressures will be generated internally by military factions that become increasingly divided over developmental choices and how much repression can appropriately be used. As the military rulers confront policy failures, growing hostility from the civilian sector, expanding internal problems concerning how to reward and promote officers for their military and/or political activities, there are increasing pressures from within the military to withdraw from the direct control of the government. Since governing inevitably conflicts with the maintenance of military unity, the military frequently retires (temporarily) to the sidelines. By comparison, Communist systems, perhaps because they are more concerned with distributive public policies, have been more successful in reconciling rationality and repression than B-A regimes.

CONCLUSION

All political sytems face conflicts over who is to rule and what public policies are to be pursued. The question for us is why do so many Latin American governments try to resolve these conflicts with state repression. The answer I am offering is that 300 years of Iberian colonialism institutionalized a style of governing in which only a few had a great power and wealth and the many were nonparticipants, docile subjects of a political economy that systematically exploited them. This style of governing has had enormous difficulty in adjusting to the changes wrought by modernization: the elite now is larger, more complex, and can no longer rely solely on personal connections to maintain their power and privilege; the class and group structure of society is now more complex, less docile, and eager to participate and influence public policies. By not resolving the legitimacy question in the nineteenth century, many Latin American nations are now confronted *simultaneously* with the problems of illegitimate governments trying to promote economic growth and distributive justice and of successfully handling the challenge of increasing political participation. The fragmented political cultures of the region have meant a lack of consensus of both the type of regime and the set of policies best suited to promote the development of the nation. Because the stakes of winning or losing power are so high, the governing elite have felt the need to develop and substitute the repressive capabilities of the state for the political capabilities necessary to allow a more complex society to influence policy and reconcile group conflict. One can hypothesize that the more a country develops its repressive capabilities, the less it develops its political capabilities in setting up communication and bargaining networks between government and society. To oversimplify, most of the countries have developed their militaries as more potent power contenders than their political parties.

Enforcement terrorism is designed to defend the interests of those who are controlling the state, but as exemplified by conditions in Argentina, Guatemala, and El Salvador, it inevitably destroys the morality of society. The tragedy for those who believe in democratic reforms is that governmental terrorism may be more effective in eradicating such beliefs than in eliminating left-wing guerrillas. The tragedy for Latin America is that the combination of the colonial legacy, the greed and "back-to-the-wall" mentality of the elites, the intractability of many developmental problems (unemployment, inflation, economic dependence), the utopian and ruthless behavior of leftist guerrillas, and the anti-politics perspective of the military are causing many of these countries to develop a more efficient infrastructure of state repression rather than a political infrastructure to resolve problems peacefully. Even the more economically advanced Latin American states have not been able successfully to combine "rationality and repression."

NOTES

1. Ernest Duff and John McCamant, *Violence and Repression in Latin America: A Quantitative and Historical Analysis* (New York: Free Press, 1976), p. 24.

2. Howard Wiarda, "Corporative Origins of the Iberian and Latin American Labor Relations Systems," *Studies in Comparative International Development* 13 (Spring 1978), p. 12.

3. Louis Wolf Goodman, "Legal Controls on Union Activity in Latin America," in *Workers and Managers in Latin America*, ed. Stanley M. Davis and Louis W. Goodman (Lexington, Mass.: D. C. Heath, 1972), p. 232.

4. Edward C. Epstein, "Anti-Inflationary Policies in Argentina and Chile: Or Who Pays the Costs?" *Comparative Political Studies* 11 (July 1978), p. 223.

5. "Final Report of Mission to Chile" (London: Amnesty International, 1974), p. 12.

6. Peter H. Smith, "Argentina: The Uncertain Warriors," *Current History* 78 (February 1980), p. 63.

7. Ibid., p. 62.

8. Jacobo Timerman, *Prisoner Without a Name, Cell Without a Number* (New York: Alfred A. Knopf, 1981), p. 101.

9. Ibid., p. 50.

10. Ibid., p. 17.

11. Daniel L. Permo, "Political Assassination in Guatemala: A Case of Institution-alized Terror," *Journal of Inter-American Studies* 23 (November 1981), p. 433.

12. *Amnesty International Report 1980* (London: Amnesty International Publications, 1981), p. 7.

13. Permo, "Political Assassination," p. 444.

14. Ibid., pp. 429-430.

15. Mario Vargas Llosa, "The Centralized State in Latin America," *Journal of Inter-American Studies* 23 (August 1981), pp. 349-350.

16. George Pendle, *A History of Latin America* (Baltimore, Penguin, 1963), p. 231.

17. Jack Hopkins, "Democracy and Elites in Latin America," in *The Continuing Struggle for Democracy in Latin America*, ed. Howard Wiarda (Boulder, Colo.: Westview Press, 1980), p. 148.

18. Daniel Goldrich, "Toward the Comparative Study of Politicization in Latin America," in *Contemporary Cultures and Societies of Latin America*, ed. Dwight Heath and Richard Adams (New York: Random House, 1965), p. 371.

19. Samuel P. Huntington, *Political Order in Changing Societies* (New Haven, Conn.: Yale University Press, 1968); Samuel P. Huntington and Joan M. Nelson, *No Easy Choice: Political Participation in Developing Countries* (Cambridge, Mass.: Harvard University Press, 1976); Guillermo O'Donnell, *Modernization and Bureaucratic-Authoritarianism* (Berkeley, Calif.: Institute of International Studies, University of California Press, 1973); David Collier (ed.), *The New Authoritarianism in Latin America* (Princeton, N.J.: Princeton University Press, 1979).

20. Howard Wiarda, "Latin American Development Process and the New Developmental Alternatives," *Western Political Quarterly* 25 (September 1972), p. 471.

21. John Booth and Mitchell Seligson, "Images of Political Participation in Latin America," in *Political Participation in Latin America: Citizen and State*, Vol. I, ed. John Booth and Mitchell Seligson (New York: Holmes and Meier, 1978), p. 16.

22. Barrington Moore, *Social Origins of Dictatorship and Democracy* (Boston: Beacon Press, 1966), p. 449.

23. Glenn Dealy, "The Tradition of Monistic Democracy in Latin America," *Journal of the History of Ideas* 23 (October-December 1974), p. 640.

24. Robert Kaufman, "Industrial Change and Authoritarian Rule in Latin America," in *The New Authoritarianism in Latin America*, ed. David Collier (Princeton, N.J.: Princeton University Press, 1979), p. 166.

25. Guillermo O'Donnell, "Tensions in the Bureaucratic State and the Question of Democracy," in *The New Authoritarianism in Latin America*, ed. David Collier (Princeton, N.J.: Princeton University Press, 1979), p. 296.

26. Brian Loveman and Thomas M. Davies, "The Politics of Anti-Politics," in *The Politics of Anti-Politics*, ed. Brian Loveman and Thomas M. Davies (Lincoln, Neb.: University of Nebraska Press, 1978), p. 12.

5

The Political Economy of State Repression in Argentina

David Pion-Berlin

The last decade in Latin America has been marked by the sudden and dramatic emergence of authoritarian, coercive regimes. One need not search long to find well-documented evidence that repression had become widespread throughout the region during this time. Prestigious organizations such as Amnesty International and the OAS Human Rights Commission provided voluminous reports detailing the mass executions, torture, arbitrary arrests, and disappearances of political dissidents—mainly at the hands of state military and police forces. Countries such as Chile and Uruguay, which formerly enjoyed long traditions of democratic rule and political freedom, were transformed overnight into military garrisons, with guards posted at every street corner. These countries faced no external threats: rather, the armed forces had been turned against the civilian population.

This shift from democratic to dictatorial systems of government became pronounced during the 1970s.

In an effort to understand this transition, a new body of social science literature emerged around models of corporatism, bureaucratic-authoritarianism, and militarism.[1] Curiously, these models paid little attention to political repression, despite the enormous buildup of the means of coercion at the disposal of state authorities. The presence of repression had become so widespread in this region that, for all intents and purposes, it was taken for granted. The concept seemed to rest implicitly in the discussion of regime types, seldom elevated to the stature of a topic deserving serious inquiry in its own right. A rigorous study of political repression demands that the concept

This chapter is reprinted from David Pion-Berlin, "Political Repression and Economic Doctrines: The Case of Argentina," *Comparative Political Studies*, Vol. 16, No. 1 (April 1983), © 1983 Sage Publications, Inc.

be treated as a variable factor and not as an assumed component of government. But how may we understand its variation?

In criticizing the bureaucratic-authoritarian model, a number of authors have suggested that extreme levels of coercion may have more to do with the establishment of orthodox stabilization policies than with any particular regime form.[2] These programs, which are administered ostensibly to reduce inflation and restore trade balances to equilibrium, have negative impacts on certain classes and sectors. Many of these authors suggest parenthetically that the particularly harsh social costs of these deflationary strategies propel regimes to use force against dissatisfied "marginalized" sectors.

These studies provide some interesting clues for inquiry into the causes of political repression but do not go far enough. No systematic attempt is made to establish the precise theoretical linkages between the two variables. Why should economic doctrine be related to state coercion in the first place? The notion is not intuitively obvious and runs counter to more conventional theories that trace governmental coercion to either civilian violence,[3] military intervention in government,[4] or cultural-historical forces.[5] What empirical evidence can be brought to bear to either confirm or reject the supposition that repression and orthodox economic doctrine are strongly linked? Conversely, are lower levels of repression found when rulers switch to other kinds of economic doctrines and policies? If a connection can be established, would it hold true, regardless of the type of regime in power? We will examine the evidence in the case of Argentina, particularly in reference to the repression of organized labor. Shifts in policy often take place as reactions to serious economic disorders. How do crises in the economy interact with doctrine to influence decisions by regimes to use force against perceived political rivals? Finally, it must be recognized that nation-states do not operate in a vacuum but are part of a larger world system. To what extent do external forces exert leverage on domestic policy makers?

CONCEPTUAL DEFINITIONS

Political repression can be generally defined as the "use of governmental coercion to control or eliminate actual or potential political opposition."[6] *Coercion* refers to force or physical deprivation, or threats of same, to prevent resistance from the opposition. This kind of interaction between the authorities and their adversaries is analytically distinct from noncoercive, yet highly controlled, interactions. In the latter case, political dissent may be effectively curtailed by government's use of positive inducements rather than negative sanctions.

Political repression can be directed at various sectors, groups, and classes in society, at both institutional and personal levels. This study centers upon the repression of organized labor, given that group's importance as a strong opposition and a likely target for stabilization measures, in the more highly developed Latin American countries.

Stabilization plans administered in the lesser developed countries, often under the watchful eye of the International Monetary Fund, share two basic postulates with conventional monetarist economics: Inflation and balance of payments deficits are rooted in the excessive growth of the money supply, and noninflationary economic growth can be attained only if the market is left to operate freely.[7]

Regarding the first, the monetarists contend that where the supply expands too quickly, it generates demands that exceed supply capabilities, forcing prices up. Monetary expansion is in turn fueled by government deficit spending and liberal credit schemes and indirectly by real wage gains beyond levels of productivity. The monetarists, or "liberals" as they are sometimes called, are proponents of laissez-faire economics, preaching the sins of government intervention to control prices or in other ways to tamper with market forces. In line with the second postulate, they believe that price distortions create bottlenecks in the economy, preventing the rational allocation of resources into productive sectors; agricultural goods are underpriced, lowering domestic food production; inefficient state-run enterprises are subsidized by the state; and currencies are kept overvalued, lowering the competitiveness of export goods and resulting in balance-of-trade deficits. These economists are convinced that there is "an attainable set of equilibrium prices which would remove these bottlenecks,"[8] if only the market were left to operate freely.

Orthodox policies usually follow predictably from doctrine. They entail restrictions on credit, higher interest rates, cuts in government spending and increases in taxes, and wage freezes.[9] To correct distortions in pricing, they call for the removal of all price and exchange controls, the abolishment of subsidies, and the devaluation of the currency, to reflect its true international market value.[10]

This is not to say that policy "packages" are always the same. It is possible to have various mixes of policy instruments for any given ideology. For instance, one plan may favor cutbacks in government current expenditure, and another may press for increases in income and property taxes. Both help reduce the government deficit but affect different classes. Policy flexibility, then, may hinge on the political predispositions or class biases of the authorities. We can safely say that stabilization doctrine can account for a large part of the variation in stabilization policy but by no means all of it.[11]

POLICY OUTCOMES

There are various growth and distributional effects of these different stabilization plans. Critics of the orthodox programs contend that these policies bring on severe recessions and cannot lay the basis for economic recovery.[12] Interestingly, many of the advocates of the "liberal" approach admit some recession is likely during the lag time between implementation and recovery. What are the contributing factors to such a decline?

The raising of interest rates, in real terms, and the devaluation of the currency will respectively cut down on local business's capacity to invest and import vital capital goods. Declining investment will lead to lower aggregate demand. Second, the freezing of prices and the freezing of wages will produce an imbalance between supply and demand, creating excess capacity and subsequent decline in output. Foreign investors—who have a comparative advantage due to the greater availability of external credit—could logically provide compensation for the fall in domestic production, but excess capacity is no incentive for prospective investors. On balance, the empirical evidence seems to confirm the critic's position: GDP growth rates decline during orthodox deflationary programs.[13] These changes are noted for the case of Argentina in Table 5.1.

The distribution of "costs" under orthodox programs is generally unequal, hurting wage earners more than owners of capital. There have been substantial uniform declines of wages, both in absolute terms (in some cases 20-40 percent; see Table 5.2) and in relative terms (represented by declining wage shares of national income).[14] Should wage earners comprise a greater percentage of people in the lower income deciles than do capital owners, inequalities in returns to factors of production will produce inequalities in income distribution overall. When wage shares decline, profit shares rise, but evenly. The distribution of capital becomes more highly skewed as it becomes more concentrated. Concentration of capital occurs when foreign-owned conglomerates—profiting from devaluations and ample supplies of external credit—buy out smaller local businesses suffering from tight credit restrictions locally. These profit-sector inequalities have an adverse effect on overall income distribution.[15]

Wage income suffers not only from government-imposed freezes but from devaluation. When a large percentage of wage goods are tradeable items, a devaluation will raise their price and cause real incomes to decline. When government current expenditures are cut (as is often the case with orthodox plans), programs that have a progressive effect on income distribution—including health, education, and housing—will suffer. Cuts in the state payroll will also throw wage and salary earners out of work and possibly lower the wage rates of those who remain, therefore further contributing to greater inequality.

THEORETICAL CONSIDERATIONS

Repression: Response to Protest

Given the nature of the orthodox doctrine, its policies, and distributional outcomes, what arguments can be used to explain the rise of state coercion during stabilization periods?

In the literature on political violence, coercion has often been treated as a response to manifest conflict, violence, or protest in society. Several social scientists have borrowed concepts from psychology in offering frustration-aggression hypotheses of civil strife.[16] Ted Gurr has argued that as the discrepancy between a person's value expectations and value achievements widens, relative deprivation intensifies, and frustration builds. Given the presence of certain

Table 5.1 GDP per Capita in Argentina, 1955-1980

Year	GDP per capita (constant $ 1970)	% Annual Change
1955	858	+4.7
1956	867	+1.1
1957	896	+3.3
1958	935	+4.3
1959	860	-8.0
1960	912	+6.1
1961	962	+5.5
1962	932	-3.1
*1963	897	-3.8
1964	975	+8.7
1965	1049	+7.6
1966	1041	- .8
1967	1060	+1.8
1968	1085	+2.4
1969	1162	+7.1
*1970	1208	+4.0
1971	1249	+3.4
1972	1271	+1.8
1973	1331	+4.7
1974	1399	+5.1
1975	1369	-2.1
1976	1328	-2.9
1977	1376	+3.6
1978	1312	-4.6
1979	1401	+6.8
1980	1417	+1.1

Underlined figures denote orthodox stabilization years. Asterisks indicate that stabilization plans terminated in mid-year.

Source: GDP per capita 1955-78 from Statistical Abstract of Latin America, Vol. 21, 1981, p. 276; 1979, 1980 data from Inter-American Development Bank, "Economic and Social Progress in Latin America, 1980-81 Report." Annual changes in GDP per capita computed from data.

intervening structural and cultural variables, frustration would give rise to political protest and provoke government to respond with force.[17] Gurr used GNP growth rates (among other gauges of economic performance) to measure short-term value discrepancies, but a similar case may be made using real wages. Let us assume (as is often the case) that real wages for labor were either constant or increasing before prestabilization crises (see Table 5.2). Given a sudden and

Table 5.2 Repression, Wages, Inflation, and Total Reserves for Argentina, 1955-1980

Policy[a]	Year[b]	Political Repression[c]	Real Wages[d]	Inflation Rate	Total Reserves (mill. SDRs)
	1955	-	42.4	12.5	294
S-R	1956	-	43.0	12.8	382
	1957	-	45.9	25.0	286
	*1958	6.8	49.0	31.4	130
	1959	8.3	36.2	111.1	276
O-S	1960	7.4	39.1	28.4	525
	1961	4.9	42.1	13.1	386
	1962	5.8	41.0	26.2	115
	1963	3.1	40.4	25.9	270
	1964	2.6	42.8	22.4	153
S-R	1965	3.0	44.1	28.6	236
	*1966	5.3	45.6	31.9	216
	1967	8.2	45.6	29.3	727
O-S	1968	8.7	40.9	16.2	760
	1969	15.5	41.8	7.6	538
	1970	5.9	44.8	13.5	673
	1971	4.9	45.7	34.8	267
S-R	1972	2.9	42.1	58.4	429
	1973	.9	46.1	61.3	1092
	1974	4.7	49.1	23.5	1075
	*1975	4.6	47.1	182.3	386
	1976	24.7	26.5	443.2	1383
	1977	20.3	20.7	176.1	2742
O-S	1978	16.3	-	175.5	3962
	1979	17.8	-	159.5	7279
	1980	17.3	-	100.8	5421

[a] S-R denotes Structuralist-Reformist policies; O-S denotes Orthodox Stabilization policies.
[b] Asterisks refer to crisis years.
[c] Political repression scores are weighted and standardized.
[d] Hourly industrial wage.

SOURCE: Political repression scores computed from information found in the NEW YORK TIMES and Amnesty International; Real wages computed from International labor Organization Yearbook, 1956-1980; Inflation rates taken from International Monetary Fund, International Financial Statistics Yearbooks, 1978, 1981; Total reserves also from IMF Financial Statistics Yearbook, 1981.

substantial loss of real wages during the deflationary phase, laborers would experience an incongruity between actual and expected income. Worker dissatisfaction would spill over into protest (given organizational capabilities) and precipitate state violence. A similar argument could be made for relative income losses, where workers who had made previous gains become frustrated by the growing gap between their share of national income and that of capital owners.

In one sense, orthodox stabilization programs are perfect candidates for these theories, given the severity of absolute and relative inequalities observed during these times. However, conceptual questions can be raised with regard to either of these approaches. In a sense, the analytical framework is too broad for our purposes. Presumably, real wage losses or relative income inequalities should precipitate political violence and repression wherever they occur. Yet if we want to argue that high levels of coercion are found only during stabilization programs, we need an explanation that discriminates between these and other programs.

The relative deprivation theses generally predict strong linear correlations between manifest protest and governmental coercion.[18] Here, coercion may be a measured response to civilian disturbance. It is also plausible that governments may anticipate working-class disturbances and *preemptively* coerce. Should political repression be imposed swiftly and severely, latent hostilities may never materialize, and hence no correlation would be observed.[19] In any event, this theory does assume that levels of preemptive coercion are calculated based on a rational assessment of the magnitude of violence. Alternatively, it can be posited that governments "strike first," regardless of the opposition's propensity to protest. The question then becomes, can levels of repression vary independently of the magnitude of opposition?

Repression and Economic Doctrine

One way to examine this idea is to focus on the principles upon which the stabilization plans are based. The following proposition might be made: The monetarist doctrine provides a framework for assigning blame for previous economic misfortunes. Organized labor becomes a likely target for repression since it is identified as the principal social force behind excess demand. Furthermore, when inflationary spirals lead to economic crises, the near collapse of the economy becomes associated with that sector's determination to gain higher income and benefits. Conversely, when government is guided by a different set of economic principles, which do not cast blame on wage earners, political repression of labor should be lower, if all else is equal. To clarify this argument, we will examine the differences between the "structuralist" school and the "orthodox" school, in reference to perceptions regarding the causes of inflationary crises.

Policy makers in Latin America have often been guided by structuralist economics. Born largely out of the work of the Economic Commission for Latin America (ECLA) in the mid-late 1950s, the structuralists rejected the conventional "demand-pull" and "cost-push" explanations for inflation, instead identifying more deep-rooted problems in the organization of agricultural and industrial life. Structuralism is less of a uniform theory and more of a collection of varied approaches. Nonetheless, there are some fundamental continuities to this brand of economics. The structuralists contend there are three major bottlenecks in the economy: food, foreign exchange, and finance.[20] Large landowners, they claim, resist the introduction of new advanced technologies. This prevents supplies from keeping pace with the growing demands of a swelling urban labor force, and prices inevitably are pushed up.

Second, inelasticities in foreign demand for primary products limit the growth of export revenue. Import substitution industries, highly dependent on external sources of capital and intermediate goods, generate growing demands for foreign exchange; the foreign exchange gap leads to the devaluation of currency and the increase in domestic prices and wages. Finally, the structuralists maintain that low internal rates of saving in the private sector leave government with no recourse but to provide finance capital to industry through inflationary spending and to absorb the surplus labor pool (which could not be hired in the stagnant private sector) through expanded state payrolls.

If food, foreign exchange, and finance bottlenecks were the root causes of inflation, increased wages and government deficit spending were "propagating mechanisms" that aggravated the inflation rate. It follows that for the ECLA school, there were no short-term solutions to the problem. Governments could not simply press fiscal and monetary levers in hopes of eliminating distortions in the economy, as the monetarists had advocated. Rather, the structuralists called for longer-term measures that included land reform to raise agricultural output, noninflationary government investment in infrastructure and capital-creating industries, and in some cases greater foreign investment.[21]

The structuralists also applied short-term remedies. Recognizing the dangers of wage-price spirals, they often called for selective controls. They were seldom enforced by the reformist and populist governments who embraced structuralist doctrines. Wage claims were seen by these regimes as "defensive reactions" to structural inflation and were in that sense legitimate. The income-shares approach, which Rosemary Thorp described as a variation of the structural school and which carried weight with many of these policy makers, claimed that different groups were "forced into battle" to maintain their shares of the pie, in the face of endemic inflation and slow growth.[22] To restrain demand, as the "liberals" suggested, would create social tension and political instability and would not get at the underlying causes of inflation. The reformists recognized the inflationary impact of real wage gains but claimed that the elimination of supply rigidities was the only solution in the long run. In the interim, latent social frustration would have to be worked out nonviolently through the mechanism of inflation.

This "social peace" is short-lived, however. Wage-price spirals will fuel inflation and contribute to an overvalued currency and balance-of-payments deficits. Export revenues will decline, as will foreign exchange reserves, which will limit the country's capacity to import vital capital goods. Declining growth rates will result and foster a "zero-sum" mentality among labor and capital. Each side believes the other's gain is their loss and thus grabs for larger and larger shares. Demands increase beyond the system's capacity to fulfill them, resulting in mounting frustrations and political turmoil.

It is at this juncture that a shift from structuralist to monetarist ideology often takes place. Carl Schmitt, a famed Nazi lawyer, once said, "Sovereign is he who decides the emergency situation."[23] Crisis management is needed, and the short-run prescriptions of the orthodox school seem infinitely more preferable to the long-term solutions of the structuralists, given the regime's precarious political and economic situation. Consequently, governments under pressure from anti-populist sectors (including the military) will reshuffle their cabinets, hiring economists trained in and committed to monetarist principles of economic planning. In other instances, incumbents may give way altogether to new administrations staffed by orthodox ideologues. In either scenario, the adoption of "liberal" economic ideology brings with it a new set of assumptions concerning the causes of the economic crisis.

The monetarists, as previously noted, traced both inflation and balance-of-payments problems to excess demand and growth of the money supply. Governments become culpable for borrowing credit to cover their deficits; organized labor is guilty of pushing nominal wages beyond anticipated price levels; both generate pressures to increase the money supply and hence aggravate inflation.

In fact, the state and organized labor become primary targets for harsh orthodox measures. They are not purely economic matters. Rather, it is thought that the orthodox planners are guided by a hidden political agenda in their selective attack on excess demand. For them, government deficit spending is a function of the power of unions to compel the state to serve a welfare role, to offer social services below cost, to provide employment, and to raise living standards by increasing salaries and wages. As the urban labor force becomes more mobilized, its demands accelerate the growth of state bureaucracies and payrolls, which in turn foster credit expansion.

If labor demands are legitimate within the ideological framework of the "income shares" school, they are clearly illegitimate under the orthodox doctrine. Reformist regimes tolerated demand pressures, lacking the economic rationale to do otherwise. We would predict a low predisposition to repress labor in these circumstances. Liberal regimes attribute inflationary economic crises to wage and government-spending demands; organized labor becomes a credible threat to economic stability and therefore to the authorities themselves. Hence we would predict a higher predisposition to coerce under these administrations.

Theoretically, other groups could be blamed for inflationary spirals as well. For instance, capital owners who lobby for liberal credit schemes could contribute to the growth of the money supply. Why then do we assume that labor will be singled out? The answer lies in the fact that orthodox ideologues in Latin America have been influenced by political doctrines that associate labor groups as threats to national development. In particular, ruling elites have embraced a national security doctrine.[24] Fashioned in part by U.S.-trained counterinsurgency advisors, this doctrine argues that political tranquility is a prerequisite for efficient economic growth. Groups that appear to undermine the established order pose threats to development and to the regime in power. In countries like Argentina, organized labor has had a history of militancy and is often labeled "subversive." This provides the state with a strong ideological rationale for repression that serves as a political counterpart to orthodox economic doctrine.

Cost of Repression and International Finance

I have argued that orthodox stabilization doctrines predispose a regime toward repression. There are nonetheless enormous political costs to pursuing such a strategy. Rulers must anticipate a loss of public confidence and support. Governments that repress can rarely be so selective as to avoid harming individuals outside of the principal opposition. Peasants, small businessmen, students, members of the clergy—people from all walks of life are bound to get caught up in the web of arbitrary assault, arrest, and execution. Where democratic channels are still available, citizens will use them to try to regain their rights and freedoms. To overcome these pressures, regimes must either distance themselves from the dissatisfied public or begin to make concessions. The decision to hold firm is made easier as the state links itself with international financial institutions.

The International Monetary Fund (IMF) is the "hub" of this finance network. Since its inception in 1944 the Fund has been a zealous advocate of laissez-faire stabilization measures as a cure-all for inflation and balance-of-payments shortfalls. The reward for compliance with IMF prescriptions is a quick transfusion of foreign credit—precisely the medicine that governments with foreign exchange crises require.

The Fund itself is limited in its capacity to loan but can open doors to private, multilateral, and governmental sources of finance by deeming prospective borrowers as "credit-worthy." The IMF "stamp of approval" is a powerful inducement for regimes to embrace the "liberal" approach.[25] Governments already converted to monetarist thinking will find ready allies in the Fund, who provide psychological as well as financial support. These internal technocrats reinforce the notion that despite a regime's tenuous political hold, it is working to revitalize the economy.

Anyway, should the government adhere to the program, it will rekindle old class alliances as economic performance creates believers out of skeptics. Should the program fail, the government has the relief of sharing the burden with its foreign conspirators. The Fund thus indirectly encourages policy makers to insulate themselves from political pressures. As government's links to the international financial community are strengthened, it more easily resists losses of domestic legitimation, having opted for a different support group. The costs of repression are consequently lowered.

Similarly, the costs of toleration (of labor dissent in particular) are raised. Should labor disruptions threaten the viability of anti-inflationary strategies, the government may become in danger of breeching its agreement with the IMF.[26] It may lose future IMF credit and jeopardize its status with international finance as a whole. The costs of toleration grow as the country's external debt grows. Service payments on previous loans accrue, and the government will be in the position of having loans to repay but with no revenue coming in. International creditors will usually condition their willingness to reschedule or refinance debts on the borrower's adherence to stabilization guidelines. Accordingly, the government must strengthen its resolve to resist labor pressures coercively or face credit boycotts.

TEST CASE: ARGENTINA

Is there some statistical evidence, using Argentina as a case study, linking the stabilization doctrine and international financial support with political repression? If so, can historical evidence buttress that statistical result by establishing the precise timing and sequence of events that precipitated the use of coercion?

First, political repression of labor was measured by a composite set of indices. Each index gauged levels of coercion directed at organizations or individuals and included the following eight factors: rank-and-file workers arrested, killed; union leaders arrested, killed; union members disappeared; unions intervened; prohibitions on organizational activities (strikes, protests); and outlawing of pro-union political parties.

Coercive acts in each category were totalled annually, and ranked on a scale from 0 to 5. Different phenomena were coded in different ways. For example, arrests were noted according to the numbers affected per million in the population. Organizational restrictions were computed by the representativeness of the group multiplied by the duration of the restriction. To standardize these measures, common z score transformations were used.

To demonstrate unidimensionally between these eight variables, a correlation matrix was run, and the covariations between factors were found to be significantly positive. The scores of each of the measures were summed to produce final annual figures on overall repression, shown in Table 5.2. The scores have been plotted in Figure 5.1. It is immediately evident by the graph that the sharpest increases in coercion come close to the beginning of stabilization periods. Levels then subside, falling off dramatically upon the termination of these programs. It can also be observed that each subsequent orthodox program brings with it progressively higher amounts of political repression. I postulate that this reflects a "learning curve" on the part of government leaders. Future administrations recall past crises and the failures of the authorities to quell labor uprisings

Figure 5.1 Political Repression, Real Wages, and Stabilization in Argentina, 1955-1980

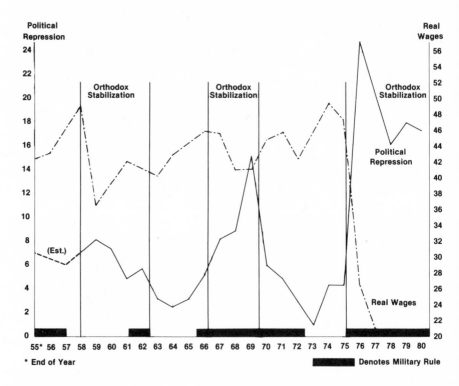

successfully. To ensure that policies can be completed, succeeding governments resort to much higher levels of repression.

A longitudinal or diachronic study has been chosen as the principal research method. Simple and multiple regression analysis has been performed on time-series data to determine the influence of stabilization plans and international financial assistance on political repression. This approach was feasible and desirable for a number of reasons. Enough information existed to compute annual scores on each of the variables. The data spanned a considerable time—twenty-three years—which afforded a large enough sample size to perform regression analysis without sacrificing too many degrees of freedom.

The multiple regression analysis in particular offered the further advantage of testing alternative rival hypotheses. For instance, it could be argued that a statistical relation between repression and economic doctrine is "spurious" and ascribed to the influence of military intervention in government. To determine the validity of this claim, I have introduced the military-rule variable into the equation. Should the beta term for the economic doctrine regressor remain sig-

Table 5.3 International Credit to Argentina, 1958-1980[a]

Year	Total (Mil. $U.S.)	Year	Total (Mil. $U.S.)
1958	304.0	1970	196.7
1959	350.0	1971	303.2
1960	113.7	1972	411.5
1961	293.2	1973	125.8
1962	282.0	1974	306.8
1963	78.2	1975	728.4
1964	4.8	1976	1783.6
1965	50.4	1977	1326.8
1966	53.6	1978	1499.9
1967	530.8	1979	2147.8
1968	530.4	1980	1426.0
1969	312.8		

[a] International Credit includes loans/aid from: U.S. Treasury Department, Agency for International Development, World Bank and Inter-American Development Bank, Eximbank, International Monetary Fund, and private sources.

SOURCES: U.S. Treasury loans from Wall Street Journal, Bank of London and South America Quarterly Review and B.O.L.S.A. Review; AID, World Bank, IDB, and Export-Import Bank data from Agency for International Development, "U.S. Foreign Assistance and Assistance from International Organizations: Obligations and Loan Authorizations," annual reports from 1962-1980; IMF loans from IMF Annual Reports; Private bank loans from B.O.L.S.A. Review and Wall Street Journal.

nificant, we would reject the idea that its influence on the dependent variable was false.

The stabilization and regime-type variables were treated dichotomously, through the use of "dummy" variables. Stabilization years and military rule years received scores of 1; nonstabilization years and civilian govenments had scores of 0. International financial support was handled as a continuous variable, using a simple monetary measure of annual, multilateral, private, and government assistance. Aid levels were those *authorized* and not actually sent. The foreign assistance data appears in Table 5.3. The Cochrane-Orcutt Iterative procedure was employed to correct for serial correlation in the error term and dependent variable.[27] Once the correction was made (as indicated by the Durbin-Watson statistic), the coefficients in the regression equations could be interpreted normally, as is done in ordinary least squares regression. Table 5.4 reports the results of the analysis.

All three independent variables contribute significantly to an explanation of political repression, when regressed individually. In the first multiple regression equation, the influence of stabilization doctrine on coercion remains positive

Table 5.4 Regression Equations for Political Repression

Independent Variables	Constant	Beta	Standard Error	R^2	F Stat.	Durbin Watson	Sig. Level*
Single Regression Equations							
Stabilization	5.0	6.70	2.25	.57	29.0	2.13	.01
Military Rule	5.53	6.10	2.28	.55	27.0	2.05	.01
International Assistance	3.43	.01	.001	.73	58.61	1.91	.01
Multiple Regression Equations							
A. Stabilization	3.31	5.04	2.32	.62			.05
Military Rule	3.31	4.31	2.32		17.98	2.14	.05
B. Stabilization	1.46	4.0	1.49	.80			.01
Military Rule	1.46	1.35	1.49				not sig.
International Assistance	1.46	.01	.001	.80	29.09	2.05	.01

* 1 - tailed test; N = 23.

when holding constant for military rule. The significance of the beta terms does decline owing to the presence of some multicolinearity between the independent variables. The variables were not highly colinear however, since the coefficient of determination increased from 0.57 to 0.62, and the standard error of the beta term rose only slightly. Some covariance between the independent variables was to be expected. Proponents of orthodox programs who depend on the military to carry out repression will often urge them to assume power as well. Hence military rule and orthodox policy formulation will at times converge. This is not always so, since the authorities can use the coercive capabilities of the armed forces while retaining civilian control of government, as evidenced from 1958 to 1962 in Argentina (see Figure 5.1).

With the introduction of the international assistance variable into the second multiple regression equation, the R^2 increases dramatically. The stabilization and international assistance terms are highly significant, but that is no longer the case for the military rule coefficient. Its influence is now captured by the other two independent variables. Multicolinearity between the terms is present but not extensive, as evidenced by the lower standard errors. Some colinearity is again predictable owing to the affinity that is shared between international financial elites and monetarist technocrats who administer policy. Together the variables account for 80 percent of the variation in political repression. These results provide a strong statistical confirmation of the theoretical propositions advanced in this study. They indicate that economic doctrine and international alliances can serve as powerful predictors of the use of coercion. Although regime types cannot be discounted, the results suggest this variable holds less power in offering similar predictions. Of course, the regression analysis does not establish causal connections between the factors but does provide a guideline for historical work. Three transition periods in modern Argentine history, corresponding to the points on the graph where dramatic upswings in coercion occur, provide a greater depth of explanation and understanding of the precise sequence of events leading up to a coercive state of affairs.

The Aramburu-Frondizi Years

The military government of General Pedro Aramburu deposed Juan Perón in 1955 and ruled through to the beginning of 1958. It was counseled in economics by the structuralist school's chief architect, Raul Prebisch. Faced with sizeable trade deficits and low productivity in agriculture, Prebisch proposed a policy of export promotion. State investment in agriculture would boost productivity; price incentives would be granted to farmers in the form of devaluations. The government was aware of the dangers of a wage-price spiral but stopped short of fully implementing a regressive wage policy, heeding Prebisch's advice not to penalize labor unjustly. Not only were cost-of-living adjustments tolerated but food subsidies were retained. A major devaluation was enacted in 1955 but none thereafter due to the adverse impact on workers of such measures.

Inflationary pressures mounted during the Aramburu years, creating an over-valued currency, balance-of-trade deficits, and loss in foreign exchange. The government received a modicum of support from international creditors (having affiliated with the Paris Club in 1956), which temporarily relieved its reserve shortfall. But these sums were insufficient, and the IMF was unwilling to commit larger amounts until the authorities agreed to implement a strict orthodox anti-inflation plan. Fearful that a complete switch to a free-market-oriented economy would provoke massive social unrest, Aramburu refused to go along.

The military returned Argentina to civilian rule in 1958 and left President Arturo Frondizi with continued high inflation, low growth, trade deficits, and foreign exchange shortages. Like his predecessor, Frondizi invoked the struc-turalist critique, albeit of a different variety. Under the guidance of his ECLA-trained team of economists and his chief advisor, Rogelio Frigerio, Frondizi rejected the export-led growth model and opted for an import substitution policy instead. He contended that long-term deteriorations in the terms of trade were limiting Argentina's ability to generate sufficient foreign exchange to support capital imports. His strategy was to bolster the country's internal supply of capital by attracting foreign investment and credit.[28] Frondizi laid the groundwork for development by building up the nation's petroleum, steel, and chemical indus-tries. He also fulfilled his campaign pledge to redistribute income to wage earners by granting a 60 percent pay hike in the early part of 1958.[29] Labor was pleased, but the peace between Frondizi and his Peronist rivals was short lived. Long-term capital investment projects could not offset the short-term loss of export revenues and rapid depletion of foreign exchange. The peso's rate abroad was being reduced, but rather than risk political turmoil with a devaluation, Frondizi imposed certain import controls that had a depressing effect on economic growth.

By the fall of 1958, Argentina was in imminent danger of economic collapse due to its inability to pay for vital capital imports. The country was in desperate need of foreign credit, but an IMF team, visiting the country in July 1958, laid down strict conditions for the release of international funds: wages must be frozen, government deficits cut, money supply restricted, price and exchange controls lifted, and the peso devalued.

In November 1958, Frondizi agreed to these basic terms, rupturing his pact with the Peronists. He also alienated his support within the General Economic Confederation (CGE)—an important association of small businessmen—who objected to the IMF's credit restrictions. Frondizi's switch did garner support from the larger industrialists and landowners, who figured to prosper from sta-bilization. On December 29, the largest single aid program ever devised for a Latin American nation was formulated. Argentina would receive $329 million in aid from multinational, governmental, and private sources.[30] Frondizi formally launched his orthodox plan that evening.

Political repression, which had been moderate during the Aramburu admin-istration, and low during the first eight months under Frondizi, suddenly rose dramatically in the fall of 1958, as delicate negotiations between the government and the IMF neared completion. According to one report, the government thought that its use of force to end a railroad strike in November would enhance its chances of gaining IMF credit.[31] Apparently it was right. As predicted by our model, preemptive coercion escalated to new heights in 1959, as the austerity plan was implemented. Real wages plummeted 26 percent from the year past, and inflation skyrocketed to 111 percent. In response, the working class became increasingly mobilized. Argentina had a record number of strikes in 1959. Frondizi responded with the mass arrest of union leaders and rank and file and the outlawing of the Peronist and Communist parties.

The Illia-Ongania Transition

The interim military government that followed the Frondizi administration allowed for limited elections in 1963 that excluded Peronist participation. Arturo Illia, the choice of the People's Radical Party (UCRP), came to power with a weak political mandate and a host of economic troubles, including a large budget deficit, persistent unemployment, high inflation, and a huge foreign debt. At the advice of his ECLA team of economists, Illia abandoned the "shock-treatment" of Frondizi and chose a reformist-nationalist strategy for economic recovery. With the help of government financing and liberated credit schemes, domestically owned industries would, according to his plan, be supported at the expense of larger, more efficient multinationals. Prices would be controlled while raising wages to generate demand. The peso would be devalued incrementally, to boost exports, while softening the blow on consumers.[32]

Illia defied the IMF by cancelling a standby loan and refusing to discuss the Fund's inflation remedies any further. It was not surprising that international loans to Argentina fell drastically during the Illia years.

Illia's nationalist strategy achieved promising results during the first two years, with steady growth and low inflation. These gains were illusory and short lived, however. Deficits on the capital account grew, as a result of repayments on outstanding loans, and a flight of capital due to Illia's nationalist posture. By September 1965, gold and foreign exchange holdings were in a precarious position, and Illia was forced to go to the Paris Club of creditors for debt relief.

Inflationary pressures continued to build, compelling the government to tighten the money supply and ask for voluntary wage restraint. Labor refused to cooperate, and rather than retaliate with coercion, Illia acquiesced. Angered over his failure to deal firmly with the Peronists, the military overthrew Illia on June 29, 1966.

Many observers of the political scene at the time expected a swift return to the rule of force with the installation of the military regime headed by General Juan Carlos Ongania. Indeed, Ongania set the tone for his administration early on by suggesting that political tranquility was the price Argentina would pay for economic vitality and growth. It is therefore curious that during the first eight months of military rule, levels of coercion were mild. What would account for this?

First, no recognizable development plan had emerged from the ministry of economy during this period. Labor seemed unperturbed. A wage increase had been granted and the General Confederation of Labor (GCL) leadership found Ongania in broad general agreement with many of its demands. The military's attitude toward labor seemed to shift suddenly in February and March 1967. Ongania ordered the banning of several unions, the freezing of syndicate accounts, and the use of troops to quell a GCL strike. On March 13, 1967, Dr. Adalbert Krieger Vasena, the newly appointed minister of the economy, went before national television to announce his "Grand Transformation" of the economy. The program included a sharp devaluation of the peso, a relaxation of import duties, incentives for foreign investors, an expansion of money and credit, and a freeze on wages.[33] Except for the relaxation of credit controls, Vasena's plan had the ring of a stabilization strategy. Finally, in May, it became apparent that in the months preceding, the military had been in consultation with IMF. On May 18, 1967, Vasena made public a letter of intent sent previously to the Fund, outlining his government's intention to pursue a free-market plan. Argentina was quickly rewarded with an international aid package totaling approximately $400 million.[34] The government's strange turnabout in late February now seemed comprehensible in the context of policy formation: preemptive coercion had been used to prepare the unions for the austerity measures to follow. High levels of coercion persisted throughout the Ongania years: unions were infiltrated; several of the largest unions, representing over 700,000 workers (of an estimated work force of 2.5 million), were banned and their funds frozen; and an anti-Communist decree was enforced under which hundreds of rank-and-file workers were arrested.

From Peronism to Videla

With the election of Hector Campora, March 11, 1973, the Peronists were restored to power for the first time in eighteen years. The government pursued a "nationalistic" stabilization program aimed at satisfying local rather than international demand. A "social contract" was formalized between labor, industry, and government in June of that year. The contract had the support of both conservative industrialists and more liberal businessmen. It established an across-the-board wage hike and price freeze, to be followed by a two-year voluntary wage freeze and selected price increases.[35] The sequential nature of the plan was devised to prevent wage-price spiraling.

Initially, the pact seemed successful, as most economic indicators registered improvements. Juan Perón assumed the presidency from Hector Campora in a special election that fall, lending greater legitimacy to the agreement. But in 1974 external and internal problems surfaced that threatened the viability of the pact. The sudden increase in the price of oil in 1973 raised Argentina's import bill significantly the following year. Profit margins that had been hurt by the price freeze were narrowed even further for businesses that depended on costly imports.

The freeze was abandoned in the fall of that year. The move unleashed latent inflationary pressures fueled by massive government spending. Labor exerted heavy pressure on the Peronist government to suspend the wage restrictions; the government subsequently obliged. Inflation rose and the export sector suffered. The government refused to devalue, fearing that such a move would trigger new inflationary forces. To support the peso at its then present value, the Peronist authorities sold off foreign exchange in the forward market; reserves dropped 75 percent in 1975. Faced with a growing debt burden and the likelihood of default, Isabel Perón (who had replaced her husband upon his death in July 1974) ended her nation's isolation with international creditors and commenced negotiations with the IMF.

The Fund helped Argentina secure some short-term credits but refused to offer any standby loans given Perón's reluctance to cut wages and the deficit. Pressures from creditors and from large industrialists contributed to a right-wing, anti-labor shift in the Peronist cabinet. José Gelbard, the minister of economy and former CGE president, was dismissed and replaced by a more conservative official. Lopez-Rega, a right-winger who had maneuvered himself into a position as Perón's chief advisor, replaced other cabinet members with anti-union officials. The social pact came unhinged and austerity measures were announced in June 1975.

During the first one and one-half years of Peronist rule, Argentina enjoyed its lowest levels of political repression in some time: few arrests were recorded; hundreds of political prisoners were released; unions and parties operated freely and the state of siege that had been in effect for four years was lifted. With the shift in policy away from the social pact toward more orthodox solutions, levels of repression increased, particularly in the fall of 1974. The Argentine Anti-Communist Alliance (AAA), a right-wing death squad that operated with the tacit consent of Lopez-Rega, stepped up its attacks on radical labor organizers. A state of siege was reinvoked, and hundreds of "guerrilla" suspects were detained.

Political repression was largely ineffective during 1975. For the first time in Argentine history, the General Confederation of Labor called a general strike against a Peronist adminstration, demanding an end to persecution and a greater share in national income. But demands had now exceeded the government's capacity to fulfill them. To contain her highly mobilized opposition, Isabel Perón would not escalate political repression any further.

The situation deteriorated further in early 1976, as the Perón government, in a last-ditch effort to salvage the economy, agreed in principle to an IMF stabilization package in exchange for a sizeable loan. Perón never had a chance to complete her negotiations, since the military overthrew her government on March 23, 1976.

Six days after the coup, economic minister José Alfredo Martinez de Hoz outlined an orthodox stabilization plan that his government would zealously pursue.[36] Hoz quickly cut wages by 30 percent from their 1975 level (by 1977, wages had sunk to 44 percent of their 1975 level). He reduced social welfare expenditures, lifted price controls, devalued the peso, and provided handsome incentives to foreign investors.

Not unexpectedly, the international credit came pouring in: the IMF came through with a $127 million standby loan; in the first two years under the military dictatorship of Jorge Videla, Argentina received more than $1 billion in private bank credits alone.[37]

With the implementation of the monetarist "shock treatment" political repression escalated to its highest levels in Argentine history. In the first four months under the military regime, more than 4,000 arrests were reported, and torture of detainees was commonplace. By early 1979, it was estimated that 5,000 guerrilla suspects had been killed since the coup. Many of them were thought to be labor organizers. According to Argentine human rights groups, 15,000 people "disappeared" at the hands of the security forces in the first three years under Videla. It has been estimated that 1 out of 4 was a worker.[38]

The historical account of Argentine troubles clearly parallels the discussions in the earlier part of this chapter: structuralist-oriented regimes propose development strategies but cannot address short-term crises; wages, prices, and government deficits aggravate the inflation rate, but these regimes are unwilling to restrain demand through force; foreign exchange dwindles, since international creditors are unreceptive to government's requests for aid; crises worsen and precipitate changes in economic doctrine from structuralist to orthodox; international aid is granted, political repression rises sharply, and income inequality worsens.

CONCLUSION AND SUMMARY

I began by suggesting an alternative framework for analyzing variations in political repression in the more economically developed Latin American countries. It was proposed that coercion may have more to do with particular doctrines, in the context of economic crises, than with certain forms of governance. International finance was identified as an additional critical variable in explaining the relation. A partial statistical confirmation of the suppositions was offered, along with an historical narrative that strengthened the case.

This study has not provided "universally" valid results in any sense. But the observation of strong correlations here should warrant further testing of the model in the context of other countries. Would one observe significantly higher levels of state coercion wherever monetarist doctrines and policies were in place? Would that hold true only for a stratified sample of economically advanced Latin American societies, or does the model have more general applicability? If the relationship is found not to hold true in certain circumstances, what reasons could one advance to explain the discrepancies?

Most observers would agree that state terror in Argentina has not been atypical of government behavior in Latin America in recent years. But it would not take a great "leap of faith" to assert also that the use of coercion has often paralleled the implementation of stabilization measures. For instance, Chile and Uruguay were traditionally noted as bastions of democracy in the Western Hemisphere. Since the adoption of free-market economies, the violations of human rights at the hands of Chilean and Uruguayan security forces and secret police have been unprecedented. The revolutionary military government that seized power in Peru in 1968 began with a commitment to satisfy popular demands for structural change. But beginning in 1975, internal and external factors caused Peru to abandon many of its reforms in favor of austerity measures. The state's use of force against the dissatisfied masses rose dramatically.[39]

These changes, which have become pronounced over the last decade, have not been unrelated to changes in the international environment during this time. The oil price hike of 1973, and the stagflationary crisis that ensued in the advanced industrial states, contributed to the severity of balance-of-trade deficits and inflation among nonoil-producing less developed countries (LDCs). The rapid expansion of international liquidity following the gains made by OPEC brought unlimited opportunities for credit extension on the part of private banks, and urgent requests for borrowing on the part of LDCs faced with foreign exchange depletion. As LDC borrowing increased, so did its external debt, wedding these regimes to internal policies that would better their chances for the refinancing or rescheduling of outstanding loans. Governments became more willing to use force to guarantee the longevity of those programs most favored by their international creditors. Orthodox stabilization measures usually topped the "most-favored" list.

Governments have doggedly pursued these policies despite their dismal results. Under stabilization plans in Chile (1973-present), Argentina (1976-present), and Uruguay (1974-present), there has been prolonged economic stagnation, persistently high inflation, mass unemployment, and severe income inequalities. Foreign businessmen have been reluctant to invest, despite strenuous efforts by these governments to provide every sort of incentive. Nonetheless, international creditors seem pleased with the efforts made by the authorities to satisfy their needs for repayment of loans, even at the cost of economic decay. The persistent and effective use of high levels of state coercion has prevented the popular sectors from overturning these policies and the regimes that made them.

NOTES

1. Among the most noteworthy contributions to these fields are Guillermo O'Donnell, *Modernization and Bureaucratic-Authoritarianism: Studies in South American Politics* (Berkeley, Calif.: Institute of International Studies, University of California Press, 1973);

Philippe C. Schmitter, "Still the Century of Corporatism?" in *The New Corporatism: Social-Political Structures in the Iberian World*, ed. F. Pike and T. Stritch (London and Notre Dame: University of Notre Dame Press, 1974); Alfred Stepan, "The New Professionalism of Internal Warfare and Military Role Expansion," in *Authoritarian Brazil*, ed. Alfred Stepan (New Haven, Conn.: Yale University Press, 1973).

2. Albert O. Hirschman, "The Turn to Authoritarianism in Latin America and the Search for Its Economic Determinants," in *The New Authoritarianism in Latin America*, ed. David Collier (Princeton, N.J.: Princeton University Press, 1979); Robert R. Kaufman, "Industrial Change and Authoritarian Rule," in *The New Authoritarianism in Latin America*; John Sheahan, "Market-Oriented Economic Policies and Political Repression in Latin America," *Economic Development and Cultural Change* 28 (1980):267-291; Thomas Skidmore, "The Politics of Economic Stabilization in Postwar Latin America, *Authoritarianism and Corporatism in Latin America*, ed. J. Malloy (Pittsburgh: University of Pittsburgh Press, 1977); Barbara Stallings, "Peru and the U.S. Banks: Privatization of Financial Relations," in *Capitalism and the State in U.S.-Latin American Relations*, ed. R. Fagen (Stanford, Calif.: Stanford University Press, 1979).

3. Ivo K. Feierabend et al., *Violence and Politics: Theories and Research* (Englewood Cliffs, N.J.: Prentice-Hall, 1972).

4. Fernando H. Cardoso, "On the Characterization of Authoritarian Regimes in Latin America," in *The New Authoritarianism in Latin America*.

5. Howard J. Wiarda, *Corporatism and National Development in Latin America* (Boulder, Colo.: Westview Press, 1981).

6. John McCamant and Ernest A. Duff, *Violence and Repression in Latin America: A Quantitative and Historical Analysis* (New York: The Free Press, 1976), p. 184.

7. Rosemary Thorp, "Inflation and the Financing of Economic Development," in *Financing Development in Latin America*, ed. K. Griffin (London: Macmillan and Co., 1971), pp. 191-93.

8. David Felix, "Monetarist, Structuralist, and Import-Substituting Industrialization: A Critical Appraisal," in *Inflation and Growth in Latin America*, ed W. Baer and I. Kerstenetzky (Homewood, Ill.: Richard D. Irwin Co., 1964).

9. Ironically, the orthodox proponents do not object to government-imposed wage freezes, despite the clear violation of free-market principles.

10. IMF-styled stabilization plans combine monetary as well as fiscal and income measures and in that sense are not strictly monetarist. The monetarist doctrine, as typified by the work of Milton Friedman, says that only the supply of money should be regulated to bring an economy into equilibrium. See Milton Friedman, "The Role of Monetary Policy," *The American Economic Review* 58 (March 1968).

11. It should be added that these free-market advocates do not pretend that their plans are long-term development strategies; instead they see them as short-run recovery programs and necessary preludes to further growth.

12. David Felix, "An Alternative View of the 'Monetarist'-'Structural' Controversy," in *Latin American Issues: Essays and Comments*, ed. A. O. Hirschman (New York: The Twentieth Century Fund, 1961).

13. Alejandro Foxley, "Stabilization Policies and Their Effects on Employment and Income Distribution: A Latin American Perspective," in *Economic Stabilization in Developing Countries*, ed. W. R. Cline and S. Weintraub (Washington D.C.: Brookings Institution, 1981), pp. 200-201.

14. Ibid., pp. 201-4.

15. Ibid., p. 215.

16. See various articles on this subject in Ivo K. Feierabend, Rosalind L. Feierabend, and Ted R. Gurr, eds., *Anger, Violence and Politics: Theories and Research* (Englewood Cliffs, N.J.: Prentice-Hall, 1972).

17. Ivo K. Feierabend and Rosalind L. Feierabend, "Systematic Conditions of Political Aggression: An Application of Frustration-Aggression Theory" in *Anger, Violence and Politics*, p. 156.

18. E. Zimmerman, "Macro-Comparative Research on Political Protest," in *Handbook of Political Conflict*, ed. T. R. Gurr (New York: The Free Press, 1980).

19. Ted Gurr and others hypothesized a curvilinear relationship between coercion and protest, whereby protest would be extensive when government used moderate levels of force, but would decline significantly when very high levels of coercion were used. See Ted Gurr, *Why Men Rebel* (Princeton, N.J.: Princeton University Press, 1970), pp. 232-51.

20. Thorp, "Inflation and the Financing of Economic Development," p. 187.

21. More radical versions of structuralism, such as dependency theory, oppose foreign investment on grounds that it denies the host country sovereignty over resources, capital, and labor and extracts a surplus that is repatriated to the home country.

22. Thorp, "Inflation and the Financing of Economic Development," p. 191.

23. Franz Neumann, *The Democratic and the Authoritarian State: Essays in Political and Legal Theory* (Glencoe, Ill.: The Free Press, 1957), p. 17.

24. Alfred Stepan, "The New Professionalism of Internal Warfare and Military Role Expansion," in *Authoritarian Brazil*, ed. Alfred Stepan (New Haven, Conn.: Yale University Press, 1973).

25. Anthony Sampson, *The Money Lenders: Bankers and a World of Turmoil* (New York: Viking Press, 1981).

26. In 1952, the Fund initiated a system of standby arrangements whereby countries could draw on higher credit tranches, should that be necessary. With the signing of a standby loan, the borrower will send the IMF a letter of intent, promising to oblige by the terms of a stabilization agreement.

27. D. Cochrane and G. H. Orcutt, "Application of Least Squares Regression to Relationships Containing Auto Correlated Error Terms," *Journal of the American Statistical Association* 44 (1949):32-61.

28. Gary Wynia, *Argentina in the Postwar Era: Politics and Economic Policy Making in a Divided Society* (Albuquerque: University of New Mexico Press, 1978), pp. 87-88.

29. Ibid., p. 89.

30. "Argentina Gets $329 Million in Aid," *New York Times*, 30 December 1958, p. 1.

31. "Economic Reform Set in Argentina," *New York Times*, 1 December 1958, p. 17.

32. Wynia, *Argentina in the Postwar Era*, pp. 116-17.

33. Ibid., pp. 169-79.

34. *Pick's Currency Guide*, 1967, p. 59.

35. For a full discussion on the Peronist stabilization plan, see Guido Di Tella, "The Economic Policies of Argentina's Labour-Based Government (1973-76)," in *Inflation and Stabilization in Latin America*, ed. R. Thorp and L. Whitehead (New York: Holmes and Meier Publishers, 1979).

36. "Argentine Chief Videla Sworn In," *New York Times*, 30 March 1976, p. 7.

37. Julian Martel, "Domination by Debt: Finance Capital in Argentina," *NACLA Report on the Americas: Public Debt and Private Profit* 12 (July-August 1978): 32-34.

38. "The Disappeared of Argentina: List of Cases Reported to Amnesty International," *Amnesty International*, May 1979.

39. Barbara Stallings, "Peru and the U.S. Banks: Privatization of Financial Relations," in *Capitalism and the State in U.S.-Latin American Relations*, pp. 246-47.

6

Militarism and Repression in the Philippines

Jim Zwick

In September, 1972, President Ferdinand Marcos placed the entire Republic of the Philippines under martial law and called out the military to restore "law and order" and to "enforce obedience to all the laws and decrees, orders and regulations promulgated by [him] personally or upon [his] direction."[1] Although Marcos likened the declaration of martial law to a "revolution from the center," the repression that followed it was to recall memories of colonization rather than liberation.

In declaring martial law, Marcos was responding to a wave of political activism that began in the late 1960s in response to increasing awareness of the internal inequalities, corruption in government, and external domination of the country's economic and political affairs that had continued since the country's colonial period. Following a series of protests organized by students, workers, and peasants, the Communist party of the Philippines regrouped under more militant leadership in 1968, and its military branch, the New People's Army, was formed in 1969. At the same time, the Muslim Filipinos were engaged in sporadic warfare with the Armed Forces of the Philippines in an attempt to defend their homelands in Mindanao and the Sulu Islands from the government's policy of resettling landless "Christian" peasants on the Muslim's ancestral territory.

In short, the internal political instability Marcos was responding to when he declared martial law was a result of gross regional and sectoral inequalities accentuated by a lack of national integration and awareness among many sectors of the population that the nation was being politically and economically dominated by foreign countries—especially the United States, although Japan was

This chapter is a substantially revised and condensed version of a paper which was published as Jim Zwick, *Militarism and Repression in the Philippines*, Working Paper Series (now McGill Studies in International Development) No. 31 (Montreal: Centre for Developing-Area Studies, McGill University, 1982).

also very much involved in the Philippine economy by that time. It would thus be unfair to state that repression in the Philippines began with the declaration of martial law or even with the Marcos presidency. What can be said is that the increased militarization of the country following the declaration of martial law has greatly increased it.

This chapter explores the structures and processes of militarism and militarization in the Philippines during the martial law period as a means of illuminating the links between militarism and repression, not only in terms of their effect on extreme forms of repression such as those that characterized the martial law period but also in terms of their effect on reinforcing and contributing to already existing repressive structures within the society.

MILITARISM AND MILITARIZATION

Militarism is a dynamic process operating on both national and international levels to mobilize people and resources for organized warfare that acts in such a way as to expand the role of the military over civilian affairs. The specific characteristics of this mobilization will differ somewhat between countries, but whether its purpose is to deter invasion or attack, to engage in war with an external or internal foe, or to gain prestige and credibility within a system of alliances, its form is becoming increasingly common: the establishment or expansion of highly technological military systems and an increasing reliance on military force in all aspects of political affairs. Marek Thee has described this condition as subsuming symptoms such as "a rush to armaments, the growing role of the military (understood as the military establishment) in national and international affairs, the use of force as an instrument of prevalence and political power, and the increasing influence of the military in civilian affairs."[2]

I will employ a definition of militarism that follows Thee's but includes only those aspects of military influence over civilian life that result either from direct military intervention in the people's lives and behavior (arrests, relocations, indiscriminate warfare, and so on) or indirect structural involvement in political and economic affairs (increasing military expenditures at the expense of civilian needs, military-oriented industries, and so on). Militarization will then denote the spread of military values and structures (discipline and conformity, centralization of authority, hierarchization, and so on) into the mainstream of national economic and socio-political life. *Militarism* is distinguished as being of a more material and physical quality (the rush to arms) and *militarization* is predominately the spread of an ideological orientation, often leading to military leadership of civilian organizations and institutions.

The most commonly used indicators of the degree of militarism of any one society are the proportion of a country's GNP used for military purposes over time and the corresponding figures for health and education expenditures. They are often inaccurate, however, because there is usually a positive correlation between economic growth and the growth of defense budgets in the Third World.

In a country with rapid economic growth, the percentage of GNP used in military expenditures is likely to show a much slower increase than the actual figures for military spending. With this and other problems in mind, the alternative of comparing military expenditures (Milex) with central government expenditures (CGE) over time has been proposed as the most accurate indicator.[3] Although a country's GNP is not fully available for investment purposes, CGE figures indicate actual expenditures and are thus a more accurate indicator of government priorities. For this reason, I rely predominately on this method while also making use of several other indicators to point out the actual quantitative and qualitative changes they represent.

REPRESSION

In this chapter I use *repression* to denote the purposeful denial of basic political and economic rights by direct or indirect governmental or inter-governmental sanction or policy or by systemic or structural means such as the perpetuation of unjust structures within the society.

Several attempts have been made to measure differences in degrees of repression, but they are fraught with ambiguities, inconsistencies, and biases, and to my knowledge, no method has yet been found that adequately accounts for the many variables involved.[4] Therefore, I will not attempt a statistical evaluation of repression in the Philippines or to put its conditions in relation to other countries as the main means of determining the existence of repressive conditions. Rather, I will concentrate on those aspects of political and economic repression that have been influenced or created by militarism. Data will be used to indicate trends, but they will be placed into the wider context of other political developments and first-hand accounts of human rights violations. It should be kept in mind, though, that such measures can be used only as rough and tentative assessments of actual conditions.

THE LINKS

Michael Randle pointed out two central relationships between militarism and repression: the instrumental and the structural.[5] At the instrumental level, the military is not only the major arm of repression but also threatens the liberties of the people through the very process of raising and maintaining a highly centralized military. Examples are the restrictions on freedom of information, discussion, and association common in national security states; the militarization of internal security forces; and the use of military justice. Instrumental links may also be seen operating at the international level through colonial forms of intervention and major power involvement in local conflicts and in the spread of military techniques and ideology through international military training programs.

The structural level refers to the influence of militarism on economic and socio-political affairs that tends to make repression more likely. In the Third World, militarism contributes to and perpetuates unjust class structures, reinforcing patterns of dependency within the societies. On the international level, militarism maintains an unequal global division of labor and demands for cheap sources of energy and other raw materials and produces many of the conditions that lead to military intervention in the Third World to protect political and economic interests.

It should be noted that links between militarism and repression do not have a one-to-one correspondence. As Randle pointed out: "Militarism is only one of a number of factors which influence the political, economic and social climate. What can be said is that the influence is a negative one and that it interacts with others to create or reinforce those situations in which repression occurs."[6]

INSTRUMENTAL LINKS

Martial Law: Creating the National Security State

When Ferdinand Marcos placed the Philippines under martial law, he exercised his constitutional right as president to call out the military, suspend the writ of habeas corpus, and place all or part of the Philippines under martial law in time of invasion, insurrection, or other national emergency.

There was, in fact, a threat of insurrection. The New People's Army (NPA) and the Muslims were engaged in intermittent warfare with the Armed Forces of the Philippines (AFP) and were both seen as a threat. So too were labor organizations and student, youth, and other mass organizations. All were seen as heavily infiltrated and controlled by Communist elements. Nor were the military, government officials, or the judiciary free from attack. Corruption was to be weeded out in all areas, and the judiciary, "unable to administer justice," lost its traditional autonomy as military courts were set up. To prevent the media from becoming "tools of the oligarchs," several publishers and journalists were immediately arrested; newspapers, magazines, and journals were forced to halt publication; and radio and television stations run by Marcos's political opponents were permanently closed.

Throughout all, however, Marcos insisted that the declaration of martial law did not represent a military takeover of civil government functions. "The government of the Republic of the Philippines. . .continues," he repeatedly assured the people.[7] Later, to an interviewer from the *Far Eastern Economic Review*, he said: "From the very beginning it was understood that the military would do the bidding of the civil authority."[8]

It is questionable, though, that such a distinction between civil and military authority can be made under martial law. Through it Marcos institutionalized the military as the dominant force in Philippine society. They were not only to enforce his decrees, orders, and regulations, but were the model for his conception of the "New Society." He saw the military as playing a "revolutionary role" in the creation of the "New Society" and as the "sentinel of [their] political sovereignty."[9] Adrian Cristobal, a spokesman for the Marcos regime, described the importance of the military in this way: "Since we [in the Marcos administration] have adopted discipline as a necessary element of national progress, and since discipline has long been associated in our minds with the military way of life, it is but natural that the military now looms so vividly in our thinking."[10]

Thus discipline, restraint, centralization of power, and other aspects of traditional military ideology were to be the cornerstones of the New Society. With the declaration of martial law, the threat to national security, both real and exaggerated, was defined in its broadest terms, creating an atmosphere of xenophobia that primed the country for the rash of presidential directives, decrees, and proclamations; the aggrandizement of the military; and the increased military control over civilian life that was to follow.

Constitutional Change

The constitutional change that Marcos pushed through as a referendum in 1973 gave the president unprecedented powers over the entire governmental structure and is a prime example of the militarization of socio-political life that took place under martial law. It permitted Marcos to remain in power indefinitely as both president and prime minister and enabled him to replace arbitrarily any or all government officials, including members of the judiciary, simply by naming their successors.[11] This gave Marcos full power over all government offices by ensuring that he could control or replace all who held government posts.

The Constitution also provided for the continuation of "all proclamations, orders, decrees, instructions, and acts promulgated, issued or done by the *incumbent* president" as part of the "law of the land" unless nullified by Marcos himself or by the regular National Assembly.[12] In other words, all proclamations, decrees, and so on issued by Marcos under martial law would remain in effect after martial law was lifted unless repealed by Marcos or the National Assembly. Since Marcos had the power to disband the interim National Assembly, there was no chance for civilian check on his and the military's power during martial law. Also, since only Marcos could lift martial law, and the military who monitored the need for it, there was slim chance of civilian powers being restored until the president and the military were assured of continuing control over the society.

The Sixth Amendment to the 1973 Constitution, passed by referendum in 1976, further consolidated Marcos's power over the governmental structure by allowing him to declare an "unidentified emergency" and to legislate by decree even after the lifting of martial law. Among the "emergencies" that would warrant legislation by decree is "when the interim or regular legislature 'fails or is unable to act adequately on any matter for any reason that in the President's judgement requires immediate action.' "[13]

Constitutional change in the Philippines led to the militarization of traditionally autonomous government structures through the centralization and hierarchization of control under one person. There was no allowance for civilian opposition to Marcos's or the military' actions and policies since they could lead either to charges of subversion or prompt removal from office through the naming of a successor. By allowing the continuation of Marcos's decrees and orders beyond the lifting of martial law, the 1973 Constitution ensured that any moves to reorder the government along more democratic and less repressive lines would involve a long and arduous legal process in the National Assembly. The "institution-alization of the revolution," as Marcos wrote of the Constitution in 1973, represents, in fact, the institutionalization of militarization in the country.[14]

Increased Military Control over Civilian Life

The declaration of martial law and the rash of anti-terrorist orders that accompanied it gave the military a degree of control over civilian life and behavior unprecedented in Philippine history. Although technically the military did not rule the country, increases in the military's power and prestige, size, and wealth were nonetheless evident.

Martial law gave the military virtually unlimited powers for the search, arrest, and detention of civilians. Through the suspension of the writ of habeas corpus, the responsibility for proving an individual's guilt, or even to provide legal counsel, was removed. In addition, military tribunals were set up throughout the country to handle cases concerning "national security" and the civilian judiciary lost most of its power and autonomy. Amnesty International stated in 1976 that "the rule of law under martial law is authoritarian presidential-military rule, unchecked by constitutional guarantee or limitations."[15]

The expanded influence of the military in business and political roles has also increased its influence over the society as a whole. The secretary of national defense and other top military officers have worked directly with the president since 1972. Marcos appointed officers to manage several corporations and the military was ordered to control all public utilities, the media, and transportation services. Presidential representatives on development, many of which are military officers, were established to supervise regional development projects, reducing the authority of local officials.

This trend of growing military influence in national policy making combined with an increase in military officers moving into high-level positions in business is connected to the spread of military ideology into the civilian sector. The U.S. International Military Education and Training Program, for instance, is designed to promote military leadership and forms of organization in national development processes. One result, implied in Adrian Cristobal's statement about the importance of the military, is that military values and goals such as law and order, discipline, and centralization of power become the driving force behind both government and business policies and structures.

The aggrandizement of the military also expanded the influence of the military over the society. Although the full ramifications of the increases in the military's size and financial support will be discussed in the next section, it is important to point out here that the dramatic increases that occurred during martial law had a substantial effect on the regime's ability to carry out the repressive sanctions on the population discussed below.

The militarization of internal security forces also played a large role in augmenting the repressive power of the Marcos regime. Although the fundamental aspects of Philippine internal security forces were present before martial law was declared, the Philippine Constabulary (PC) and the Local Self-Defense Force were not fully mobilized under direct AFP control until 1973. The Integrated National Police, under direct PC control, was not established until 1975. The results of these developments have been described by Walden Bello: "Both the army and the constabulary are now the prime police agencies in the country, with local police activity having virtually disappeared in insurgency zones and playing a secondary role elsewhere. Political intelligence and security functions have been centralized to a degree unparalleled in Philippine history, with the military-dominated National Intelligence and Security Agency (NISA) forming the apex of a structure of interlocking army and constabulary agencies."[16] Thus the military values of centralization and hierarchization can be seen as thoroughly pervading the internal security forces, eliminating local control over police activities.

The effects that these forms of militarization have on creating the stimuli for repressive practices has been explained by the Study Group on Militarization of the International Peace Research Association. Pointing out that although militarization leads to *more* respect for law and order among the population in general, due in part to fear of severe sanctions, it leads to *less* respect for law and order among the political and economic elite. They concluded that "this contradictory situation is probably due to the fact that the reciprocal interaction between various groups of a society in a democratic system tends to be eliminated in a militarized system, making it more possible for the authorities to control the people and less possible for the people to control the authorities."[17]

Figures from Amnesty International (AI) and the International Commission of Jurists (ICJ) indicate the impact this has had on repression: more than 60,000 people were arrested between 1972 and 1977, many of them for political reasons. In 1977 AI estimated that at least 2,000 of these political prisoners were still being detained without trial.

Another effect of the lack of civilian control over the military was the frequent cases of torture performed on political prisoners by the military. Although AI, the ICJ, and Task Force Detainees Philippines (TFDP) all compiled documented lists of military personnel who actively participated in the torture of prisoners, none has been convicted. Some have been acquitted by military courts; the trials of others have been postponed indefinitely.[18]

Although TFDP reported that cases of torture decreased slightly from 1978 through early 1980 compared with previous years, they noted that this trend was accompanied by a marked increase in the number of "salvagings" and "disappearances." As many as 303 cases of substantiated "salvagings" and 233 "disappearances" have been recorded by TFDP from 1975 to early 1980.[19] Other military abuses include declaring barrios a "no man's land," where anyone seen may be shot on sight; extortion; burning of houses and produce; strafing; abuse of women; and the forced relocation of whole villages into "strategic hamlets."

These internationally condemned repressive practices were nurtured by the atmosphere of urgency within the national security state and the free reign given the military to restore "peace and order." These conditions, however, have increased the range of opposition to the government and have virtually forced the people into acceptance of violent revolution, since all other means of protest (demonstrations, use of the media, boycotts, strikes, and so on) have been outlawed by presidential decrees and orders. This has been one of the important factors in the formation of a united National Democratic Front that coordinates the efforts of diverse groups such as the NPA and the Catholic clergy. The constitutional change, which eliminated all chances for electoral opposition to the Marcos regime, also contributed to this by radicalizing segments of the urban and opposition political elite.[20]

STRUCTURAL LINKS

It should be noted again here at the outset that there is a considerable overlap between the instrumental and structural links between militarism and repression. They interact to a large degree and, although they can be isolated somewhat for discussion, should not be considered as separate from each other. They are, by their very nature, mutually reinforcing.

Rising Military Expenditures

In the discussion of increased military control over civilian life above, the general trend of increasing military expenditures was pointed out, and this was tied to the regime's ability to carry out repressive sanctions against the population. This instrumental link to political repression is matched by a structural link to economic repression because of the vast quantity of government expenditures and raw materials used by the military that could otherwise be put toward meeting civilian needs and reducing regional inequalities.

A rapid increase in military expenditures (Milex) took place following the declaration of martial law. Milex in constant 1976 dollars increased from US$198 million in 1972 to US$597 million in 1977. The rate of the increase has outpaced growth in central government expenditures (CGE), clearly indicating a strong preference toward Milex over other services. Although the Milex/CGE ratio was relatively high at 10.1 percent in 1972, by 1977 it had nearly doubled to 19.8 percent, a trend that has not only had an effect on building the regime's repressive powers but also on depriving the population from urgently needed government expenditures.

The latter effect can be seen in the comparison of Milex with public health expenditures (PHE) and public education expenditures (PEE). Although combined PHE and PEE declined in the 1973-1977 period relative to the previous five years, there was a dramatic increase in Milex to the point where in 1976, the last year figures for all three categories are available, Milex accounted for US$176 million more than both PHE and PEE combined.[21] Likewise, although the number of armed forces per 1,000 people more than doubled in the 1973-1977 period from 1.55 to 3.45 per 1,000 people, numbers of physicians and teachers declined.

In the Philippines it cannot be said that these priorities on military spending are justified because the people's needs for health and education services have been met. Figures gathered by Ruth Sivard indicate that there is a need for greater emphasis in both of these areas. In 1976 there were 54 school-age Filipinos per teacher, only 56 percent of the school-age population in school, and a literacy rate of 80 percent. Health figures show a similar trend for 1976: 3,154 people per physician, 650 people per hospital bed, an infant mortality rate of 80 per 1,000 children in the first year of life, a life expectancy of only 58 years, far below standard nutritional levels and only 50 percent of the population with a safe water supply.[22] Compounding the impact of neglect of these crucial needs is the fact that the services that are available differ greatly from region to region.[23]

Although rising military expenditures did not create the conditions of rural/urban inequalities in access to basic needs, they reinforced them by channeling funds away from programs that would benefit the majority of the civilian population. The potential for meeting people's needs certainly increased during the 1970s since the country's GNP grew larger than it had ever been. Unfortunately, military priorities work against the needs of the civilian population. Marcos argued that the restoration of law and order must precede other goals in the establishment of the New Society. This may be true since increases in health and education expenditures would mean little if schools and clinics were continually surrounded by warfare, disrupting normal daily activities. It cannot be assumed, however, that increased military spending alone can restore law and order since it aggravates the very conditions the people revolt against, not only in terms of access to basic needs but in the orientation of the economy toward rapid industrialization and external dependence.

Arms Imports and Domestic Military Industries

The effects of arms imports and the development of domestic military industries on the economy can be seen in two inter-related areas: in strengthening economic and technological dependence on developed countries and in rein-forcing the export-orientation of the domestic economy for the accumulation of internationally acceptable currency needed for the import of arms and other commodities. The effect of both factors is to orient the economy toward meeting the needs of the developed countries rather than those of the domestic population.

Arms imports strengthen economic and technological dependence, because they set in motion a chain of supplementary import demands, thus predisposing that future CGE will also be put toward military imports from developed coun-tries. Spare parts, technological assistance, and special housing arrangements for foreign specialists represent only some of the extra demands caused by imports of military technology. The extent of the effects this pattern can have on tying up future CGE can be seen in the Philippine Air Force's (PAF) 1977 estimate that the ten-year, life-cycle cost of the twenty-five Vought F-8H "Crusader Fighters" ordered that year would be US$4.39 million each, or approximately 3.25 times the initial acquisition price, despite the fact that ten F-8Hs for spare parts were included in the acquisition price. A 1980 PAF report pointed out that life-cycle cost is actually much higher than originally estimated due to unforeseen maintenance and operational costs, many of which result from a lack of local mechanics with the skills necessary to work on the F-8Hs.[24] When it is considered that Philippine arms imports from 1973-1977 more than doubled those for the previous five years, it is safe to assume that there was a corresponding increase in dependence on future military expenditures.

The development of domestic military industries also increases external de-pendence. The Philippines has begun an ambitious arms industry program in hopes of becoming self-sufficient in production of military equipment. They currently produce light aircraft, helicopters, missiles and rockets, and small arms and ammunition. All of the programs, however, consist of licensed production with technological assistance, the technology needed to produce the items being retained by the licenser.

There are many factors that work against Third World countries in development of domestic arms industries: increasing research and development (R&D) ex-penditures, resulting in more complex weapon systems; fast rates of innovation, leading to rapid technological obsolescence; increasing requirements for specially adapted infrastructure to create the operational conditions for major weapon systems, resulting in large indirect costs; rapid increases of product and life-cycle costs, leading to shorter production runs; and increasing complexity of weapon systems, allowing effective control of the technology by the licenser over a considerable period of time.[25]

Although production of arms that are competitive in the world market is essential if a country is to be able to maintain economies of scale in production of weapons and use arms exports to defray R&D and production costs, it is unlikely that the Philippines will be able to acquire technology quickly enough to keep pace with countries that already have expansive arms producing capa-bilities and global markets for their products. These difficulties will maintain the country's dependence on imports of military technology over a considerable period, reinforcing the economy's export orientation as the need for foreign currencies continues.

It is not only production of advanced weapon systems that leads to external dependence but small arms production as well. The Philippines has experienced this since 1974 when it began developing an M-16 rifle facility in cooperation with Colt Industries using Foreign Military Sales Credits totaling US$21.8 million. U.S. government figures indicate that this and similar M-16 projects in other countries have had to rely heavily on foreign imports for production of the rifles. Imports in the countries, including Taiwan and South Korea, have accounted for 53 percent to more than 80 percent of the programs' total costs.[26] Since technology for such programs is retained by the licenser, and imports of foreign-produced parts still account for over half of the programs' costs, it is unlikely that the benefits of domestic arms production can justify the many costs in human terms that are incurred upon the nation.

An example of the effects that the development of arms industries has on the economic development of the country and thus on the population as a whole is the reorientation of industrial goals that such industries demand. Because the Philippines lacks sufficient economies of scale and since civilian applications for highly specialized industrial techniques and products do not exist, the development of military industries tends to dominate industrial development in such a way as to cause a considerable waste of energy and capital when compared with civilian priorities. Specialized development goals such as the manufacture of high-quality steel and special alloys that are necessary for many military products but unnecessary for civilian use are added "civilian" costs of military industrial programs. In a country like the Philippines where schools, hospitals, roads, irrigation, and housing are all in short supply, the added costs of industrial and construction projects that must use militarily specified materials hinder attempts to meet civilian needs. They work, therefore, to reinforce existing conditions of unequal access to basic needs: the conditions that promote internal unrest.

The export orientation of the economy for the accumulation of internationally acceptable currency is reinforced by arms imports and the development of military industries because of the external dependence they promote. The process of raising funds to pay for military imports reduces the chances of the country's moving away from the import-substitution, export-promotion industrialization program it has been pursuing. The effects of this industrialization program have been described by Robin Luckham:

1) Conflicts between industrial/urban centers and rural/agricultural peripheries, intensified to the extent that the latter subsidize the process of industrialization. 2) Conflicts between capital and labor in the industrial sector, intensified to the extent that profits and investment are subsidized by low wages. 3) Marginalization, creation of a "reserve army of unemployed" by industrialization/urbanization process. 4) Crises created by exhaustion of

process of import substitution. Cycle of foreign exchange shortages, inflation, unrest, repression, military spending and more shortages, inflation, etc.[27]

Export promotion further exacerbates this pattern by requiring sufficiently low wages to attract foreign investment, and the vulnerability of the economy to crises in international markets is also heightened. These conditions, in turn, dictate repressive policies such as the outlawing of strikes and demonstrations in the urban areas, increased military presence in the rural areas to quell revolts and protect foreign investments, and increased military control over the civilian population in general. The added costs of these military operations lead to further foreign exchange shortages and the cycle outlined by Luckham is intensified.

It should not be surprising, then, that although the government has established that a family's annual income must be at least 15,000 pesos to lead a "decent life," 83 percent of all Filipino families earn less than 8,000 pesos a year, and an additional 12 percent earn less than 15,000 pesos annually.[28] Export-oriented industrialization, which is both cause and consequence of militarism, dictates such conditions by requiring low wages both to make Philippine products competitive in world markets and to attract foreign investment.

THE INTERNATIONAL CONNECTION

Militarism and repression in the Philippines should not be viewed apart from the general pattern of global militarism. There are many links between the militarism of the United States, Western Europe, and the Asian countries and the political and economic trends in the Philippines described above. The subject is far too broad to cover completely here, but three general areas indicate the extent of these connections: national security thinking, military and economic aid, and international arms marketing.

National Security Thinking

National security thinking has played a role in cementing the interests of the elite across national borders and has contributed to continued international support for the Marcos regime despite international recognition of gross violations of human rights within the country.

Although the cross-national ideological struggle between communist and capitalist countries is an obvious aspect of the elite alliance, U.S. dependence on trade with Asia and the Persian Gulf is another main reason for U.S. unwillingness to relinquish control of its military bases in the Philippines. They are not so much oriented toward defense of the Philippines as toward military operations throughout the western Pacific and Indian Ocean/Persian Gulf regions.

Since the United States is one of the world's largest importers of energy and other raw materials, it is not surprising that access to resources and markets in Asia and the Persian Gulf and protection of the sea lines of communication over which the resources are transported are a major aspect of U.S. economic and military objectives for those regions. Control of the military bases and military assistance programs are used to secure these objectives because the U.S. government believes that military presence reinforces trade patterns and willingness to accept direct foreign investment and retards protectionist pressures that would affect U.S. markets.[29]

In the post-World War II era, *national security* has come to be defined in broad terms, including not only military threat but also ideological and economic threats. This has made effective curtailment of arms transfers increasingly difficult and has contributed to militarism in the Third World by increasing the stakes involved for an arms supplier in refusing an arms transfer. In the U.S.-Philippine relationship the political and economic stakes have involved control of the U.S. military bases, leading to continued support for a pro-U.S. authoritarian regime to avoid having a strongly nationalist or a Communist regime come to power, either of which would demand the nationalization of the bases.

Military and Economic Aid

The link national security thinking has with militarism and repression in the Philippines is that the United States' stake in maintaining the military bases and political stability in the region for the sake of expanding markets plays a major role in determining that U.S. policy puts greater emphasis on national security criteria (leading to increased arms transfers to the country) than on human rights considerations. Hence dramatic increases occurred in both the Foreign Military Sales (FMS) and Foreign Military Sales Financing Program (FMSFP) categories from 1973 to 1978 during the preceding six-year period, and only slight reductions occurred in the International Military Education and Training (IMET) and Military Assistance Program (MAP) categories (see Table 6.1).

Although the U.S. Congress passed a law in 1977 limiting U.S. military assistance to the Philippines on human rights grounds, the perceived necessity of controlling the bases in the Philippines led President Carter to concede to Marcos's pressure for $100 million a year in military and economic aid in exchange for continued U.S. control of the bases. The marked increase in FMSFP appropriations beginning in 1980 is a result of this Philippine Bases Agreement signed by President Carter in 1979.

Although total U.S. military assistance represents only a part of Philippine military acquisitions, it still represents a formidable source of support for the regime both in its effect on strengthening the military and in the tacit support for authoritarian rule it exhibits in the political realm.

Military and economic aid plays an even further role in determining Philippine domestic policies. The 1978 U.S. Foreign Assistance and Related Programs Appropriations Act states that ''the president can deny assistance to the government of any less developed country which has failed to enter into an agreement with the U.S to institute an investment guarantee program providing against

Table 6.1 Official U.S. Military Assistance to the Philippines, FY 1955-1982 (in thousands of dollars)[a]

Fiscal Year	IMET	MAP	FMSFP	FMS (agreements)
1955-66	23,871	327,250	0	4,646
1967	910	28,129	0	439
1968	1,327	21,319	0	237
1969	1,051	18,279	0	454
1970	795	15,600	0	852
1971	824	14,622	0	1,107
1972	994	13,156	0	468
1967-72	5,901	111,105	0	3,557
1973	813	16,141	0	1,159
1974	579	14,626	8,600	4,339
1975	410	19,465	14,000	32,006
1976	825	21,590	17,400	35,347
1977	614	16,499	20,000	67,919
1978	704	18,100	18,500	33,250
1973-78	3,945	106,421	78,500	174,020
1979	650	17,100	15,600	17,100
1980	539	25,000	50,000	20,000b
1981	600	25,000	50,000	10,000b
1982c	1,300	1,466d	50,000	NA

a Sources: U.S. Congress, Senate, Committee on Foreign Relations, Indonesia, Thailand, the Philippines and Taiwan (Washington, D.C.: U.S. Government Printing Office, 1980), p. 44; U.S. Department of State, Country Reports on Human Rights Practices for 1981 (Washington, D.C.: U.S. Government Printing Office, 1982), p. 674; U.S. Congress, House, Committee on Foreign Relations, Subcommittee on Asian & Pacific Affairs, Foreign Assistance Legislation for Fiscal Year 1982 (Part 5), (Washington, D.C.: U.S. Government Printing Office, 1981), p. xix.

b Projected   c Subcommittee recommendations   d FY 1982 figure is for windup costs for programs voted in past years NA Not Available

IMET - International Military Education and Training program; MAP - Military Assistance Program; FMSFP - Foreign Military Sales Financing Program; FMS - Foreign Military Sales inconvertibility, expropriation, or confiscation."[30] Thus if the Philippines had implemented a decision handed down by the Philippine Supreme Court in August, 1972, that all acquisitions of agricultural lands by Americans after 1946 were illegal, they would have risked discontinuation of all economic and military assistance to the country from the United States, which would have meant a vital loss in dependable foreign reserves. After declaring martial law, Marcos moved quickly to overturn the Supreme Court's decision, first by presidential decree and then through the 1973 Constitution.[31]

The IMET program is perhaps one of the strongest links between militarism in the United States and the Philippines. Ernest W. Lefever has described the program as a "low-cost, low-risk foreign policy instrument that has served the United States' interest in interstate stability and has provided a valuable channel of communication and influence with a significant elite, especially in the Third World."[32]

The IMET program proliferates both military skills and ideology. In the program officers are taught that the military is the best organization to lead their countries through a phase of rapid industrialization. Peter Lock and Herbert Wulf pointed out that U.S. leaders have promoted this, because they see the military as the "most important modern, rational, and bureaucratically organized institution in traditional under-developed societies."[33] They have therefore relied upon this training as a way of speeding up development and guiding the countries' political systems along acceptable paths. In this respect, the IMET program is an excellent example of the role of military ideology in international affairs.

From 1950 to 1979, 16,363 Filipino officers received training through the IMET program.[34] U.S. training of Philippine military personnel has also taken the forms of integrated operations against the Huks in the 1950s, joint training exercises, and the continued presence of the Joint U.S. Military Advisory Group (JUSMAG).[35]

There are many links between this training and both the repressive practices carried out by the military and the increasing prevalence of the military in the country's economic and political affairs. The Philippines were used as the testing ground for U.S. counterinsurgency doctrine in the 1950s, and the "strategic hamlet" technique mentioned above was a direct adoption of tactics the United States used in Vietnam. JUSMAG is also primarily responsible for many of the structures of the Philippine military as well as the introduction of the "civic action" role for the military that Marcos has incorporated into his counterinsurgency efforts through the expansion of the Local Self-Defense Forces. IMET training may also account for the increased prominence of high-ranking military personnel in national decision-making roles as well as the promotion of increased centralization and hierarchization of power under the president and military in areas where civilian autonomy traditionally prevailed.

International Arms Marketing

International arms marketing has been promoted as a way of reducing balance of trade deficits and defraying R&D expenses and has contributed to the proliferation of arms and military technology to the Philippines.

A major factor in the willingness of developed countries to engage in transfers of military technology to the Philippines is the competitive nature of the American and European arms industries. Competition for export markets has led to a rate of proliferation of military industries to the Third World equal to that of actual transfers of arms. Lock and Wulf pointed out that developed countries are willing to undertake licensing programs such as those in the Philippines because it allows them to penetrate otherwise inaccessible markets; they may gain tax-exemption or other low-cost production inputs such as cheap labor for production of labor-intensive components; there is a possibility of increasing total sales to the country since reexport of locally produced components may attract the local government; and the existence of export restrictions may make it necessary to transfer production or assembly facilities to the country.[36]

The Philippines has such licensing arrangements with Great Britain, the Federal Republic of Germany, Australia, and the United States. Since the former three countries share only a small fraction of Philippine trade, it is likely that they have been drawn into licensing programs through the need to penetrate the market and to make their products competitive with those from the United States that enjoy preferential trade status in country. The other factors may also play contributing roles, but an examination of Philippine trade relations with all three countries is beyond the scope of this chapter.

It is important to reemphasize here that the dynamic of militarism in the First World plays a crucial role in fostering militarism in the Philippines and that it has contributed at both instrumental and structural levels to the repressive nature of the Marcos regime. The export of military technology and ideology and pressures for an export-oriented Philippine economy have reinforced both the country's internal inequalities and external dependence while providing both the means and ideology for suppressing domestic opposition. U.S. reliance on the military bases in the Philippines for securing its political and economic objectives has also motivated continued international support for the Marcos regime despite recognition that the government is engaged in gross violations of human rights in its attempt to secure the stable political environment that is required to encourage foreign investment.

CONCLUSION

Militarism and militarization have resulted in the proliferation of both conventional and nuclear weapons, increasing destructive power of major weapon systems, the rapid depletion of scarce natural resources consumed in the global arms race, and the continuation of colonial patterns of dominance and dependency. Most importantly for the concerns of this volume, they have led to the subjugation of human beings to below subsistence levels of existence and inhumane treatment.

Marcos has justified militarism and militarization in the Philippines as the only means for securing ''national security'' (understood by Marcos as political stability and uninterrupted economic development). As we have seen, however, militarism, and the external dependence and misuse of resources it promotes, reinforces many of the causes of political and economic instability it is intended to eliminate. Therefore, it should not be assumed that militarism and militarization effectively reduce threats to national security.

By promoting political repression and channeling vast sums of money away from social services at a time when GNP is expanding, it may even increase political instability as the people become aware of the increasing injustices with which they are faced. That this has happened in the Philippines can be seen in the increasing polarization of political forces within the country during martial law and in the formation of the National Democratic Front that brought together many groups that previously had little or no contact with one another. The formation of this broadly based coalition would not have been possible without the high degree of repression that has characterized the Marcos regime. Likewise, the import of arms and military technology have not only further impoverished the Filipino people but have reinforced the country's dependence on production of exports for the accumulation of international currencies. This has heightened the vulnerability of the economy to crises in international markets and reduced national control over the economy.

Repression in the Philippines is not an isolated phenomenon, however. It is linked at both instrumental and structural levels to militarism in the countries with which it has military and economic ties. The colonial pattern of dominance between the United States and the Philippines, for instance, is maintained by both countries' tendency toward militarism as a means of addressing pressing economic and socio-political issues. This, in turn, leads to higher levels of technological sophistication in weapons systems, inequalities in access to advanced technology, reinforced patterns of economic dominance and dependence, perceived threats to national security from movements for political and economic change, militarism, and so on.

This cycle is also reinforced through the mutual interests of the elite in both the First and Third Worlds. As has been pointed out, the political, economic, and military goals of the Filipino elite have closely paralleled those of the U.S. government. National security thinking and other aspects of military ideology help to forge this bond. The IMET program, for instance, is designed primarily for this purpose. The dominance of the United States over the Philippine economy has also played a crucial role in this area.

It is not true, however, that the bond between the elite and the United States is necessarily stable when an authoritarian regime is involved. The two traditionally dominant forces in Philippine society, the Catholic Church and the premartial law political elite, have become increasingly alienated from the United States because of the continued military support the United States has provided the Marcos regime. The stability of the relationship now rests on the continuation in power of only one political faction and the military rather than of the whole political elite as was the case before martial law. This severely limits U.S.

options in its relations with the Philippines and, in the long-run, is bound to lead to an unstable relationship.

Because of the interaction of the world military order and militarism and repression in the Third World, any attempt to understand fully the dynamics of repression in a country such as the Philippines must also take into account both the global context in which it occurs and its long-term effects. The interaction of national and global trends described in this chapter indicates that this sort of approach will be necessary if repression in the Third World is to be addressed in an effective manner.

NOTES

1. "Proclamation No. 1081, Proclaiming a State of Martial Law in the Philippines," in *Marcos and Martial Law in the Philippines*, ed. David A. Rosenberg (Ithaca, N.Y.: Cornell University Press, 1979), p. 240.

2. "Militarism and Militarization in Contemporary International Relations," *Bulletin of Peace Proposals* 9 (1978): 296.

3. See Milton Leitenberg and Nicole Ball, "The Military Expenditures of Less Developed Nations," *Bulletin of Peace Proposals* 8 (1977): 310-315.

4. Ernest A. Duff and John F. McCamant, *Violence and Repression in Latin America: A Quantitative and Historical Analysis* (New York: Free Press, 1976), is the most ambitious attempt to date, but see also Stanley J. Heginbotham, "Measuring Social and Economic Human Rights Conditions," in *Human Rights Conditions in Selected Countries and the U.S. Response*. U.S. Congress, House, Committee on International Relations, Subcommittee on International Organizations (Washington, D.C.: U.S. Government Printing Office, 1978), pp. 359-372.

5. "Militarism and Repression," *Alternatives* 7 (Summer, 1981): 67-82.

6. Ibid., p. 67.

7. "Statement of President Ferdinand E. Marcos on the Declaration of Martial Law," in *Marcos and Martial Law*, ed. Rosenberg, p. 219.

8. "Ferdinand Marcos on a Fateful Move," *Far Eastern Economic Review*, September 30, 1972, p. 12.

9. Ferdinand E. Marcos, *Notes on the New Society of the Philippines* (Manila: Marcos Foundation, 1973), p. vii.

10. Cited in José Veloso Abueva, "Ideology and Practice in the New Society," in *Marcos and Martial Law*, ed. Rosenberg, p. 39.

11. Philippines, "'Constitution of the Republic of the Philippines (1973)," in *New Society*, by Marcos, p. 225.

12. Ibid., p. 224. Emphasis in original.

13. Harvey Stockwin, "The Marcos Recipe for Democracy," *Far Eastern Economic Review*, October 29, 1976, p. 19.

14. Marcos, *New Society*, pp. 165-166. Not surprisingly, then, the lifting of martial law in Janaury, 1981, produced few prospects for the democratization of the government: See Richard Vokey, "Anxiety Over the Army's Role," *Far Eastern Economic Review*, January 30, 1981, pp. 28-31; and Sheila Ocampo, "A Stronger Strongman," *Far Eastern Economic Review*, March 20, 1981, pp. 24-25.

15. *Report of an Amnesty International Mission to the Republic of the Philippines, 22 November-5 December, 1975*, 2nd ed. (London: Amnesty International, 1977), p. 56.

16. "The Logistics of Repression," in *The Logistics of Repression and Other Essays*, ed. Walden Bello and Severina Rivera (Washington, D.C.: Friends of the Filipino People, 1977), pp. 41-42.

17. "The Impact of Militarization on Development and Human Rights," *Bulletin of Peace Proposals* 9 (1978): 179.

18. U.S. Congress, *Human Rights Conditions*, pp. 200-203.

19. Task Force Detainees Philippines, *Pumipiglas: Political Detention and Military Atrocities in the Philippines* (n.p.: Association of Major Religious Superiors in the Philippines, 1980), pp. 3, 36.

20. See Larry A. Niksch and Marjorie Niehaus, *The Internal Situation in the Philippines: Current Trends and Future Prospects* (Washington, D.C.: Congressional Research Service, Library of Congress, 1981), pp. 36-37, 64-99; Joel Rocamora, "The United Front in the Philippines," *Southeast Asia Chronicle*, May-June, 1978, pp. 8-13.

21. The PHE and PEE/Milex ration declined from 204.3 percent to 68.3 percent from 1972 to 1976. Data in this section are from U.S. Arms Control and Disarmament Agency, *World Military Expenditures and Arms Transfers, 1968-1977* (Washington, D.C.: U.S. Arms Control and Disarmament Agency, 1979), pp. 57, 100.

22. Ruth Leger Sivard, *World Military and Social Expenditures* (Leesburg, Va.: World Priorities, 1979), pp. 30-31.

23. See World Bank, "The World Bank Philippine Poverty Report" (Confidential first-draft version obtained by the Congress Task Force and *Counterspy Magazine*), pp. 21-44.

24. Michael Westlake, "The Crusader's Tale," *Far Eastern Economic Review*, October 16, 1981, p. 29.

25. Peter Lock and Herbert Wulf, "The Economic Consequences of the Transfer of Military-Oriented Technology," in *The World Military Order: The Impact of Military Technology on the Third World*, ed. Mary Kaldor and Asbjorn Eide (New York: Praeger Publishers, 1979), p. 218.

26. Ibid., p. 220; "Logistics," in *Logistics*, ed. Bello and Rivera, p. 17.

27. "Militarism: Force Class and International Conflict," in *World Military Order*, ed. Kaldor and Eide, pp. 248-249.

28. 1979 Wage Commission figures cited in José W. Diokno, "Philippine Society and the Challenge of the Eighty's" (Talk given to the Convocation Seminar held at Manila on March 28, 1980, by Kapatiran Kaunlaran Foundation, Inc.), pp. 2-3.

29. U.S. Congress, Senate, Committee on Foreign Relations, *United States Foreign Policy Objectives and Overseas Military Installations* (Washington, D.C.: U.S. Government Printing Office, 1979), pp. 138-144, 147-150, 155.

30. Cited in U.S. Congress, House, Committee on International Relations, Subcommittee on Europe and the Middle East, *United States Arms Transfer and Security Assistance Programs* (Washington, D.C.: U.S. Government Printing Office, 1978), p. 25.

31. Stephen Rosskamm Shalom, *The United States and the Philippines: A Study of Neocolonialism* (Philadelphia: Institute for the Study of Human Issues, 1981), pp. 169, 176.

32. Cited in U.S. Congress, *Security Assistance*, p. 45.

33. Lock and Wulf, "Economic Consequences," p. 211.

34. Michael T. Klare and Cynthia Arnson, *Supplying Repression: U.S. Support for*

Authoritarian Regimes Abroad, revised ed. (Washington, D.C.: Institute for Policy Studies, 1981), p. 48.

35. Shalom, *United States and the Philippines*, includes an excellent account of JUSMAG activities; see pp. 65-66, 74-82, 104-106. See also "Logistics," in *Logistics*, ed. Bellow and Rivera, pp. 14-16, 24-31.

36. Lock and Wulf, "Economic Consequences," p. 217.

7

South African State Terror: The Costs of Continuing Repression

Robert A. Denemark and Howard P. Lehman

Most theoretical and practical works on revolution tend to attribute the act to an uprising by the masses. Whether the theorist points to social breakdown and a resulting anomie, relative deprivation and a resulting frustration-aggression reaction, or an increasing alienation and a resulting class consciousness and militarization, rarely is more than a spark seen as necessary to send a revolution-prone society into the throes of violence.[1] South Africa is a state that would certainly have to be included in any list of revolution-prone social systems. The gross inequalities that exist between the 16 percent of the population that is white and the rest of the population, especially the 70 percent black majority, provide a veritable catalogue of the conditions of which revolutions are born. The state has left no stone and relatively few pebbles unturned in its attempts to concretize the inferior position of the nonwhite, be it through the provision of inequitable social services or through the actual creation of pseudo-nation-states designed to make the blacks "foreigners" in their own country. Yet some two decades after the great movement toward independence overtook the rest of the continent, roughly half a decade after the successful conclusion of violent revolutions in the "front-line" states of Angola, Mozambique, and Zimbabwe, and after some rather convincing false starts in places like Sharpeville and Soweto, South Africa remains a bastion of white racist rule in Africa and a stable one at that. How are we to understand this?

We suggest that there are two closely related points that can help us in dealing with the problems involved here. The first entails the way in which we view the process of revolution. The second regards the efficacy of various methods of political repression that are at the disposal of the state and that include the use of state terror.

One of the few theorists to question the "bottom-up" nature of the development of revolutionary violence is Theda Skocpol. In *States and Social Revolutions* she criticized those who would argue that social and political upheaval is primarily voluntaristic and based on the loss of support for the government by the masses.[2] Although not denying the importance of such phenomena, she argued for a more structural perspective:

To explain social revolutions, one must find problematic, first, the emergence (not "making") of a revolutionary situation within an old regime. Then, one must be able to identify the objectively conditioned and complex intermeshing of the various actions of the diversely situated groups—an intermeshing that shapes the revolutionary process and gives rise to the new regime. One can begin to make sense of such complexity only by focusing simultaneously upon the institutionally determined situations and relations of groups within society and upon the inter-relations of societies within world-historically developing international structures. To take such an impersonal and nonsubjective viewpoint—one that emphasizes patterns of relationships among groups and societies—is to work from what may in some generic sense be called a structural perspective on sociohistorical reality. Such a perspective is essential for the analysis of social revolutions.[3]

Thus the state's position in a wider world system (both political and economic) must also be considered to gain a better understanding of the evolution of physical violence.

Our second point regards the ability of the state to maintain itself in power through the use of the coercive forces at its disposal. Skocpol cited Russell's important work on the ability of states to survive based on their use of force. The efficacy of repression may have been understated in previous analyses of potential political violence. Part of the repressive repertoire of the state includes methods that may be viewed as terroristic. Thus state terror may play an important role toward maintaining in power the governments of some states, South Africa among them.

THE SOUTH AFRICAN CONTEXT

The development of repression in South Africa has been conditioned by the contradiction between the need for nonwhite labor and the ideological and political necessity for racial separation. Wide-scale state repression (and its ideological foundation) is the result of the state's attempt to reconcile these conflicting interests. In its early efforts the state encouraged a migrant-labor system and, eventually, institutionalized this new relationship into the policy of apartheid. Apartheid is not the cause of a segmented and polarized environment but rather a result of attempts to institutionalize it. The fundamental basis of this structure remains the need to manage and control labor.

Such a system both rests upon and engenders violence. The state seeks to instill fear in those it has the need to control to make its task easier. The "controlled" will ultimately act (eventually violently), and the state's reaction must then be even more forceful. Thus violence and the conditions that give rise to its increase are perpetuated. This situation is further exacerbated by the superimposition of racial and economic cleavages that increase social polarization and thus influence the potential intensity of social conflict.[4] As Leo Kuper noted, within a society inflicted with social polarization, "the dichotomy of values is pervasive, unresolved conflicts cumulate, and minor, seemingly isolated issues quickly escalate to the level of the total society."[5]

This polarized environment is a product of a long series of historical interaction between Africans and the ruling whites. Each movement by the state initiated a reaction on the part of the African opposition that again gave rise to actions by the state. This action-reaction process has been most clearly analyzed by Peter Walshe and documented by Muriel Horrell.[6] The mechanisms to ensure white domination gradually emerged as white settlers manipulated and developed the African labor force. After the discovery of diamonds and gold in the 1860s and 1880s, a scarcity of labor elicited efforts by the state to create a ready pool of inexpensive labor. Such attempts were formalized by laws, including the 1913 Natives Land Act, which created labor reserves and special native reserve areas. Not only did the reserves provide a large floating pool of labor, they served to keep the Africans in a state of permanent disorientation, minimized the costs of social welfare by allowing Africans to maintain some traditional lands, and built the rural proletariat into a quasi-consumer class.

The period from 1924 to the 1948 national election witnessed a growing convergence of capitalist interests and the institutionalization of racial separation.[7] The emergence of a unified Afrikaner elite signaled increased competition against English mining interests and, later, collaboration with them to reinforce their mutually held interests. The political ramifications of this new relationship included the National party's victory in 1948. This alliance, and the National party that represented it, became instrumental in the post-1948 era, and the party platform came to represent the dominant political ideology. To appease the influential interests of both white groups, the ruling party sought to advance capital accumulation, protect the interests of white workers, and strengthen the capitalist system. This era also became South Africa's most active period for the promulgation of security legislation. The legal system that emerged after 1948 has led one scholar to describe South Africa's governing process "not as the rule *of* law—but as a rule *by* law."[8] The Suppression of Communism Act (1950) dissolved the Communist party, provided severe penalties for any member of this or other outlawed organizations, and broadly defined *statutory communism*. The definition subsumes any doctrine that aims at bringing about any political, industrial, social, or economic change by the promotion, threat, or conduct of acts of disturbance or disorder. In the aftermath of the 1960 Sharpeville massacre, the government passed the Unlawful Organizations Act, which dissolved the main African nationalist groups, the African National Congress (ANC), and the Pan-African Congress (PAC). The stifling of formal and collective opposition extended into individual opposition as well as an attempt to thwart all resistance to the white regime. Bannings, detentions, and banishments are all instruments in the legal arsenal of the state. The cornerstone of state repression, reference books and passes, is most clearly related to the state's need to control the movement of labor. It was an all-encompassing law, and one study concluded that the government prosecuted 5.8 million persons for pass law violations between 1966 and 1975.[9] A more recent study noted that there were 272,887 arrests for similar offenses in 1978 alone.[10]

Coinciding with the changing needs for control over black mobility, the state has sought to resettle Africans away from highly congested and potentially disruptive urban areas to the "independent" homelands. A similar program calls for the removal of Africans concentrated in "white" rural regions. Gwendolen Carter reported that the displacement of "black spots" has resulted in the resettlement of 996,000 tenants and squatters between 1960 and 1970.[11] A 1967 government circular noted by Ernest Harsch provides the rationale behind the forced resettlement efforts: "It is accepted Government policy that the Bantus are only temporarily resident in the European areas of the Republic, for as long as they offer their labor there. As soon as they become, for some reason or another, no longer fit for work or superfluous in the labor market, they are expected to return to their country of origin or the territory of their national unit where they fit in ethnically if they were not born and bred in the homeland."[12]

More recent events signal a new expansion of state repression. After the dissolution of the ANC and PAC, these opposition groups guided their efforts from locations outside South Africa. In response, Amnesty International noted that in early 1981 South African military forces entered Mozambique, destroying houses occupied by ANC members and killing fifteen people.[13]

Fresh buildups of internal African opposition tend to prompt a series of repressive actions by the state. The harshest government response against black opposition since Sharpeville occurred in June 1976 in Soweto. Within ten days after schoolchildren had taken to the streets to protest the introduction of a rule requiring the mandatory use of Afrikaans in the schools, 175 people had died. By the end of the year most accounts placed the death toll around 500. Another change in governmental policy resulted in an increased number of deaths among individuals held in detention. Among the 20 political detainees who died in security police custody between August 1976 and September 1977 was Steven Biko, leader of the Black Consciousness Movement.[14]

Elements of violence have, through the medium of state repression, penetrated every level and every sector of society. As the needs of the South African economy have evolved, singular acts of repression have formed into a systematic network that includes the use of terror.

The current system may be viewed as repressive in its economic, political, and social forms. The most fundamental component, economic, constitutes the foundation upon which rests the structure of repression. As we have noted earlier, the drive to control labor is the dominant theme of the South African social structure. The job and wage color bars, the migratory labor system, and the resettlement of Africans from so-called "black spots" are important components of economic repression. Political repression, on the other hand, is perhaps the most visible arm of systematic repression. Under this category attention may be focused upon the political institutions created by apartheid such as the "homeland" system and the structure and content of the judicial system. South Africa's vast system of internal security is designed to enforce the laws of apartheid. The third component, social repression, contains policies that ensure racial separation on a daily basis. The control over labor mobility extends into residential, educational, and athletic segregation. Laws including the Group Areas Act and the Bantu Education Act formalize racial separation to such an extent that social movement and participation, white as well as black, are severely restricted. State repression can thus be viewed as an all-encompassing dynamic force whose specific elements modify in relation to the changing historical context.

ELEMENTS OF TERROR

Any attempt to specify elements of state terror within the context of such generalized repression confronts us with a number of analytical and definitional difficulties. As we have observed, levels of repression in South Africa are extremely high and encompass all aspects of social interaction. Repression may be viewed both as a method by which to control labor and an attempt to regulate or eliminate actual or potential opposition to the rule of the state. Repression in the South African context affects nearly all individuals through the use of structural and administrative as well as physical actions. *Repression* is a more general and pervasive phenomenon that systematically and structurally molds the individual. *State terror*, on the other hand, may be viewed as the more precise and deliberate act of inflicting harm on an individual or group in order to change the nature of their behavior and/or instill fear in other individuals or groups. Terror is a more direct method of behavior modification that seeks a more direct effect. However, any attempt to establish a strict line of demarcation between terror and repression proves difficult. More fear may result from overnight detentions due to pass law violations than from detention deaths and military attacks on civilians, and, indeed, the former is probably a much more salient concern. Since there is only the thinnest of qualititative lines separating repression and terror, we prefer to deal with state terror as a relatively amorphous extreme on the continuum of repression.

Due to their level of institutionalization and the resulting hardships inflicted upon the African population, three principal elements of state terror can be distinguished: the internal security and enforcement component, the military component, and the resettlement program. Although other facets of state terror can be identified, the effects of these elements extend deeply into the lives of all individuals in South Africa and effectively underpin the South African social structure. It is for this reason that we focus our attention upon them.

The first is based on the broad spectrum of laws regarding "security" and imprisonment. Political imprisonment itself cannot be branded as an act of terrorism. However, in South Africa the laws are so broadly defined as to offer no real safeguards against arbitrary or inequitable sanctions. Furthermore, as Amnesty International reported, "the burden of proof is placed upon the accused to show the innocence of their intentions rather than on the state to prove their guilt."[15] Under the Terrorism Act of 1967 the state defined *terrorism* as any activity that may "endanger the maintenance of law and order." The act covers not only the activities that result in the disturbance or disorder of society but those that lead to the "embarrassment" of "the administration of the affairs of the State." Section Six of the Terrorism Act allows the indefinite detention without charge or trial of anyone suspected of being a terrorist.

Another legal mechanism underpinning the system is the General Law Amendment Act of 1962, which defines the offense of "sabotage" in similarly vague style. The breadth of this term facilitates application to many intended and unintended acts.

The Internal Security Act of 1976 provides for preventive detentions, the detention of potential state witnesses in political trials, and the expansion of terms under which banning orders may be imposed. Unlike the more specific Suppression of Communism Act, which it replaced, the Internal Security Act gave authorization to impose banning orders on any individual who "engages in activities which endanger or are calculated to endanger the security of the State of the maintenance of public order."[16]

A great number of individuals pass through the prison system each year. Albie Sachs estimated that one African adult in every three could have been expected to serve a prison sentence during the 1970s.[17] The level of terror to which these individuals are subjected cannot be accurately known, but most analysts acknowledge that torture is a general method for the extraction of information and that deaths of political detainees are not rare. According to Amnesty International, some twenty-two detainees died between 1963 and 1972, and another twenty died under similar conditions between August 1976 and September 1977.[18] Ernest Harsch estimated that from 1963 to 1979 at least fifty political prisoners died under mysterious circumstances.[19] General prison conditions, if reports leaking from places like Robben Island are at all true, include the kind of degradation and physical abuse most closely associated with terror.

Finally, even the least physically harmful of these "security" sanctions, namely bannings, may be considered an act of terror. The fear instilled in an individual confronted with a lengthy sentence as a nonperson may be greater than that of facing short-term physical violence. Amnesty International noted that "the imposition of a banning order not only condemns an individual to stifling restrictions and a life outside the limits of normal society, it also employs the police to invade every sphere of life."[20]

A second element of state terror focuses attention on the role of the military. A clear delineation separating the external acts of the armed forces from internal events can no longer be maintained. Two reasons for this can be noted. First, an increase in military influence and power within the government is evidenced by the rapid growth of defense outlays. Second, the "internal" South African Police Force has become "a wing of the SADF (South African Defense Force) with additional training in crime prevention.''[21] It is only for analytical reasons, then, that we discuss military terror in two areas.

First, we should observe the use of the military in confronting the large-scale disturbances that occur during strikes or in the context of general demonstrations. It seems to matter little to the state whether it faces striking workers or frustrated schoolchildren; general disturbances are met with brutal military force. Almost 1,000 "political sanctions" are listed as having occurred in South Africa between 1948 and 1977 in the *World Handbook of Political and Social Indicators* (III) (giving it a ranking of seven out of the 122 states reporting), and more than 1,700 "deaths from domestic group violence" are documented. Almost half of them occurred in 1960 (Sharpeville) and 1976 (Soweto) alone. The lesson of history is clear: when threatened, the level of state terror rises both in general terms and as a percentage of the overall repression in use.

An allusion has already been made to the second component of military terror. In recent months military incursions into surrounding areas have increased with the expressed intent of killing individuals viewed as a threat to the state. Although ground forces might conceivably be able to select their victims, it is difficult to believe this of air strikes. Such actions have caused the deaths of hundreds of civilians and noncombatants and can also be considered terroristic.

The process of removing and resettling large numbers of rural Africans is the final component of state terror. The instrumental policies of the "grand design" of separate development—influx control, resettlement, and the eradication of "black spots"—have all necessitated the forced displacement of millions of persons, disrupting if not dislocating their lives and creating a general fear throughout society. Hence we may label this process an act of terror. Harsch estimated that between 1960 and 1970, 1.9 million Africans were resettled, of whom the majority were rural squatters working and living on white-owned farms. The white regime also has dispossessed many Africans of their plots within the reserves. According to Harsch, nearly 6.0 million Africans have been moved as a result of the homeland program.[22] Another million have recently been informed that they and their land are being ceded to Swaziland in a security-related move that has led even the conservative leaders of the homeland movement to predict violence.[23]

From this we may conclude that elements of state terror within the general context of repression pervade South African society. Especially when challenged, the South African state has shown a particular quickness in using terror to control its populace. The question this poses to scholars and policy makers interested in such repression and terror is the price that the maintenance of such a system exacts.

SOCIAL COSTS

The maintenance of such a large, complex, and active apparatus designed to repress, if not terrorize, its populace entails both social and monetary costs. The military, judicial, and administrative components of state terror operate on budgets large enough to threaten the economic stability of the state. The costs of this repressive apparatus continue to rise even during periods of economic decline. One of the by-products of this decline is an increase in disorder, which is, in part, responsible for the increased expenditures on the part of the state, and these expenditures further add to existing economic problems.

Any examination of the "maintenance costs" of such a system is confronted with several difficulties. Foremost among them is the question of evaluation. Certainly, dollar (or Rand) outlays on the military and other institutions are the most directly calculable. Political, social, and indirect economic costs, however, influence a cost-benefit relationship that does not fit neatly into any simple formula. Savage, in his study of the costs of the pass system, lists a dozen areas that necessitate careful assessment including expenditures for things such as the provision of separate schools and amenities.[24] A complete analysis would also consider intangibles such as the low productivity of black workers given their lack of incentive to produce. Of course, all of this would then have to be weighed against the benefits accrued from having a large labor force that works at or near subsistence wage levels and requires a minimal outlay for social services.

Even if such costs and benefits could be calculated from available data, there are serious questions about the reliability of state-supplied information on items such as resettlement costs. Finally, hidden costs (such as the value of the oil stockpiled by the state in anticipation of an embargo) cannot always even be identified. In this section, therefore, we hope to outline the monetary costs of maintaining the repressive apparatus as best we can determine. Although we recognize that this both simplifies the problem and does not account for the fact that some of these expenses would be necessary even if the state were black-ruled, we do contend that a study of the magnitude and direction of these costs will indeed suggest some things about the viability of the state.[25]

In terms of overall disbursements, the security-force budget is the most significant component of the repressive apparatus. The South African Defense Force can call on nearly half a million soldiers if one includes reservists, commandos, and paramilitary forces. This represents a sixfold increase since 1960 while during that same twenty-year period the population rose by 77.0 percent.[26] The International Defence and Aid Fund (IDAF) estimates that the South African Police alone has at its disposal about 72,000 men.[27] Coinciding with this buildup in military strength is, of course, a substantial increase in expenditures. Frank Barnaby reported that between 1967 and 1977 South Africa's military disbursements (in constant prices) jumped 3.5 times.[28] Although the South African government proudly reported that defense expenditures have declined as a percentage of the GNP since 1977-1978, when they reached 5.1 percent of that figure and 19.0 percent of all state expenditures, this belies the great per capita increases that the booming price for South African exports allowed to be hidden in the "percentage of GNP" figure. Official figures place per capita defense spending at R2.75 per person in 1960, R11.79 in 1970, and R79.5 in 1980.

This is an increase of about 3,000.0 percent over the past two decades or 733.0 percent in the last ten years. Even taking inflation into account, the rate of per capita spending on defense has increased an average of 30.0 percent a year since 1970.

A good example of the expense of military operations may be found by looking at the border war in Namibia and Angola. Gwendolen Carter estimated that South Africa had some 20,000 to 30,000 troops fighting South West African People's Organization (SWAPO) incursions in Namibia.[29] The maintenance of this defense force in Namibia cost the government approximately $1 million a day.[30] Furthermore, an IDAF study warned that in assessing full military costs, the construction of new military bases (by the Department of Public Works), the housing of SDAF personnel (financed by the Department of Community Development), and the gathering of intelligence (by the Treasury Vote) must also be taken into account.[31] Therefore, the figures provided by the government in the form of the defense budget should be treated as a conservative and partial total.

The point is that defense expenditures have been rising consistently. Although part of this increase can certainly be viewed as a function of the rising fortunes of the state, a good argument can be made for the increasing "need" for (and the increasing unit costs of) defense expenditures. The end of the massive five-year buildup announced in 1974-1975 came in 1978-1979; yet expenditures rose again in 1979-1980 and accounted for 16.6 percent of all state spending. Both South Africa's internal and international position points to an ever increasing need for defense spending.

The next principal area of maintenance costs focuses on the cornerstone of apartheid, the pass law system. Michael Savage provided the most notable and complete study of the costs necessary to sustain this instrumental network of state terror. He arrived at a total of R112,825,237 ($169,237,854) for 1974-1975, and even this figure is considered conservative.[32] Numerous hidden costs obscure calculations of the more realistic sum necessary to maintain the pass laws. Savage offered examples of costs in the areas of transportation, labor replacement, and labor time lost to updating pass documents. The costs of this system rise, of course, during times of unrest when many more infractions must be dealt with.

In our third area we are faced with limited reliable source material. The resettlement program has, as we have seen, permeated into the marrow of the rural black population as well as into semiurban areas such as Crossroads. Although affecting hundreds of thousands of people, the total cost to the state has not been made publicly available. The *Christian Science Monitor* reported that one element of the resettlement policy, land purchases in rural reserves, had resulted in expenditures of $592.0 million as of early 1982.[33] Since the resettlement and homeland programs will maintain their central position within the structure of apartheid, state expenditures supporting these programs are likely to rise. Data on homeland budgets support this contention. A Rockefeller Foundation Commission reported that the dependence of the homelands on South

Africa for funds to pay for their public services has been increasing. If defense costs are included, the homelands contributed only 5 percent to their overall operating costs during the 1970s.[34] Official government figures also suggest that recent state expenditures for homeland "development" have been increasing at an average annual rate of 10 percent. Indeed, this budget has risen from R95.0 million in 1970 to R1,108.7 million in 1979.[35]

Although these expenditures only partially indicate the wide range of differing costs associated with operating the broad system of state terror, they do suggest a tendency toward increased spending and a profound commitment to the continuation of terrorist policies. If one considers more than simply the defense fund vote, the magnitude of this spending is greatly increased. We estimate that in 1979 spending on defense, the pass system, resettlement, and the homeland movement equalled about R3.6 billion or R151 per person. This is about 40 percent of the yearly wage of many black workers.[36] Maintaining the system is clearly a very expensive and an increasingly more expensive task.

Given these growing costs, Savage has suggested that South Africa "must prepare to move onto a war footing and continue to implement apartheid, or dismantle segregation and use South Africa's resources to deal with the human needs of its population for housing, education, food, and for all that is involved in a just social system."[37] The choice, of course, is not as simple as Savage suggested. Recent events in South Africa may signal the rise of reformist policies if for no other reason than to lower the costs of apartheid while maintaining its benefits. Among the most significant of these consequences is the disruption arising from state manipulation. Not only does the rigid labor structure restrict black productivity, but many whites find constant military callups undermining their careers. Carter noted that more than 3,000 English-speaking and Jewish youth left South Africa in 1978 due to what they considered excessive military obligations.[38]

At a more macro level, the economic structure may no longer be able to provide the gains to whites it once did. As T. Hanf and others suggested, "as the rate of inflation started to rise and export markets to shrink, South Africa was also sucked into the vortex of world-wide stagflation."[39] The level of real wages has been simply unable to keep up with the rate of inflation. With falling real incomes, the state must confront the dilemma of policy trade-offs. Signs of economic retrenchment have, however, increased political divisiveness and infighting. In 1979 the National party suffered a narrow defeat in a Johannesburg by-election. This was an early indication of the decisive split between Botha and more militant and racist factions that occurred in early 1982. The expulsion of sixteen of Andries Treurnicht's followers from the National party, the electoral gain of the Progressive Federal party in 1981, and the formation by Treurnicht of the South African Conservative party will test the sincerity, strength, and adaptability of the reformist elements in the National party. When conservative whites begin to perceive an increase in the severity of economic life along with a greater displacement of benefits to the black population, we may look for sharper polarization and more dissension from within the ranks of the white community.

POLITICAL ECONOMY

South Africa's European community was not to be forever content with the great agricultural and mineral wealth that the tip of the continent provided. An industrial capitalism sprang to life around the turn of the century, and as it grew so did the need for investment capital, technology, and markets in which to dispose of manufactured goods. The only commodity South Africa did not lack was an ample supply of cheap labor. But the process of industrial development that South Africa decided to tie itself to was by no means an easy one. Manufacturing became the largest single component of the GDP by 1945, but the import-substitution industrialization boom of the 1940s and 1950s was largely over by 1960;[40] so too was the South African's ability to "hide" among the white-ruled colonies of Africa. The decolonization of Africa began in 1957, and by 1963 most of West, Central, and Eastern Africa had gained or been granted independence. Although the Portuguese and Rhodesians had assured that the same would not happen just yet in southern Africa, apartheid was soon to serve as the center of internal, regional, and world attention.

The end of the import-substitution industrialization boom about 1960 left future industrial development and the rate of growth in South Africa dependent, as in many states in the same predicament, on its ability to export its raw materials and manufactured goods and on its attractiveness to foreign investors. South Africa was extremely well apportioned in terms of mineral wealth, whose exports accounted for some 30.0 percent of the GDP in 1960. Unlike many other states, which in the wake of a colonial heritage had only one major cash crop or mineral export whose price structure could be extremely volatile, South Africa had a diversity of stable or increasingly valuable assets. Foremost among them was gold, the price of which remained unchanged between 1934 and 1968. Gold exports constituted a majority of South Africa's foreign exchange earnings until 1950, after which it remained a stable 30.0 to 40.0 percent of all exports through 1971. South Africa also produced a great percentage of the world's rough gem diamonds, the price of which had not dropped in real terms between 1934 and 1981. In 1978 diamonds constituted 14.0 percent of all exports or about 4.2 percent of the GDP. Other raw materials, food, canned fruit, and metals such as copper and uranium constituted an additional 21.8 percent of all merchandise exports or about 5.5 percent of the GDP.

South African manufacturing exports faired less well. In 1960 only 11.85 percent of all merchandise exports were of the manufactured type. More importantly, it was Great Britain, the European Economic Community (EEC), and the United States that received the vast majority of these goods. South Africa's "natural market," and the one that was most important to it in the long run, was the rest of Africa. This area, however, had never really opened to its products. In 1960, for example, only 17.6 percent of South Africa's nongold exports stayed in Africa. That figure declined dramatically in the following three years and did not again reach its 1960 magnitude until 1971.[41]

The third lynchpin in the South African system was its ability to attract foreign investment, and it was here where South Africa's political system caused it considerable trouble. Specifically, the strictness with which apartheid was applied brought an inevitable black response. In 1960 it came at Sharpeville where the killing of 67 Africans caused an exodus of foreign and domestic capital that was large enough to turn the R305 million trade surplus of 1960 into a foreign exchange loss in the year that actually threatened the state with bankruptcy. By virtue of the fact that order was quickly restored, however, investor confidence returned shortly. The 1961 trade surplus and the slowing of capital flight signaled a return to relatively high rates of growth. But the point had been well taken.

In the absence of social reform South African society (or more specifically, the South African economy), would have to provide for a number of things. It would have to maintain a system affluent enough to be able to afford the extensive and expensive system of repression necessary to impose stability on such a social system. It would also have to provide for an expanding economy capable of employing a significant percentage of its growing black population. The matter of black employment is perhaps the most central. South Africa maintains a large pool of unemployed reserve labor and even among those securely employed, few are allowed to consider themselves permanent residents in "white" areas. Furthermore, "permanent" residents with secure jobs may be considered a labor aristocracy of sorts. Such workers will, on occasion (and at the urging of the government), engage in pro-government counterdemonstrations. More important, however, is the reluctance of this vulnerable group to oppose government policy violently. The threat of violence is much more pronounced if unemployment hits this group, for not only would this serve to help radicalize a very stable and important sector of the economy, it would affect individuals who are not so easily removed to remote homeland areas. Today some 200,000 young blacks enter the job market every year. It has been estimated that a growth rate of about 5.5 percent a year would be necessary to employ them all.[42] Although full employment is probably not necessary, certainly enough of these newcomers must be employed (and those already established cannot be faced too closely with unemployment) if stability, and thus a reduced need for overt oppression, is to be maintained. Thus affluence and growth may be viewed as central to the continued stability of the state.

In his excellent work on South Africa, R. W. Johnson outlined three strategies by which the government has sought to assure its continued affluence: an attempt to open large, and especially African, markets for its manufactured goods; an attempt to increase the price of its raw materials exports, especially gold; and a buildup of South Africa's ability to survive in an isolated environment coupled with a policy of avoidance where costly, large-scale military involvement in surrounding areas is concerned.[43]

The first of these strategies has met with the least amount of success. Any economic system bent on industrial development requires a market area sufficient to make manufacturing profitable. Yet it also requires the (sometimes contradictory) maintenance of low labor costs. Thus the internal market may not be sufficient to provide the economies of scale necessary to make large-scale manufacturing profitable. The obvious solution is to find export markets for the goods involved. In 1962 this market consisted primarily of the United Kingdon (33.2 percent), the EEC (21.0 percent), and the United States (9.9 percent), which together received almost 65.0 percent of all South African nongold exports. But even the government realized that the greatest potential for expansion was in Africa itself. Johnson suggested that "the whole of the White Establishment felt the pull of the African market"[44] and cited a government study that noted: "Our economic and political objectives in Southern Africa are to harness all natural and human resources from Table Mountain to the border of the Congo River....Member countries of the Common Market could complement one another. For example, the Republic of South Africa could manufacture machinery, chemicals and electrical appliances—while the Transkei could produce jute, Swaziland sugar, Botswana beef, and Lesotho water."[45] In the service of this grand scheme stood a number of conservative Africa leaders ready to consider ties with South Africa. By 1970 the state was acting to bring Zambia, Malagasy, and the Ivory Coast (with whom it had negotiated reexport agreements) more openly into its favor. This, it was hoped, would lead other African conservatives to come to terms, at least economically, with South Africa. But such was not to be. A coup in Malagasy, along with immense pressure on the part of both the more radical states and more radical elements within those states, turned the tide distinctly against any open economic normalization. From 1971 to 1978 the amount of trade South Africa did with "developing Africa" was stable, but its percentage of all trade with that area declined significantly.

During this same period some ominous clouds were gathering in the "developed" world as well that boded ill for South Africa's economic strategy. Under considerable pressure, South Africa had to withdraw from the Commonwealth in 1961. The United Kingdom still served as South Africa's key customer, but two factors were to threaten this market. The first was the great decline in the vibrancy of the British economy, which greatly reduced Britain's role as a dependable trading partner. A second and more critical problem was the British request for membership in the EEC. Having withdrawn from the Commonwealth, South Africa would not be granted special EEC status and its exports stood to decline. Furthermore, British entry into the EEC stood to worsen Portugal's economic and political position and thus its ability to hold Angola and Mozambique. The oil crisis of 1972-1973 may well have been the last straw. A worldwide inflation and recession served to show South Africa (if not the rest of the world) that attempts at economic development through industrialization could be hazardous. This became most obvious to South Africa in 1971. The trade surpluses of the 1960s had turned into a substantial deficit by that year.

Devaluations followed as did a slowing of the rate of growth and an actual decline in real per capita income. Great increases in inflation coupled with this downturn led very quickly to serious labor disorder. Strikes spread, and the number of protest demonstrations in 1970 alone fell just two instances short of all those taking place between 1963 and 1969.[46] The wave of illegal strikes lasted some two years and included up to 60,000 workers at a time. In 1973 wage increases of 15 to 18 percent ended the strikes for a short period. Labor unrest soon resumed, however, due to persistence in the rate of inflation.

Even these moderate wage increases were only possible given increases in commodities prices, which will be discussed shortly. Most importantly, the existence of the state had been jeopardized by the tenuous position of its manufacturing sector in the international market. Johnson concluded that this failure to increase significantly its manufacturing exports was of "critical importance." The volume of South Africa's imports, due to both the structure of its economy and its military needs, grew at a rapid rate. Without an expanding export sector South Africa's balance-of-payments position would suffer. Manufacturing was clearly not going to solve the state's problems. If help was to come it would have to come from its commodity wealth and, more specifically, from gold.

South Africa has a great wealth of mineral resources. It holds 83 percent of the world's platinum reserves, 25 percent of all known uranium reserves, a great percentage of the known gem diamond reserves, 25 percent of all known chrome reserves, along with significant amounts of copper, vanadium, fluorspar, iron, and coal. Of all of them, however, it is gold, of which South Africa produces 70 percent of the world's supply, that is of primary importance.[47]

The history of gold's escape from its $35 an ounce level in the late 1960s and early 1970s is long and complex and need not be reviewed here.[48] Let it suffice to say that the freeing of the market and the rise in price came at an extremely fortuitous time for Pretoria. It had been holding down gold exports to aid in the effort to raise its price, and although slow and frought with peril, gold's rise would salvage the state's financial position. Serious trade imbalances, as we have noted, developed in the late 1960s and early 1970s, and even with foreign capital investments at an all-time high, a very serious deficit, inflation, and a devaluation of the Rand were in store in 1971. By June 1972, however, the price of gold had broken free and reached the $60-70 an ounce level. Further U.S. trade deficits and the preoccupation of the U.S. government with Watergate would see the price rise to the $122 an ounce level by June 1973. The end of 1974 would see the price just under $200 an ounce before serious concerted effort on the part of a new U.S. administration pushed gold back to levels that averaged about $150 an ounce between 1974 and 1978. In August 1978 gold again reached the $200 an ounce level, but this time on its way to a January 1980 high of more than $850 an ounce. Such dizzying prices allowed the South African state a rare opportunity to bolster its position. Old mines, whose production costs had made them unprofitable to work at lower price levels, reopened and had little trouble financing their capital needs. Johnson concluded:

For South Africa the gold war opened up a whole new promised land. The value of her gold output rose from R775 million in 1967 (the last full year under the ancien regime of $35 an ounce) to R847 million in 1969, R922 million in 1971, R1161 million in 1972. . .and R2560 million in 1974. Her reserves soared. The Rand was upwardly revalued to $1.49. Every $10 on the average annual price of gold meant an increase of 1% in her GNP. These fabulous figures were achieved despite a falling gold output, indeed, as we have seen, largely because of it.

But victory in the gold war brought gains greater than money. If, as expected, gold maintained its 1974 heights then the failure of South Africa's drive for African markets hardly mattered. The trade deficit, even allowing for the huge rise in the oil price, was clearly a thing of the past in such circumstances. Gold would make South Africa much less vulnerable to fluctuations in the level of foreign investment. It would insulate her from the world recession—while other economies slumped in 1974, South Africa's grew at a real rate of 8%. It would buy arms, it would buy self-sufficiency, it would buy détente—or, if that could not be bought, it would more than cover the cost of isolation. The cliché references to a "golden future" had to be taken seriously. Pretoria's planners made plain their confidence in such a future by announcing massive expansions in expenditure on the parastatals. Defence expenditure rose 40% in 1974 over the (record) 1973 level and Pretoria confidently announced that it had been decided to fulfill the ten-year Defence Plan in five years.[49]

To a certain extent the same was happening with the price of diamonds, especially investment-grade gemstones. Inflation in the Western states (and the search for hedges against it), along with a reduction in gem reserves, drove the price skyward. Increases of 1,000 percent on rough diamonds and 1,700 percent on select gem prices fueled an 865 percent increase in income derived from South African diamond sales between 1971 and 1980. On a smaller scale, much the same can be said of the price of copper and uranuim. As for the price of platinum, it rose even higher and faster than the price of gold. In fact, the value of these "secondary" minerals rose so much that gold actually decreased as a percentage of all South African raw materials sales between 1974 and 1977.

All of South Africa's major commodities increased in value through 1979 and into 1980. As long as these prices remained high, the economy would prosper.

The final strategy that Johnson suggested the South Africans adopted in trying to assure their survival is that of two-part isolationism: military self-sufficiency and foreign military noninvolvement. Military self-sufficiency became a reality during the period of high gold prices. Research in coal gasification, the storing of large emergency stocks of oil, and the expansion of parastatals in strategic industries have also been central to this effort. One problem area in this search for autarchy has been the role of foreign investment. Conditions eliciting great anxiety among investors occurred in 1960, 1976-1977, and 1980 and were followed by an exodus of such funds leading to instability. Foreign investment, however, constitutes only a small portion of gross domestic savings.[50] Although cutbacks in these funds are harmful, a true crisis would only take place should large foreign firms (especially large employers) decide to leave South Africa altogether, and this is a situation that is unlikely to occur.

Finally, before 1981 South Africa had been extremely hesitant about committing its military forces anywhere outside the state itself. Mozambique, Zimbabwe, and Angola all fell to radical black regimes with only a minimum of direct military interference (and that in Angola at the urging of the French and the United States), even though these regimes were viewed as direct threats to the security of the South African state. The government clearly decided that military intervention in what would have essentially been a series of foreign wars would be too dangerous. Such wars would have the potential to increase fear and disillusionment among the white minority and among foreign investors and would inevitably serve as a constant drain on resources, given the protracted nature of such conflicts. Thus even in places where intervention could easily have succeeded (for example, Southern Mozambique), it has not been generally attempted and this (especially in Zimbabwe) at no small political cost to the regime.

The net result of these three strategies has been the successful, if not stable, maintenance of South African affluence and security. Violence by the state is least likely, as we have noted, in such a context. But recent events have threatened this affluence and will lead, we believe, to an increase in state terror.

The development of African markets for South African manufactured goods has yet to develop. Even with an increase in purchases from states like Japan and Argentina, merchandise exports have not grown quickly enough to offset growing imports, given the recent volatility in the prices for the raw materials that make up a significant percentage of South Africa's total export package. Real problems have developed as a result of recent price fluctuations. Gold has declined in value by more than 40.0 percent between January 1980 and July 1982, reducing the value of the Rand, creating a new balance-of-payments crisis (a $3.7 billion shortfall in 1981—an amount equal to roughly 9.0 percent of the total GDP), cutting the 1981 growth rate to half the 1980 figure (4.0 percent down from 8.0 percent), and likely to half it again during 1982.[51] Inflation rose to 15.0 percent during 1981 with prime interest rates at the 17.0 percent level. The South African economy must grow at a rate of about 5.5 percent, as we have noted, to keep pace with black employment needs. This decrease in the price of gold has thus threatened the very viability of the state, especially if one also considers the effect such a downturn will have on the numerous businesses (engineering, construction, services, and so on) that depend on the mining sector. Given this reduction in prices, some mines have had to close and others cut back production. Figure 7.1 plots the cost per ounce of producing gold from about thirty-five major South African mines and the reserves available in those mines. A line representing the breakeven point would be located between 15.0 and 17.0 percent to the right of the cost of production line.Thus we may estimate the reduction in exploitable reserves that occurs as the price of gold is reduced. Very serious repercussions would be the result if gold prices slumped under the $250 an ounce level.

Gold is not the only commodity in trouble. Copper and platinum have both

Figure 7.1 South African Gold Reserves Exploitable at Various Costs of Production

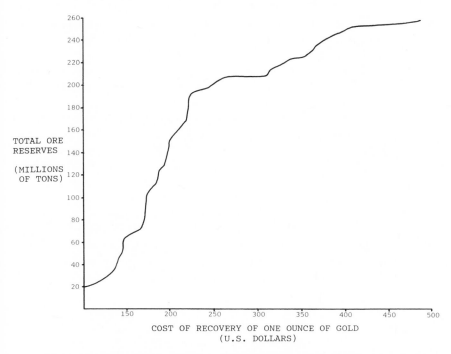

TOTAL ORE
RESERVES

(MILLIONS
OF TONS)

COST OF RECOVERY OF ONE OUNCE OF GOLD
(U.S. DOLLARS)

Source: *Mining Journal*, "Analysis of Rand and O.F.S.
Quarterlies," August 6, 1981, November 6,
1981, and January 29, 1982. Average costs
of production and known reserves were
calculated from July, September and December
1980 and 1981 data from about 35 major mines.

fallen in value to levels so low that copper producers, for one, are cutting back production.Even diamonds, a commodity with a 46 year history of growth, have decreased in value dramatically. DeBeers had literally stopped selling gem quality rough to try to counter the drop. A major scandal in the Israeli cutters market, however, along with the announcement of a major new find in Australia (with industrial-quality reserves reported to be larger than those of all of Africa), a decrease in the rate of inflation in the West, and the Soviet's use of diamonds (along with gold) to help cover costs incurred in Poland and Afghanistan, have served to depress prices to levels not seen since the mid-1970s.[52] The first ten months of 1980 witnessed a 37 percent drop in the value of South African diamond exports. The value of median-size and grade-investment diamonds dropped about 300 percent during that same period even though South African production in 1980 was cut to one-sixteenth its 1979 level. *Mining Journal* provided the following summary: "Statistics from the South African Minerals

Bureau show that in the first seven months of 1981, the value of total mineral sales fell about 11.7%, with earnings from gold down 20%, those from diamonds 42% lower, and other minerals (which includes platinum, uranium and vanadium) 39% lower than in the corresponding period of 1980. At the same time, base metal prices have remained at depressed... levels."[53]

In this same period, imports, led by machinery and industrial supplies, were still rising both in unit costs and as a percentage of the South African GDP. As a result, the South Africans again faced serious balance-of-payments problems in 1982, the fourth year in a row in which the balance-of-payments deficit stood at nearly R3 billion.

To make matters worse, South Africa now finds itself more and more unable to refrain from taking a more active military role in Namibia and Angola. Although recent actions do not necessarily signal a reversal in the strategy of noninvolvement, they do suggest that short run, although certainly expensive, incursions are deemed necessary under the current situation.

The implications of the decline in affluence for South Africa should be clear. As the costs of repression rise, the economic situation is simultaneously increasing the bases of dissension and undercutting the ability of the state to absorb them. The structural prerequisites of stability are thus breaking down, and the result will be an increase in violence and state terror.

CONCLUSION

Internally, the pressure for change is growing and will continue to grow. Increasing black unemployment means more and more pass law violations, more dissension among the unemployed, and more fear on the part of the whites. Political activity of all sorts becomes more likely. Anti-state terror, both from black organizations and from the far Right (which accounted for some 1,600 incidents of terror between 1960 and December, 1980, according to the *African Research Bulletin*), has increased and so too has state terror. Although no national-level data is available to substantiate these claims, it is known that state terror increased both in real terms and as a percentage of overall repression during the crises of 1960 and 1976, and there is no reason to expect otherwise in this newest precrisis period. Given the position of the state in the world system during the past 18 months, larger scale state terror can be expected. Recent increases in violence, including the deaths of eight individuals in mining-sector wage disputes, also suggests that this analysis is on the right track.[54] One may also note the state's perceived need to step up attacks in Namibia and Angola. This too leads to an increase in state terror.

State terror is, as noted, a very difficult phenomenon to deal with explicitly. But some general conclusions can be drawn from the South African situation. Both state and anti-state terror do seem to emanate from the condition of the state itself and not simply from the disgruntled masses. Granted, it has not been

Figure 7.2 Average Monthly Price for Gold, Platinum, and Copper, 1975-1982

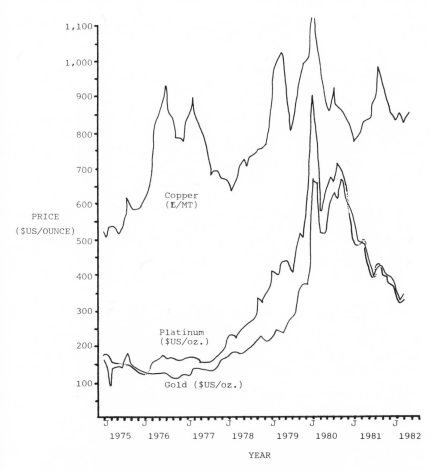

Sources: 1981 Commodity Yearbook (New York: Commodity Research Bureau), and Metals Week (New York: McGraw-Hill). Gold prices expressed in U.S. dollars per troy ounce as reported by the U.S. Bureau of Mines. Platinum prices expressed in U.S. dollars per troy ounce on the New York Exchange.

possible to show a one-to-one relationship between declining state fortunes and upsurges in state terror. South Africa so uses repression and so shrouds that use that any truly sensitive measurement is out of the question. Recent larger scale incidents such as those at Sharpeville and Soweto, however, do lend support to

Figure 7.3 South African Import Costs

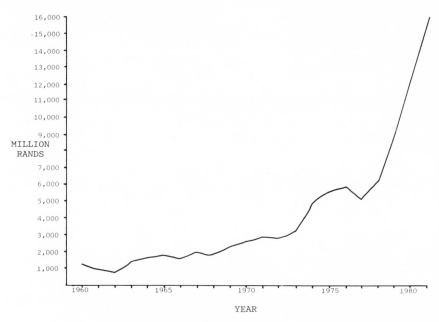

Sources: United Nations Yearbook of International
            Trade Statistics, 1979, (New York: United
            Nations Publications) and South Africa: 1982
            An Official Yearbook of the Republic of
            South Africa, (Johannesburg, Chris van
            Rensburg).

such an hypothesis. The reaction to the current crisis situation, if it evolves as
we have predicted, will lend even more support.

South Africa is a state whose government has successfully relied on repression
and terror to keep itself in power. As its ability to provide the structural requirements of stability (employment and affluence) decline, it will be faced with
a greater need to employ both repression and terror. Concomitantly, however,
as employment and affluence decline, the state's ability to afford increasing
repression and terror also declines. This tends to increase the ''terror'' component
of that repression as ''desperate circumstances warrant desperate measures.''
These waves of ''desperate measures'' will end only when the state is weakened
enough, and its opponents become strong enough, to turn general state repression
and terror into general revolution.

NOTES

1. Theories of this nature may be found in Chalmers Johnson, *Revolutionary Change*
(Boston: Little, Brown, 1966); Ted Gurr, *Why Men Rebel* (Princeton, N.J.: Princeton
University Press, 1970); and in various works by Marx and his followers.

2. Theda Skocpol, *States and Social Revolutions* (New York: Cambridge University Press, 1978).

3. Ibid., p. 18.

4. Ralf Dahrendorf, *Class and Class Conflict in Industrial Society* (Stanford, Calif.: Stanford University Press, 1959).

5. Leo Kuper, *Race, Class and Power* (London: Duckworth, 1974), p. 6.

6. Peter Walshe, *The Rise of African Nationalism in South Africa* (Berkeley, Calif.: University of California Press, 1971); and Muriel Horrell, *Action, Reaction, and Counteraction*, 3rd ed. (Johannesburg: South African Institute of Race Relations, 1971).

7. Bernard Magubane, *The Political Economy of Race and Class in South Africa* (New York: Monthly Review Press, 1979).

8. Gwendolen Carter, *Which Way Is South Africa Going?* (Bloomington, Ind.: Indiana University Press, 1980), p. 13.

9. Michael Savage, "Costs of Enforcing Apartheid and Problems of Change," *African Affairs* 76, 304 (July, 1977): 295.

10. Carter, *Which Way Is South Africa Going?* p. 38.

11. Ibid., p. 34.

12. Ernest Harsch, *South Africa: White Rule, Black Revolt* (New York: Monad Press, 1980), p. 77.

13. Amnesty International, *Amnesty International Report, 1979* (London: Amnesty International Publications, 1979), p. 32.

14. Amnesty International, *Political Imprisonment in South Africa* (London: Amnesty International Publications, 1978), p. 661.

15. Ibid., p. 21.

16. Ibid., p. 23. As of July 1980 the South African government reported 154 banned persons, 119 black and 35 white. See also Committee on Foreign Relations and Committee on Foreign Affairs, *Country Reports on Human Rights Practices* (Washington, D.C.: U.S. Government Printing Office, February 2, 1981), p. 241.

17. Albie Sachs, *Justice in South Africa* (London: Sussex University Press, 1973), p. 188.

18. Amnesty International, *Political Imprisonment*, p. 66.

19. Harsch, *South Africa*, p. 138.

20. Amnesty International, *Political Imprisonment*, p. 91.

21. International Defence and Aid Fund, *The Apartheid War Machine* (London: IDAF Publications, April 1980), p. 47.

22. Harsch, *South Africa*, pp. 77-78.

23. James F. Smith, "South Africa Offers Land to Swaziland," *The Washington Times* (July 2, 1982), cited in *AF Press Clips* (Washington, D.C.: U.S. Government Printing Office, July 2, 1982): 7.

24. Savage, "Costs of Enforcing Apartheid," p. 300.

25. Ibid., p. 296. Savage, in his much more specific study of but one element in the repressive system, the pass laws, warned the reader of the precariousness of his own estimates: "It is difficult, if not impossible, to do the arithmetic necessary to assess the fiscal costs of maintaining and operating the pass system." Under such circumstances, arriving at an exact cost for overall system maintenance would be impossible.

26. Harold D. Nelson (ed.), *South Africa: A Country Study* (Washington, D.C.: U.S. Government Printing Office, 1981), p. 79.

27. International Defence and Aid Fund, *The War Machine*, p. 43.

28. Frank Barnaby, "The Militarization of South Africa," *Notes and Documents* (New York: U.N. Centre Against Apartheid, September 1978), p. 1.

29. Carter, *Which Way Is South Africa Going?* p. 114.

30. "South Africa's Military to Draft Older Whites as Namibia War Drags On," *Christian Science Monitor* (March 26, 1981): 4.

31. International Defence and Aid Fund, *The War Machine*.

32. Savage, "Costs of Enforcing Apartheid," p. 296.

33. "Black Sash Lashes Out at South Africa's 'Lip Service' to Race Reform," *Christian Science Monitor* (March 23, 1981): 6.

34. The Study Commission on U.S. Policy Toward South Africa, *South Africa: Time Running Out* (Berkeley, Calif.: University of California Press, 1981), p. 152.

35. Ibid., p. 162.

36. Savage, "Costs of Enforcing Apartheid"; International Defence and Aid Fund, *The War Machine*; and South African Information Service, *South Africa: 1982 Official Yearbook of the Republic of South Africa* (Johannesburg: Chris van Rensburg, 1982).

37. Savage, "Costs of Enforcing Apartheid," p. 301.

38. Carter, *Which Way Is South Africa Going?* p. 113.

39. T. Hanf, H. Weiland, and G. Vierdag, *South Africa: The Prospects of Peaceful Change* (Bloomington, Ind.: Indiana University Press, 1981), p. 76.

40. Unless otherwise indicated, the data presented in this section were gathered from a number of World Bank, United Nations, South African, and commodities brokerage statistical sources that are noted in the tables.

41. R. W. Johnson, *How Long Will South Africa Survive?* (New York: Oxford University Press, 1977), p. 64.

42. South African Bureau for Economic Research, cited in Joseph Lelyveld, "Gold's Great Fizzle," *The New York Times* (February 14, 1982): Section 12, p. 44.

43. Johnson's work (see n. 41) was the source of a great deal of information on South African political and economic strategies.

44. Johnson, *How Long*, p. 49.

45. Charles Taylor and Michael Hudson, *World Handbook of Political and Social Indicators* (New Haven, Conn.: Yale University Press, 1972).

46. Cited in Johnson, *How Long*, p. 49.

47. Lewis Gann and Peter Duignan, *Why South Africa Will Survive* (New York: St. Martin's Press, 1981), chapter 4.

48. Johnson provided an interesting review of the "war over gold" in chapter 4 of *How Long*, pp. 67-82.

49. Ibid., pp. 65-66.

50. Gann and Duignan, *Why South Africa Will Survive*, p. 161.

51. Lelyveld, "Gold's Great Fizzle," p. 44.

52. The Soviet Union is the world's leading producer of rough diamonds and the second largest producer of gold. The use of such instruments to cover one's debts, however, is not as easy as one might guess. Sales of large amounts of either of these commodities, particularly the former, can greatly reduce the value of stocks still held and thus jeopardize future revenues. Where diamonds are concerned the Soviets had appeared to be willing to sell exclusively through the Central Selling Organization of the DeBeers conglomerate and allow that organization's monopoly position to maintain the price. Under extreme pressure, however, large-scale direct sales of gold and diamonds are possible. The twin problems of war in Afghanistan and financial collapse in Poland

seem to have elicited such a condition. Although no exact data are available, a number of brokers suggest that recent downturns in diamond prices can be traced, in part, to large Soviet sales. Also, a Consolidated Gold Fields Ltd. analyst has unofficially estimated Soviet gold sales as having tripled between 1980 and 1981. Note "Drop in Gold Prices Laid to Rise in Sales by Soviets, South Africa," in the *Baltimore Sun* (January 7, 1982), cited in *AF Press Clips* (January 15, 1982): 12.

53. "South Africa: The Rate of Change," *Mining Journal* (November 20, 1981): 382.

54. "New Unrest Among Black Miners Shuts a Gold Mine in South Africa," *The New York Times* (July 6, 1982): 3.

8

Government Terror in the United States: An Exploration of Containment Policy

Frederick D. Homer

This chapter explores U.S. government terrorism by analyzing it as an offshoot of a broader perspective on American politics. The broad perspective is suggested by the writings of Alexis de Tocqueville and sees terror as one of the consequences of a majority of Americans trying to maintain social peace and their own personal safety. This policy, containment, is ongoing in the American experience, operates through different levels of government, and, although continual, enjoys alternating periods of higher and lower visibility. Containment is carried out by government through what I call intrusion and indifference. *Intrusion* is aggressive action to maintain peace and personal safety for the majority, and *indifference* represents government inaction if the majority is not threatened. In existential terms, indifference means that minorities may have only themselves to turn to in times of danger and fear.

Initially, this chapter explores some useful distinctions others have drawn that pertain to our analysis of containment. Once these distinctions have been sifted through we may rest the concept of containment in the context of existing literature on terror. Containment will provide us with an empirical description of government terror as a manifestation of majoritarian tendencies so sharply noted by Alexis de Tocqueville.[1] Containment can then be brought into bolder relief by comparison with contemporary criticisms of American government and society: Marxism, liberalism, neo-conservatism, and existentialism. This contrast will help fill out the description of containment as well as suggesting some normative solutions to U.S. government terror.

PRELIMINARY DISTINCTIONS—GOVERNMENT TERROR

Analysts who study terror label actions by the state to subdue the general population a "reign of terror," "establishment terrorism," "terror from above," or the term we will use, "government terror."[2] These concepts define acts of violence by those in power against those out of power. What differentiates acts of terror from those of force or violence is the message the acts of violence convey to those who are not harmed directly. Acts of terror include a message to others that the government may act in similar or equally drastic ways toward them in the future.[3]

Difficulties immediately arise with these preliminary definitions. Most all acts of violence by governments have a general deterrent effect as well as one of specific deterrence. In an open society, news of arrest travels quickly. Even in a closed society, the disappearance of a citizen, an act of violence, causes rumor and concern and has a general deterrent effect. If it is difficult enough to determine from the people what the generalized effect of a specific act of violence is, it is often as difficult if we try to judge the subjective intentions of the government actors. In the latter instance was the unjustice done to frighten others, to punish the one dissident, or was it a confused or mistaken bureaucratic directive?

One also has difficulty deciding whether an act must be illegal to constitute a terrorist act. In certain countries where insurgency is constantly threatened, preventive detention may be legal. Civil liberties may be loosened under emergency powers legally granted in a government's constitution.[4] Yet even if an action is legal, it may constitute for the aggrieved, or for his or her friends, a gross violation of human rights. On the other side of the argument, friends of the government may show extreme reluctance to label any actions by government as anything but their right of self-protection. Sidney Hook, for example, said "A government has the moral right to protect itself." He did not want to call the actions used by government to protect itself "violence" or "terror" but "force."[5]

When attempting to define *government terror*, it depends on the side you are on or the perspective you use as to whether you label a government act "terrorist." Did Abraham Lincoln save the Union or was he a terrorist? Are the police terrorizing or preventing unjustified insurrection? We have to come to some resolution of these questions if we are going to speak of containment and terror.

One way out would be to apply the standards of Amnesty International to our government and concentrate on those acts they label "terror." (We would probably sidestep the debates about justifications of those standards and accept them as given, something social scientists are reluctant to do.) In their 1980 report, Amnesty International wanted to see the abolition of the death penalty in the United States; they reported several trials that did not adhere to our own standards of justice, and they reported the murder and mistreatment of Mexican immigrants at border crossings.[6] How can we decide what is government *terror*? Hook excluded the word from the democratic lexicon, and Amnesty International let us, as a country, off too easy.

If we move to a comparative context, we run into difficulties as well. As many authors have noted, there is often more overt insurgency in democratic nations, especially weak ones, than in totalitarian nations. Democratic nations may openly display terrorist tactics; their opponents may draw world attention to them. The terrorist machinery of totalitarian regimes, although the regimes have shown themselves clumsy at times, is more covert, one that Saul Bellow has called a "hierarchy of terrors." Here we get into an argument about whether conditions are worse in El Salvador, the USSR, Chicago, or Argentina. Conditions may be bad in all places, and to decide which is worse may lead us to excuse activities in another place. This attitude may be countered by what I call a "parity of terrors." Here it is equally unfair to lump all countries together with respect to terror, to find them all equally culpable, even if one is Nazi Germany, the other is the United States, and a third is El Salvador. Although it is arbitrary and difficult to make normative judgments with respect to a particular system, it may be appropriate to expect more from one's own country, to demand more. This is the arbitrary tactic I will follow here.

If there is no agreed-upon standard we are free to look at our perspective and to define terror in the way we please, consistent with that perspective. The measure I will use does not exonerate the U.S. government through a comparative hierarchy of terror or overindict it with a parity of terrors. The American government should apply its laws equally to all citizens; allow for a maximum of free speech, assembly, and movement; be free of arbitrary abuses of authority; and keep the use of laws that convey extraordinary powers to a minimum. These standards applied in this country stem from our professed ideals of due process. Abuses in these areas will occur when containment policy is used in this country. I will leave it to others, if they wish, to operationalize these statements and establish cutoff points between accepted procedures and terror. I am more interested in describing the perspective from which most terror arises.

PRELIMINARY DISTINCTIONS—SCOPE OF GOVERNMENT TERROR

Most of the literature on terror concentrates on "insurgency," "terror from below," where the message the terrorists try to convey is that existing government is brutal and corrupt.[7] Analysts often point out that no response or a minimum response to the demands of terrorists is the most effective way to combat terror and prevent governments from becoming what insurgents want—terrorist. Others demand policies of non-negotiation or limited negotiation with terrorists. Yet if we narrow our discussion of government terror only to the response or lack of response to insurgent groups, we narrow considerably what we would consider as government terror. Government terror, in our definition, will include more than actions in response to deliberate insurgency.

The scope of our definition of *government terror* is dependent upon our definition of *political crime*. Alan F. Sewell suggested that the "most common definition of political crime concerns actions intended to disrupt or destroy the integrity of a governmental system."[8]

If we accept this definition, government terror is only our response to deliberate insurgency. Stephen Schafer cast a definition that better suits our purposes. It allows us to consider much more to fall under the label of "government terror." For instance, just because we may have no deliberate insurgency, we cannot assume that government terror is nonexistent. Schafer said, "In the broadest sense, it may be agreed that all crimes are political inasmuch as all prohibitions with penal sanctions represent the defense of a given value system or morality in which the prevailing social power believes."[9] One might go further in suggesting that government terror may occur whenever people are perceived as committing crimes, whether or not they are actually in violation of the law. A person may be carrying a picket thinking he or she is exercising a right, when a police officer grabs the sign and throws the individual to the ground. In this officer's mind, the protestor may be inciting his or her friends and threatening social stability. We will accept a broad definition of *government terror*. It is not merely the reaction against deliberate insurgency but reactions on the government's part to all actions the government believes are detrimental to the social order. To be an act of terror, government response, of course, would have to overreach the earlier mentioned acceptable boundaries of behavior.

NATIONAL AND INTERNATIONAL TERROR

Nations with a plurality of armed services, police forces, customs agencies, border patrols, and regulatory agencies try to divide agency labors so that they do not conflict with one another. These fiefdoms are supposed to protect the public from unwarranted intrusion by limiting the jurisdiction of each agency. In this country, one such designation is by levels of government; the army fights our wars, the FBI engages in fighting crime involving interstate commerce, and the local police may deal with a protest march for which no permit was issued. Yet in the 1960s all three agencies might have intervened in the same local protest. The division of labor often breaks down. More recently, the federal government wanted to use the Navy's radar planes to locate potential drug smugglers in south Florida. To maintain the facade of independent spheres, the navy would make no arrests. Local officials would put the cuffs on.

Words like *national security* that have been conceptually stretched by agencies, the flexibility of the commerce clause, and the sheer number of agencies involved in maintaining the public order in this country can create terror among the citizenry. In Hannah Arendt's terms it appears to be rule by nobody, and hence, to elaborate on her concept, rule by nobody degenerates into rule by everybody. It is never clear whether a citizen may be subject to surveillance, threat, or harm by agents from a multitude of agencies. We will have more to say later about terror and the plurality of agencies responsible for maintaining domestic tranquility.

In this analysis I concentrate on government terror within our borders. This is purely a convenience, and we should be mindful that agencies with their principle charge of protecting the country against external enemies may act in domestic situations.

PRELIMINARY DEFINITIONS AND CONTAINMENT POLICY

It has been duly noted that definitions of *government terror* are arbitrary stipulations. Even if a set of definitions can be agreed upon, significant disagreements about the subjective intentions of actors mean that we will have no final agreement on what we define as government terror. Given this situation of relativity and uncertainty, I have summarily fashioned a set of assumptions that accommodate the policy of containment to be developed. This perspective and these assumptions will be weighted against other perspectives and assumptions and ultimately judged by the reader. In sum, *government terror*, or *terror from above*, is a response to any perceived threat to social peace or tranquility. This terror involves not only the act but the generalized message conveyed to the public. The acts that constitute terror are not judged in comparison with other systems but by our own standards of justice and fairness. To define *justice* in a hierarchy of terrors or parity of terrors would be to render the concept of terror as a useless standard within our own system: overly permissive or overly harsh.

CONTAINMENT

The perspective of *containment* is where the majority of individuals are concerned about social peace and personal safety, and these concerns take precedence in their minds over the niceties of civil liberties. Containment resembles what Herbert Packer called the crime-control model where individual liberties are subordinated to the requisites of social order.[10] The subordination of civil liberties may pose a dilemma for those in the majority, but more often than not, liberties are either deliberately ignored or not even related in the majority's mind to a particular incident of terror. Or the rights of individuals may be rationalized away as only the privilege of the deserving. For instance, few people are able to see the following example as an attempt to redress an abridgement of rights: A reputed organized criminal went to court to ensure that the FBI, which was following him with twenty-four-hour surveillance, play at least one foursome behind him on the golf course. We are willing to be amused by such incidents, and as long as the victims are not in the mainstream of society, violations of rights are ignored, played down, rationalized away, or not thought about. Deep down, perhaps, we believe that rights are only for the deserving.

Containment is an inclusive concept that allows one to analyze the well-documented examples of "government terror" or "repression," such as the Palmer Raids after World War I, the FBI's COINTELPRO program, and the Watergate break-in.[11] As the analysis proceeds, one will see that containment also allows for consideration of many other government actions and examples of inaction that should but usually don't fall under the rubric of "government terror." I emphasize the less publicized elements of government terror and do not dwell on the known and familiar. This emphasis should not be interpreted to mean that the publicized events are less important but merely that the other elements of containment deserve to be brought to our attention.

Containment does not mean that all peoples of minorities or out-groups will be terrorized and harassed at all times. The government is intrusive only when minorities threaten (real or imagined) the social peace of majorities. Indifference is public policy when minorities or out-groups threaten only themselves. As Robert Sherrill has pointed out in *The Saturday Night Special*, most homicides occur within minorities and out-groups, and majorities shed few tears in reading of these deaths.[12] The murder of one poor ethnic by another, a gangland slaying, crimes of family passion, gang rumbles, rarely bring tears to most or cries for gun control. The government treats intra-minority or out-group crime or violence with indifference.

Containment policy is aimed at keeping crime and violence from the property and persons that constitute the majority.[13] People demand action from their government if middle-class homes are burglarized but maintain a policy of indifference to ghetto slayings, extortion rackets, and gang violence as long as they are geographically contained to one area or socially contained to one group. In William Wharton's *Dad*, father and son have just delivered a car to a Philadelphia ghetto and the son expresses the attitude of containment and hopes for its continued success. "It's hard to believe we are only five or six miles from the jungle. What's going to happen when these people over there come charging into these places? I hate to think about it. I sure as hell don't want to be there."[14]

INTRUSION AND INDIFFERENCE

Containment policy often means intrusion by the government to protect the majority from real or imagined violence and anarchy. Often the FBI has used this as an excuse to harass minorities like the Socialist Workers party, the Black Panthers, and civil rights leaders. Perhaps the most severe containment occurred in the South after the Civil War, where crime rates among blacks were high. Physical separation was not used to prevent blacks from committing crimes against whites. This has often been pointed to as liberal policy on the part of southerners. It was northern cities that suffered physical segregation. However, fear of black crime against whites, especially white women, often reached a fevered pitch. Blacks only had to look the wrong way at whites to end up on a rope.

Today, when we think of containment, we most often think of it in spatial terms. Minorities are questioned if they are in the "wrong neighborhoods"; undesirables are often given money to leave town. A group of Gypsies has portrayed their undesirability so well thay they can travel across the country with virtually no funds. Police petty cash pays for their travel to the next town. When a political convention comes to town, prostitutes are herded from the hotel district. Authorities have many ways of keeping the majorities safe.

From the victim's viewpoint, their feelings range from the feeling of terror to the feeling of harassment. To the innocent minority member stopped for the first time, strip-searched, and detained, government intrusion is an instrument of terror. The prostitute's tenth trip to the station and release without charges filed is an intrusion as well by the government. However, terror from the victim's point of view often becomes defined as harassment as incidents become repetitive. Detention, threats, physical violence, false accusations, involuntary transport, all may constitute tactics of intrusion used to reinforce containment. Whether performed on the innocent or guilty, on a person for the first time, or for the nth time, the government practices selective random terror by singling out all members of certain minorities and out-groups for ill treatment to prevent contamination of the masses by a "crime-ridden minority."

The most difficult time authorities have with containment and intrusion is with youth. A large age cohort of fourteen to twenty-one year olds in a population is enough to create crime and disorder. The only cure is when this population grows older and develops ties to family and community.[15] Containment is used with minority youth, but difficulty occurs when the enemy is within. In other words, when middle-class youth are involved in crime and/or social disruption. In the 1960s containment strategy began to run into difficulties. How could the majority contain their own? In the abstract, the youth of the 1960s were anarchists who had to be crushed. In the concrete, they were the majority's children. Today, the majority is facing ambivalence over the drug problems in schools. The majority could afford to be indifferent when it was defined as an inner-city problem. Today the schools that are supposed to contain middle-class youth are having difficulty suppressing the drug problem. If they continue to ignore it, they do not have to face the problem of the enemy within. On the other hand, intrusion may help to restore social order but stir up old memories and rekindle inter-class warfare. One such battle is symbolically being fought in a suburban Colorado school where school officials deny there is a drug problem and don't want the police on the premises. The police insist they will register some of their undercover force in the schools to arrest drug pushers.

Indifference occurs when groups are hurting themselves and not majorities. Indifference is expressed in many ways. Rookies and veterans to be punished are often sent to patrol high-crime areas. Police may hear gunshots and not respond for hours, not wanting to risk their lives. Often patrolmen will not get out of their cars; if one minority assaults another, charges may not be filed. Indifference means little fear of police by perpetrators and perpetual terror felt by actual and potential victims. The government has come to a tacit understanding; within certain groups, or among certain geographical areas, you live life at your own risk; the law is virtually inoperative. At times, authorities have so little regard for rights that they encourage informal wars within groups or territories. Police have been known to release organized criminals from custody and announce that they were found with $100,000 on their person.[16] The criminal may have trouble explaining that to his friends. Instead of arresting a drug pusher, a plainclothesman may just confiscate the merchandise and leave the pusher to explain the absence of stuff to his friends. Indifference may blend into a malicious participation in a war of attrition, one that does not unduly upset proponents of containment.

ROOTS OF CONTAINMENT POLICY

Perhaps what we fail to understand is how containment is so deeply rooted in the American experience. It is easy to cast off containment as the last vestiges of racial and ethnic prejudice, a short-term problem that will vanish with increasing tolerance. If told about containment policy, most probably would deny complicity and point to others who hold such attitudes.

Containment, however, is deeply rooted in our needs for safety and collective security. Theorists like Hobbes and Schopenhauer recognized the importance of these fears individuals have. Perhaps we all believe in ideals of altruism and self-sacrifice, but in practice safety and collective security often predominate. When one can afford it, one moves to a crime-free neighborhood. To move back across the tracks to poverty and crime rarely occurs voluntarily. As Tom Wolfe pointed out, the youth of the 1960s did move back symbolically by wearing torn jeans, T-shirts, and other run-down garments. As he so perceptively pointed out, these youth did not know those they were trying to emulate who, at the same time, were buying expensive, gaudy, flashy clothes. Also, real as opposed to symbolic masochism rarely occurs.

Alexis de Tocqueville also sees the needs for safety and collective security in America and speaks of Americans' tendency to combat individualism by the principle of self-interest rightly understood. It is not a lofty principle but is pretty clear and sure. ''They show with complacency how an enlightened regard for themselves constantly prompts them to assist one another and inclines them willingly to sacrifice a portion of their time and property to the welfare of the state.''[17] With respect to violence, Americans secure their persons and property. With respect to the problem of crime, they are willing to volunteer some time and money once they are secure. Few are willing to put their families and property directly on the line.

Windy ideals sustain altruism, but acute observations such as Tocqueville's seem to express current public morality. Containment may also be supported by a common belief, one eloquently expressed by Albert Camus. As human beings we cannot agree on what is right or what we like, but we can all agree on what we don't like. Threats to our lives and of those we love are circumstances we cannot countenance. In a more dramatic way Israeli novelist Amos Oz expressed the same sentiments. Oz criticized Martin Heidegger for describing existence as meaningless. If Heidegger had been faced with threats to his life, Oz is convinced that Heidegger would have run, hidden, or fired back on his antagonists.[18] Containment based on the need for preservation of life and property is central to the human condition and is built into the texture of American life. Whether the fears are real or imagined, the response is most often containment—the protection of one's life and property.

Intellectuals often point to nihilism in the twentieth century and suggest that there is no longer any basis for public morality. The wars, the bombs, the Holocaust, destroyed the intellectual and spiritual basis of society. Containment, although distorted in its consequences, inarticulate in its voice, is one aspect of a public morality that remains.

MAJORITIES

The difficult term here is *majorities*, and it is as difficult for us to clarify as it was for Alexis de Tocqueville. We are not only talking about political majorities and decisions, but the social power of majorities to mold opinion. "The majority in that country [U.S.], therefore, exercise a prodigious actual authority, and a power of opinion which is nearly as great; no obstacles exist which can impede or even retard its progress."[19] Tocqueville predicted that associations might be able to temper the will of majorities in much the way that aristocrats could in societies not yet overwhelmed by democracy. There are associations like the American Civil Liberties Union (ACLU) and other legal groups that do temper the abuses of majorities zealous for crime control and showing excessive concern with public safety.

In the early studies by Paul McCloskey and others on consensus, the majorities paid lip service to ideals of freedom and individual rights. Yet when faced with actual examples, they agreed that in concrete situations, rights could be abridged. Freedom of speech, fair trial, and other rights are for the deserving, not for all. The majority is willing to overlook the niceties of civil liberties to ensure social peace and individual safety.

The majority in the United States want to be free from physical harm and live in a stable polity. They expect that the government will intrude upon those who jeopardize social peace. The public views crime as the sociologist does and tends to believe that some groups are more responsible for crime than others. Ethnic minorities, age cohorts, lounging in particular hangouts, type of clothing or grooming styles, extreme political beliefs, all may be the basis for suspicion of criminality.

Containment means protection from all members of suspected groups, regardless of the numbers in those groups that may be innocent of wrongdoing or even thoughts of wrongdoing. In the lexicon of law enforcement we tend to suspect more people than would actually commit crimes. These suspected but innocent individuals are called "false positives," those who fit the social or individual profiles of criminals but who are not criminals. Containment as a policy often catches false positives in its net as a necessary price of social peace. Containment may lead to abridgement of the rights of individuals belonging to minorities or out-groups to catch the few individuals who are guilty of threatening the public order. Containment differs greatly from the "due process" model, which argues that a person is "innocent until proven guilty," and "one must be proven guilty beyond a reasonable doubt."

CONTAINMENT AS A POLICY?

I have used the word *policy* when I have spoken of containment, and the word usually implies some conscious deliberation by those involved in formulation. Containment is not part of an overarching deliberate conspiracy. It is a word I use to describe a set of consequences for the American system that stem from deep-seated utilitarian attitudes the American people hold toward their own safety and social stability. Perhaps the attitudes of Americans toward minorities and out-groups are best summed up by the major protagonist in Saul Bellow's *The Dean's December*. "Those that can be advanced into the middle class, let them be advanced. The rest? Well, we do our best by them. We don't have to do any more. They kill some of us. Mostly they kill themselves."[20] Containment is to ensure that if they kill, it's mostly themselves they kill.

There is no conspiracy. As we described, there may be centralized government, but there is decentralized administration in law enforcement. Even in the 1960s individual agencies were singled out as abusing power. Yet in discussing collusion, even the most vociferous opponents of the FBI could find no overarching conspiracy involving many agencies.[21] Agencies are querulous; their concert together is in the dreams and fears of the public. The biggest danger of this administrative pluralism was described earlier; confusing concurrent jurisdictions can leave citizens prey to a variety of agencies, many unknown to the citizens themselves.

In sum, containment describes an attitude of the people that encourages government agencies to isolate crime and instability, thereby insulating majorities. Out-groups like organized criminals and extremist political and religious groups may be terrorized by the authorities without much public outcry. Those isolated in the ghettos of our country are treated with indifference not intrusion so long as they do not threaten the majority.

I have described the policy of containment not to condone such actions but to suggest that it has deep roots in human nature in general and our culture in particular.

MARXIST POSITION

In the criminological literature Richard Quinney has popularized the Marxist position toward justice in this country.[22] Containment, although not expressly in his vocabulary, is achieved on economic foundations. The rich exploit the justice system to their own ends. In his explanations, exploitation of the masses is fairly deliberate and systematic. The position of containment, in contrast, is less deliberate and sees fear as opposed to wealth as the major divisive force. Groups may find themselves in the minority on dimensions other than economic status. We described extremist religious groups, organized criminals, gangs, middle-class delinquents, and career diplomats often finding themselves in the minority. I believe the containment policy better fits the American system in all of its seething richness and variety.

Perhaps where the two perspectives would most part ways is in suggesting modes of change. Containment is deeply rooted in the American mind and is simply not amenable to quick change by economic redistribution. Even long after a group has made it economically, the majority of the population may contain its members, preferring to suppress many to contain the few who threaten safety and stability.

A radical restructuring of society along Marxist lines does not appear in the offing, and one would only be speculating about the changes that it would bring in containment.

LIBERALISM

Perhaps liberals would be most angered by the descriptions of containment policy. Marxists have not used the word, but have described a picture somewhat in concert with containment. Liberals would feel that through intervention, containment, if it exists, could be exised by the goodwill of the citizenry. In its purest form the liberal would open the half-way house in the ghetto, join the Peace Corps or VISTA. This goes beyond self-interest rightly understood and is to be admired in the few but not to be expected from the majority.

The hypocrisy comes when liberals have no more than self-interest rightly understood, pretend they are not living under the shelter of containment, and believe their tax dollars can liberate those under siege. In the war on poverty, much money was placed in expensive, large-scale experiments. They often came to be run by bureaucrats without the integrity or reforming zeal of those who were originally willing to commit life and limb to experimentation.

At its best, liberalism backed thought with social action. At its worst, liberalism conformed completely to self-interest rightly understood but appeared as the worst form of hypocrisy: for example, the congressmen who voted for school desegregation and sent their children to private schools. Perhaps liberalism gave way to neo-conservatism not because programs did too little to integrate people into mainstream America, for they did work to a great degree; they ultimately failed because all parties to the bargain were uneasy. One would feel uneasy, even guilty, paying a form of tribute to the poor while holding to attitudes of containment, while the recipients felt no gratitude or warmth to the donees. Liberalism gave way to neo-conservatism.

NEO-CONSERVATISM

Neo-conservatism came closest to acknowledging the position of containment in society. Perhaps the first conceptualization to speak to with candor the gulf between the majority and those on the outs was "benign neglect." In the best sense of the phrase, it suggests that paternalism, noblesse oblige, may not work in reconciling differences. Others have more optimistically gone forward to try to break the grip of what I call "containment." Calls for a social revolution to strengthen family and church ties is a way to alter the threat to the majority. James Q. Wilson dealt directly with the problem of crime and violence and, along with many others, suggested that we concentrate on jailing repeat offenders, for this small minority commit the majority of crimes.[23] This certainly would be more welcome than terrorizing whole groups to isolate a few deviants. Unfortunately, Wilson's processes ignore opportunity in crime. If repeaters are jailed others will perhaps pick up on the lucrative opportunities in crime. Other problems with his solution occur as well.

Other hopes opened by neo-conservatism may lie with the Reagan trickle-down theory, which is Marxist in expectations. If, and it's a big "if," the poor benefit from Reaganomics, this distribution of wealth will lead to social tranquility. The more cynical version is that Reaganomics is a return to the nineteenth-century Darwinian notions of survival of the fittest.

Neo-conservatism may ease the majority from a position of hypocrisy, but one has the uneasy feeling that it brings us no closer to breaking the shackles of containment. In fact, during a neo-conservative era, a lack of guilt on the part of the masses may bring even swifter reprisals and terror than occurred when violence erupted in the 1960s.

CONCLUSION

If I stop here, those sympathetic to the analysis will see containment as an overwhelming stumbling block to decreasing government terror. If the reader also shares my analysis (cursory at best) of prevailing ideologies, they will fear Marxism has never worn well as a solution on our soil, liberalism has run its course, and neo-conservatism, less hypocritical, may lead to tougher containment in the future.

I need to put my two cents in, however, for I feel containment, although deeply rooted, is basically unacceptable. What follows is a prescription, sketchy, probably utopian, and definitely masochistic for me to propose. From an individualistic perspective I cannot ask myself or others to throw their lives into the fray: to go beyond self-interest rightly understood.[24] Practically, we will never see a nation of VISTA- or Peace Corps-types dominate the social landscape. From a more realistic position, however, we live behind containment's walls, but in our society we do provide almost every interest group with a dole from the public largesse. Only with the poor in the 1960s, however, did we demand such a thorough public accounting in the use of our funds. Social scientists were paid to design studies to measure the effectiveness of poverty programs, rehabilitation schemes, urban renewal, job training. We gave money to other groups— farmers, the military, for example—with more trust and less accountability. With the poor we gave money and wanted results, an accounting. Perhaps we decided the programs failed because they were not cost effective. In reformer's terms, rates of return expected were too high. If one measures social progress in financial terms, one should not expect to spend much on many for the salvation of a few souls. Social reform is tough and not subject to easy manipulation. Recipients of our aid were labeled welfare chiselers, thieves; scandals were raised because gang leaders got money. In other words, if Rabbi Maimonides is correct in saying that charity is best given anonymously we treated the poor the worst. We gave and still give to others with few questions asked. On the other hand, we let the poor know they were charity cases and never let them forget it. My solution is in line with self-interest rightly understood. If everyone else is on the dole, give to the poor with few questions asked. If a few enrich themselves, why get spiteful and demand such an accounting. Do we scrutinize so carefully when someone benefits from an army contract?

Finally, I do not mean that dropping bills off the Empire State Building is the solution. Funds should be allocated to those in disadvantaged communities who have innovative ideas for themselves or others. The mistake in our large bureaucratic society is to try and duplicate a success by enlarging the scale of a project that works, either by increasing the size of a successful enterprise or cloning many off the original. Most of these large-scale operations or clones fail, because the concept is less important than the skills the innovator brought to the project. I do not claim containment will disappear, that all small-scale programs will move us to an integrated society. I have no interest in measuring these outcomes. Holding the poor more accountable than the rest of us is demeaning to them and puts us on a double standard. The rationale for this solution is that it puts responsibility firmly in the hands of those in need, and it is consistent with self-interest rightly understood. It moves away from the altruism of liberalism, the utopianism of Marxism, and the pure self-interest regulated by market forces proposed by neo-conservatives.

NOTES

1. See in particular Alexis de Tocqueville, *Democracy in America*, Volume I (New York: Alfred A. Knopf, 1945), pp. 264-280.

2. See, for example, Walter Laqueur, ed., *The Terrorism Reader: A Historical Anthology* (New York: New American Library, 1979), p. 7; David Fromkin, "The Strategy of Terrorism," *Foreign Affairs*, Volume 53, number 4 (July 1975), p. 684; Richard Schulz, "Conceptualizing Political Terrorism: A Typology," *Journal of International Affairs*, Volume 32, number 1 (Spring/Summer 1978), pp. 9-10; and E. V. Walter, *Terror and Resistance: A Study of Political Violence* (New York: Oxford University Press, 1969).

3. See, for example, Alexander Dallin and George Breslauer, *Political Terror in Communist Systems* (Stanford, California: Stanford University Press, 1970), pp. 1-2.

4. For an excellent discussion about the permissible legal flexibility of Western societies (in particular the United States and England) to deal with extraordinary situations

of terror and violence, see Joseph W. Bishop, "Can Democracy Defend Itself Against Terrorism?" *Commentary*, Volume 65, number 5 (May 1978), pp. 55-62.

5. Sidney Hook, "The Ideology of Violence," *Encounter* Volume 24, number 4 (1963), p. 29.

6. *Amnesty International Report 1980* (London: Amnesty International Publications, 1980), pp. 162-165.

7. Marius H. Livingston, Lee Kress, and Marie Wanek, eds., *International Terrorism in the Contemporary World* (Westport, Connecticut: Greenwood Press, 1978); and M. Cherif Bassiouni, *International Terrorism and Political Crimes* (Springfield, Illinois: Charles C. Thomas, 1975). Emphasis is on insurgent terror in the majority of articles in these volumes.

8. Alan F. Sewell, "Political Crime: A Psychologist's Perspective," in M. Cherif Bassiouni, *International Terrorism*, p. 13.

9. Stephen Schafer, *The Political Criminal: The Problem of Morality and Crime* (New York: The Free Press, 1974), p. 19.

10. Herbert Packer, "Two Models of the Criminal Process," in George F. Cole, *Criminal Justice: Laws and Politics* (Boston, Massachusetts: Duxbury Press, 1972), p. 35. See also E. V. Walter's "Zones of Terror," which also resembles the concept of containment, in Walter, *Terror and Resistance*, pp. 6, 10.

11. See, for example, Alan Wolfe, *The Seamy Side of Democracy: Repression in America* (New York: David McKay and Company, 1973); Cathy Perkus, ed., *COIN-TELPRO: The FBI's Secret War on Political Freedom* (New York: Monad Press, 1975); Isidore Silver (ed.), *The Crime Control Establishment* (Englewood Cliffs, N.J.: Prentice-Hall, 1974).

12. Robert Sherrill, *The Saturday Night Special* (New York: Penguin Books, 1975), pp. 32-35.

13. Although the examples here are of majorities made up of middle- and upper-class individuals, there are instances where majorities are made up of lower-income groups, and elites may be in the minority. For instance, elites are much more concerned about kidnapping and assassination than the wider public is. Acts of violence toward domestic or international corporations appeal to the "social bandit" in most and do not engender widespread indignation. The out-groups could be a bank or a corporation.

14. William Wharton, *Dad* (New York: Alfred A. Knopf, 1981), p. 337.

15. Charles E. Silberman, *Criminal Violence, Criminal Justice* (New York: Vintage Books, 1980), pp. 43-45.

16. Many of the examples about police and organized criminals are garnered from the author's previous work, Frederick D. Homer, *Guns and Garlic: Myths and Realities of Organized Crime* (Lafayette, Indiana: Purdue University Press, 1974).

17. Alexis de Tocqueville, *Democracy in America, Volume II* (New York: Alfred A. Knopf, 1945), p. 130.

18. Amos Oz, *Touch the Water, Touch the Wind* (New York: Harcourt Brace Jovanovich, 1973), pp. 148-149.

19. Alexis de Tocqueville, *Democracy*, p. 266.

20. Saul Bellow, *The Dean's December* (New York: Harper and Row, 1982), p. 207.

21. Pat Watters and Stephen Gillers, eds., *Investigating the FBI* (New York: Ballantine Books, 1973).

22. See, for example, Richard Quinney, *The Social Reality of Crime* (Boston: Little, Brown, 1970), pp. 8-13.

23. James Q. Wilson, *Thinking about Crime* (New York: Basic Books, 1975), pp. 198-209.

24. For elaboration of this position, see Frederick D. Homer, "Character: An Individualistic Perspective on Politics" (Unpublished manuscript), 225 pgs.

9

Studying the State as Terrorist: A Conclusion and Research Agenda

George A. Lopez and Michael Stohl ___•_____

The preceding chapters have examined the causes, consequences, and dynamics of governance by force, which is called "state terror." Despite this, the authors clearly have just scratched the surface of the topic, and their efforts comprise a small number of the research directions that the scholar might choose in the analysis of government terror. We thus direct our attention here to two related issues: what should scholars interested in state terror examine, and how should the systematic study of this phenomenon of political violence proceed?

Of primary concern ought to be the movement from a purely descriptive and case-study approach presented in most of the chapters on state terror to an explanation of the phenomenon in question. In the language of normal science we need to think in terms of state terror as a dependent variable, resulting from the dynamic interaction of a number of factors. The crucial next step in this research is to postulate and test models that isolate the factors or "causes" of state terror.

In the chapters in this volume we have had hints at this but no direct grappling with the problem. Michael Stohl notes that state terror serves as a function of national security policy within a state's alternative approaches to international affairs. George Lopez outlines a number of variables that could be examined as causal, but he assigned no causality to his scheme or relative weighting of the importance of the factors, save for ideology. In the case study approaches, David Pion-Berlin came closest to assigning explanation to patterns of repressive policy in Argentina but actually used correlational techniques and quantitative analysis to cross-check results about the association of macro-economic policies with state terror. John Sloan's explanations of Latin American behavior may appear plausible but are certainly controversial because of their level of aggregation. From the chapter about the Philippines by Jim Zwick, it is clear that militarism sparks repression, but also that it interacts with a host of other factors. For South Africa, the study of Robert Denemark and Howard Lehman illustrates not causation but those important complementary or sustaining variables that permit certain policies to operate with more ease than the ruling elite may have expected. Frederick Homer's containment approach represents an outcome of societal values directed toward policy in the U.S. context but, much like Sloan's, remains at a macro level of analysis.

Where then to proceed? A number of directions come to mind. First, dynamism might be given to certain variables in the Lopez scheme, particularly the impact of changes in regime and ideology. In terms of the latter, researchers ought to pick up where Pion-Berlin and Denemark and Lehman left off to assess the linkage between macro-economic policies and the incidence of state terror. Some further direction in this area may be provided by Richard Falk's comparative analysis of authoritarian regimes. He posited different political-economic variables that give impetus to terror in different systems.[1] Furthermore, scholars might want to delve more deeply into the impact of patron-client state relations and the onset of terror. That such relationships *sustain* repression has been thoroughly analyzed, but do these linkages *stimulate* its beginning and how so? Finally, although virtually all governments employing terror will argue that necessities of state push them into positions of counterterrorism, the actual relationship between levels of civil strive and/or anti-state terrorism and rule by terror has yet to be explored. This may also uncover some important patterns for our understanding of cycles of violence within and across particular political systems.

A second major area for investigation concerns the problem of the development of terror systems. Lopez discussed alternative views and possibilities of outcomes in a classificatory manner, paying special attention to the assertions of Jeane Kirkpatrick, Luigi Bonante, and Falk.[2] All three theorists presented examples of regimes and regime change (or lack thereof) that support their general contentions about the prospects for change in totalitarian, authoritarian, and other systems. But the reality remains that each claimed "proof," without positing *a priori* to their assertions the conditions under which we might judge them correct or incorrect. These assertions, then, do not constitute proof in a strict empirical sense. Some standard of agreement about a yardstick for measuring progressive change within terror systems becomes an absolute necessity for scholars and policy makers interested in understanding such rule by force.

Other dimensions hold here as well. One of Kirkpatrick's central indicators for a "bad" terror government is that it creates refugees via its policies of economic and social transformation.[3] Conversely, if we read her argument correctly, the fewer the refugees fleeing the state, the less repressive its type of government. Obviously, there exists a number of areas for disagreeing with Kirkpatrick's claims: whether disappearance, torture, and death in detention data might not constitute a functional equivalent to "being made a refugee" for purposes of comparative analysis; or whether she is correctly reading the available data on refugees (that is, Haiti as the most notable example). But all arguments for and against the claims do little more than underline the need for more indicators of the internal state of affairs within terror polities. We suggest four areas for investigation.

The first entails a thorough and detailed study of the progress of liberalization in terror systems. Our prime candidate for study must be Brazil. The *abertura* program to which the government seems committed carries with it attacks from some rightist groups, interest and concern from industrialists worried about civil strife, and cautious optimism of the church and other liberal groups.[4] What will be the dynamics of change in this regime that epitomized authoritarian, right-wing rule for more than a decade? Will change be "blocked" inherently by the nature of the system as Bonante would lead us to believe? Will the government continue to use economic indicators as a sole determinant of the amount of reform? If rightist extremists begin violent activities against the reformist groups and/or the government, will the government depart from its path? What will the correlation be between government-stated intentions and the political and daily reality? Such is the kind of analysis that could later be applied to diverse polities such as South Korea, Poland, or the Philippines. It is imperative in the future study of state terror.

On a second level, since it is clear that liberalization of terror systems is going to be the exception rather than the norm in the contemporary world, scholars still need to know more about the logistical and political dynamic of terror and how it unfolds. In particular, we ought to have a much better sense of the implementation of terror tactics. How much of this develops simply as orders "from the top down" rather than as a shared sense of a viable way to proceed by the clear majority of the army or police? We know a good deal, from the personal accounts of "survivors" and defectors of the torture practices, detention systems, and so on, but exactly how long and under what conditions these apparatus are established is not well known. To what extent do local rivalries or hostilities give the terror policy more impetus than any directive from the national government? These analyses might tell us a great deal about the progress of state terror.

A third area of investigation would be the extent to which certain groups become politically mobilized as a result of their increased consciousness about the dynamics of state cruelty. In a number of states of Latin America this occurred in the late 1960s with the church, which for so long identified itself with the interests, if not the individual rulers, of the state. This development has been followed in these nations, and in others like South Africa, and India under martial law, with the banding together of lawyers. In Argentina, the National Bar Association has taken up the task of filing collective habeas corpus writs in response to the large number of "disappeared" persons. This has two intriguing dimensions to it. On the one hand, it tends to have a much greater impact and dramatization of the seriousness of continued government complacency about answering to the disappearances. On the other hand, the large-scale collective action tends to protect individual lawyers, save possibly the executive officers of the Bar Association, from direct reprisals by the government. The extent to which discontent with government terror mobilizes a previously inconsequential or inactive political group constitutes yet another area for future research.

As a final substantive concern, scholars of international affairs in particular must begin to explore patterns of response of international actors to state terror. On the first level, of course, is the community of nations with its international organizations and legal framework that, on the face of it, with genocide and human rights legislation ought to have the impetus to be more active in this area, thus limiting the ability of leaders of other national entities to invoke a state of war on their population. But discussions of such active stands or policies are rare among states either in bilateral conciliation or in larger forums. Similarly, the concept of sovereignty appears to continue to reign as a major value to be cherished in international affairs education in most nations.[5]

On a different level, international relations entails the actions of non-national actors as well. It is clear to virtually all analysts of state terror that without the services of Amnesty International we would not have the level of documentation necessary for a comprehensive and cross-national perspective on this phenomenon. International church groups and other nongovernment organizations are also beginning to take a more active interest in the actions of state terror systems. The question will be whether such groups are able to exercise more direct influence on the policies and practices of repressive elites than national leaders of other states, and if so, why might this be the case? To what extent should national actors, including governments interested in averting terror practice in other states, channel their actions through these transnational networks?

Underlying much of the discussion of substantive focus of state terror research in the future are issues of methodology. We would like to raise four areas for scholarly discussion: the extent of scientific inquiry possible; the problem of analyzing terror acts versus terror threats; the unit of analysis, that is, the state problem; and those other disciplines that must be involved in this research.

Certainly, our tone at the outset of this conclusion may give the impression that we are going to plead for a hard-nosed, empirical-science approach to the study of state terror. Although that may be our methodological predisposition in many cases, the real issue may rest in the fact that some of the key ingredients for doing "normal science" may never be present in the study of the phenomenon of state terror. Although we believe that McCamant's arguments should open eyes and minds to permit a proper conceptualization of terror, and perhaps the development of a theoretical framework in which to test the operation of terror systems, we worry about data and the positing of relationships.

In terms of the data issue a number of problems arise. The first and most obvious problem involves sources of data and their reliability. Certainly, studies like those issued by Amnesty International (AI) provide most of the material scholars might use, but coding yearly AI reports is not systematic inquiry. The reality of the problem is that the nature of the political acts we want to study do not, by definition, lend themselves to multiple information sources well known to the general public or scholarly community. It is possible in fact that the more successful the state terror apparatus, the less we might know about it!

A second problem develops when we try to consider operationalizing certain categories. Let us take, for example, "support mechanisms," as described by Lopez and used in different respects in a number of the case studies. We can certainly arrive at measures of arms flows, financial guarantees, and so on that serve to bolster/stimulate the mechanisms of state terror. Yet it is difficult to postulate that such support indicators measure the same things across different cultures (which is a *sine qua non* in comparative inquiry) or that in so doing we fall into the trap of having our concept and indicator "loaded" with causation to the point that the phenomenon of state terror is not different from the aid levels that support it.[6]

Beyond this are matters of positing relationships. Recall that in their study of South Africa, Denmark and Lehman spoke succinctly about the nature of repression being a "shrouded" phenomenon that defies one-to-one correspondence between independent and dependent variables. Although not all social science techniques depend on direct, linear patterns, the assumption of analysis of many usually entails being able to establish how much terrorism by the ruling elite results from the mix and change of a set of particular factors. If, in the study of this issue, such analysis "just isn't that simple," normal science is not the appropriate technique. Given these difficulties, with which we invite scholars to struggle, it appears that some combination of limited data-based analysis, directly reinforcing more detailed study, as is the style of the Pion-Berlin essay, may be in order.

A second methodological issue rekindles a controversy faced by scholars and policy makers in the United States as regards anti-state terror. In the analysis of the state as terrorist, most scholars would clearly interpret a telephone call or a visit from a government security officer in which the latter claimed that death would come to one's family if one did not cease making political speeches as not just a threat but as an act of government terror. Certainly, delivering on the threat would be a severe act, but the degree of difference would not deter our claim that any such action or threat to action is an inappropriate use of government authority or force; and that the acts of threat and then murder are separate, distinct, and punishable as such.

Yet the opposite was the thrust of argument of a number of scholars and government officials involved in group terrorism research when the Reagan administration sought in 1981 to "recode" its manner of compiling data on international anti-state activities. Basically, those closest to the research warned against the adminstration's desire to compute threats to take terrorist action as the equivalent to terror acts themselves, that is, kidnapping, bombing, and so on. In the end, the administration viewpoint won out amidst a number of resignations of analysts of such events who had been in government service.[7]

Throughout much of this volume we have been careful to document, as often as appropriate, those points at which the systematic study of state terror might benefit from concepts and approaches applied successfully to the study of anti-government terror. Such an approach is essential in building a comprehensive theory of terrorism regardless of the character of the perpetrator. Yet this is not to obscure those key areas where distinctions are warranted because the phenomenon of terror changes *in fact* due to the nature of the actor. In the area of threats to violence, we believe this clarification holds. The import of state threats vis-à-vis the normal, acceptable range of behaviors of the state, and the power of the state over the lives and welfare of its citizens, makes its threat much more serious and "terrorist" than pledges, phone calls, and so on from anti-state terrorists. These actions, and possibly others, need to be documented and translated as such in the study of regime terror.

A third concern for the study of state terror focuses on the unit and level of analysis problem in such research. The classic conceptions of this comes from Kenneth Waltz and J. David Singer,[8] in which scholars are cautioned not to make generalizations about the individual, national, or international level of world affairs unless their study has remained consistent in its analysis of behavior at that particular level. Such a problem may prove difficult for students of state terror. On the one hand, it is clear that the individuals ruling the nation and their supporters are those that develop and carry out state terror. But on the other hand, we do not seek or obtain information about individuals but about aggregate atrocities taking place within the boundaries called the state. This leads us to talk of state terror and the comparison of terror across states. Furthermore, we are ready to talk about this phenomenon as an international problem demanding international action. We must recognize the possibility that "South Africa is a repressive state," *and* that this may be a misleading and analytically inaccurate statement even if descriptively useful and powerful.

One further point can be made about the nation-state that relates to its use as a unit of analysis and our assumptions about its place in world affairs. The study of state terror presents an intriguing challenge to Western analysts of world affairs since it demands that we leave aside some of our working biases, if not world views, about the place of the state. Enthralled with scholarly analyses about the changing nature of the globe[9] and scholar-policy writings about the changing nature of world order,[10] and living in a nation imbued with a trilateralism and global linkages in a variety of areas of our life, Americans have an unconscious sense of a world of vanishing borders and the declining importance of nationalism. This may predispose us against fully comprehending not only the heightened sense of importance of the state that operates in the minds of those leaders who perpetrate terror but also their reification of the state that undergirds their style of governance.

Our final consideration involves those other disciplinary perspectives that ought to be brought to bear on the study of the state as terrorist. The chapters in this volume fall primarily in the political science tradition, with some emphasis in the Pion-Berlin and Denemark and Lehman chapters on political economy. As mentioned earlier in this essay, the contribution of the latter interdisciplinary approach cannot be understated. Political economy modes of analysis can bring to the study of state terror highly developed theories of marginal utility and cost-benefit analysis for internal dynamics of terror and theories of dependence for the assessment of external influences on terror systems. In addition, as demonstrated by the essays mentioned, key indicators of economic development and international finance help illuminate those conditions that work to sustain terrorism.

Contributions must also come from psychology and social psychology. Psychology has made important contributions to our understanding of the dynamics of political leadership, to the relationship of personality to power and world view, and to the behavior of decision makers under conditions of stress and in crisis.[11] Much the same application of patterns of inquiry is necessary for us to understand why and how leaders of nations opt for repressive measures against those who often share their language, culture, religious values, and historical experiences. Furthermore, the analysis of the impact that continual involvement in policies of kidnapping and torture have on individuals in the armed forces and police of these societies is also an important issue.

From social psychology we need an examination of the impact of terror on local and national community life. To what extent does state violence work to strengthen or destroy people's visions of their community, their future, or their deeply held values? To what extent do people as a whole perceive that they live in a nation of citizens against the government? These queries present large data-gathering problems, but are important dimensions of the reality that is state terror in a number of political systems in the world today.

One of the central dangers of all social science scholarship is that it perceives itself to be about the task of addressing *the* crucial issue of our time. Those contributors of this volume feel no less strong about the dynamics of government violence and repression. But even in our more detached and self-scrutinizing moments, we would rather fall victim to the claim of overemphasis on the importance of the topic and the work yet to be done than to leave unasked some crucial questions about one of the more underexamined phenomena of our era. This chapter and the book as a whole comprise an attempt to spark such inquiry and scholarly enthusiasm.

NOTES

1. Richard A. Falk, *A World Order Perspective on Authoritarian Tendencies*, Working Paper Number 10, The World Order Models Project (New York: The Institute for World Order, 1980).

2. See chapter 3 of this volume.

3. Jeane Kirkpatrick, "Dictatorships and Double Standards," *Commentary*, November, 1969, pp. 42-45.

4. For one of the earliest assessments of these trends and tensions, see Robert M. Levine, "Brazil: Dimensions of Democratization," *Current History*, February, 1982, pp. 60-63, 86.

5. One of the few exceptions in the United States is the debate about the role of law, the United Nations, and humanitarian intervention contained in Burns H. Weston, Richard A. Falk, and Anthony A. D'Amato, *International Law and World Order: A Problem-Oriented Coursebook* (St. Paul, Minnesota: West Publishing Co., 1980), pp. 300-386.

6. For a succinct discussion of this point in international conflict research, see J. David Singer, "Conflict Research, Political Action, and Epistemology," in Ted Robert Gurr (ed.), *Handbook of Political Conflict* (New York: The Free Press, 1980), pp. 490-499.

7. The lively debate on the data gathering and coding of insurgent terror is analyzed thoroughly in Michael Stohl, "Fashions and Fantasies in the Study of Political Terrorism" (A paper presented at the Inter-University Center for Post-Graduate Studies, Dubrovnik, Yugoslavia, and the UNESCO Symposium on Political Violence, June 29-July 3, 1981).

8. Kenneth N. Waltz, *Man, the State and War* (New York: Columbia University Press, 1959); and J. David Singer, "The Level of Analysis Problem in International Relations," in James Rosenau (ed.), *International Politics and Foreign Policy* (New York: The Free Press, 1969), pp. 90-99.

9. See, for example, Richard Cooper, *The Economics of Interdependence* (New York: McGraw-Hill, 1968); and Robert O. Keohane and Joseph S. Nye, *Power and Interdependence: World Politics in Transition* (Boston: Little, Brown and Company, 1977).

10. For example, Richard A. Falk, *A Study of Future Worlds* (New York: The Free Press, 1975); and Saul H. Mendlovitz (ed.), *On the Creation of A Just World Order* (New York: The Free Press, 1975).

11. This is demonstrated by some of the best textbook discussions in the international relations field, for example, James E. Dougherty and Robert L. Pfaltzgraff, Jr., *Contending Theories of International Relations* (New York: Harper and Row, 1981), especially chapters 7 and 11; and Michael P. Sullivan, *International Relations: Theories and Evidence* (Englewood Cliffs, N.J.: Prentice-Hall, 1976), especially chapters 3 and 7.

Bibliographic Essay

George A. Lopez and Michael Stohl _____

Given the wealth of material on repression, human rights abuses, and state terror practices, we present below only what we believe to be the most representative and useful literature in the field, and those works which inform in some way the research questions undertaken in this volume. We divide our focus into three general areas: studies of authoritarianism, studies of genocide, and data collections on state terror.

THE LITERATURE ON AUTHORITARIANISM

Since the end of World War II there has been a steady stream of social science analyses of the phenomenon of authoritarianism. As one might suspect, this has often taken the form of examinations of totalitarianism, as in Germany or the Soviet Union in the 1930s. Similarly, there have been even more detailed studies of ideologies, such as fascism, which were tied to this ruling style. In light of this, we have selected just a few of the many fine studies for comment, with the criteria being the strength of their theoretical approach and their relevance to the consideration of the larger phenomenon called state terror which this book has addressed.

The classic study in the field, by any measure, is Hannah Arendt's three-volume masterpiece, *The Origins of Totalitarianism* (Harcourt, Brace and World, 1966). First written in 1951 and then revised and updated in 1966, Arendt's volume focuses on totalitarianism, the uses of totalitarian power, and the link between terror governance and ideology. The other two volumes detail anti-Semitism and imperialism respectively and complement the development of the totalitarian theory.

In a study that stands free of contemporary examples or detailed analyses of Western political systems, E. V. Walter's anthropological study, *Terror and Resistance* (Oxford University Press, 1969), provides a solid source of theory for the analyst of state terror and authoritarian rule. Walter concentrates on the "process of terror" (within the Zulu kingdom) with special emphasis on terror tactics, the societal position of terror agents, and the relation of the terror process to the wider social realm.

Alexander Dallin and George Breslauer's *Political Terror in Communist Systems* (Stanford University Press, 1970) is especially noteworthy for its comparative approach, its categorization, and its theoretical approach. The authors examine the changing nature and function of coercion in the prepower, mobilization, and postmobilization periods of Communist rule and drive to rule. Further, their grounding in social and psychological theory permits a detailed and purposeful study.

The three volumes of Alexander Solzhenitsyn's *Gulag Archipelago 1918-1956: An Experiment in Literary Investigation* (Harper and Row, 1973), Roy A. Medvedev's *Let History Judge* (Alfred A. Knopf, 1971), R. C. Tucker's (ed.) *Stalinism: Essays on Historical Interpretation* (W. W. Norton, 1973), and Robert Conquest's *The Great Terror* (Macmillan, 1973) are all required reading on the Stalin period.

The classic defense of ''Red Terror'' is found in Leon Trotsky's *Terrorism and Communism* (reprinted by the University of Michigan Press, 1961). Trotsky's work was composed as a reply to the criticisms of the social democrat Karl Kautsky, who, while in favor of the Russian Revolution, opposed the measures that the Bolsheviks had employed in its defense. Trotsky provides useful insight into the process by which new leaders consciously defend their use of the instruments of state violence.

Among a number of books of readings in this area, the edited *Authoritarian Politics in Modern Society* of Samuel P. Huntington and Clement H. Moore (Basic Books, 1970) stands out in particular. Although the range of essays is broad, the volume aims at the particular role of one-party systems in the creation and maintenance of the authoritarian state. The analysis therefore is almost exclusively from a political science perspective. A broader approach, with a bent toward philosophical tenets of authoritarian governance, is Leonard Schapiro's *Totalitarianism* (London: Pall Mall Press, 1972). Schapiro ranges widely through history and across twentieth-century systems to support his ultimate goal of a more refined and detailed concept of totalitarianism.

The most recent study to draw attention in the tradition of these aforementioned and older works is Amos Perlmutter's *Modern Authoritarianism: A Comparative Institutional Analysis* (Yale University Press, 1981). Building on prior definitions of totalitarianism, autocracy, and authoritarianism, Perlmutter's analysis is rich in theory and historical example. The strength of the study may lie in the treatment of the ''institutions for political mobilization, control and propaganda,'' and the role of the military as a bureaucratic agency.

Standing beside these treatments has emerged a distinct set of studies in both definitional focus and geographic concentration. This literature has come to be known as the bureaucratic-authoritarian (B-A) school of thought and it has virtually all of its attention directed to the increasing dominance of this ruling style in Latin America. The classic study that provided definition to this topic of inquiry is Guillermo O'Donnell's *Modernization and Bureaucratic-Authoritarianism* (University of California Press, 1973), which focuses mainly on the prospects for regime change in Argentina.

This work was followed by two edited volumes of considerable import for the study of terror systems in Latin America. James M. Malloy's (ed.) *Authoritarianism and Corporatism in Latin America* (University of Pittsburgh Press, 1977) provides a rich mix of studies on ten Latin systems and also assesses the parameters of corporatist and authoritarian rule. David Collier's (ed.) collection, *The New Authoritarianism in Latin America* (Princeton University Press, 1979) further refines the analysis of the B-A systems and raises crucial questions about democracy and industrial change under B-A rule.

THE LITERATURE ON GENOCIDE

Those interested in the dynamics of that distinctive aspect of terror rule which aims at the systematic extermination of a particular ethnic, religious, racial, or political group, and which has come to be called genocide, will not be left wanting for research ventures in this field. Clearly there is a plethora of literature on the Nazi Holocaust of the Jews in this century and on the massacres of particular foes undertaken by Stalin in the consolidation of power in the Soviet Union. Here again, in this essay we opt not to present the definitive listing of studies in the area, but to highlight the treatments we have found most comprehensive and helpful in the continuing study of rule by force and terror.

In that vein, one must begin with three superb analyses of genocide. Norman Cohn's *Warrant for Genocide: The Myth of the Jewish World-Conspiracy and the Protocols of the Elders of Zion* (Scholars Press, 1981), although a fine case study of the Holocaust, moves beyond description to a thoughtful discussion of differences between anti-Semitism, stereotypic assessments, and the noncombative character of the Jews as victims. A final section of the work also discusses those factors that correlate with genocide.

Of the many studies one might select, Helen Fein's *Accounting for Genocide: National Response and Jewish Victimization during the Holocaust* (Free Press, 1979) may be the premier modern social science analysis of the Jewish extermination under Hitler. Not only does the author draw heavily from social theory and history to sketch the parameters of the genocide process but she integrates in a dynamic way the perspectives of survivors into the analysis.

Possibly the best study of the entire phenomenon is the comparative treatment of Leo Kuper, *Genocide: Its Political Use in the Twentieth Century* (Yale University Press, 1981). Drawing from a number of cases in this century, Kuper develops a thorough analysis of the processes, ideological commonalities, and social structures that appear to undergird the practice of genocide. An excellent complement to Kuper's work is the recently edited volume of Jack N. Porter (ed.), *Genocide and Human Rights: A Global Anthology* (University Press of America, 1982), which provides a mix of theoretical studies of genocide and case studies of particular genocide occurrences.

DATA COLLECTIONS

Social scientists' efforts to compile comprehensive empirical data sets on the occurrence and use of state violence and terrorism are in their infancy. Currently there are three broad sources of data collected that would be useful starting points for the creation of a state violence and terrorism data set.

Amnesty International has been collecting and publishing data on state abuses of prisoners and human rights since 1961. Since 1974 annual volumes, called *Annual Reports*, which review prisoner and human rights situations by country, have been published (Amnesty International, London). For the purpose of developing a comprehensive data set, the reports suffer from an unsystematic use of time periods in their construction, such that the reporting period for each volume varies from country to country, and subsequent volumes do not maintain any consistency by country either. There is often much data overlap and it becomes impossible to disaggregate data on a yearly basis. Different data are also gathered in different countries and thus it is difficult to compare countries systematically. Amnesty also publishes periodic reports on individual nations and special reports on torture, human rights abuses against children, and disappearances.

Freedom House, an organization devoted to what it perceives as the defense and vigor of free institutions in the United States and around the world, has published a yearly survey of political rights and liberties around the world since 1978 under the direction of Raymond Gastil (G. K. Hall, 1978-1981, Greenwood Press, 1982). The 1979 edition also includes a terrorism scale that is admirably suitable for comparative analysis of state behavior. The Freedom House material is quite useful but it also does not present enough raw material for the construction of a data set.

The final current data source is the United States Department of State, which is charged under sections 5:116d and 502b of the Foreign Assistance Act of 1961, as amended, to prepare County Reports on Human Rights Practices for the nations of the world. Yearly reports for 1976-1982 are currently available and may be secured from the Government Printing Office. These reports may be compared with the Amnesty International reports for the same period, with some interesting results. Using the Freedom House terror scale, one such comparison found only a .5 correlation of the reports for the years 1976 and 1981 (see Michael Stohl, David Carleton, and Steven Johnson, ''Human Rights, State Terrorism and U.S. Foreign Aid: From Nixon to Reagan,'' a paper presented to the European Consortium on Political Research, Freiburg, FRG, March 1983).

The three major data resources available are thus useful but inadequate bases for the empirical analysis of state terrorism and state violence. Perhaps social scientists will now turn their data-gathering attentions to this important area.

Index

About the Editors and Contributors

ROBERT A. DENEMARK is Assistant Professor of Political Science at Memphis State University. He co-authored (with Mary Welfling) "Terrorism in Sub-Sahara Africa," in Michael Stohl, ed., *The Politics of Terrorism* (2nd edition). His interests include political economy, comparative political development, and political violence.

FREDERICK D. HOMER is Professor of Sociology and Director of the Administration of Justice Program at the University of Wyoming. He has published on terror in the United States in Michael Stohl, ed., *The Politics of Terrorism*, and has written a number of essays on crime and violence. His *Guns and Garlic: Myths and Realities of Organized Crime* was listed by *American Scholar* as one of the outstanding university press books published in 1973-1974.

HOWARD P. LEHMAN received a B.A. in history and political science at Colorado College and is currently a graduate student in political science at the University of Minnesota. He has traveled and studied in Costa Rica, Tanzania, Rwanda, South Africa, and Eastern Europe. His research interests lie in comparative politics and political economy.

GEORGE A. LOPEZ is Associate Professor of Political Science at Earlham College, Richmond, Indiana. His research work has focused on problems of political economy, international conflict resolution, and terrorism. His publications in these areas have appeared as monographs for the Consortium for International Studies Education, and articles in *Peace and Change* and in *Terrorism: An International Journal*. He also serves on the Executive Committee of CISE and the Board of Editors of *Peace and Change*.

JOHN F. McCAMANT is Professor of Political Science and a member of the faculty of the Graduate School of International Studies at the University of

Denver. He has written about and taught in Latin America, focusing his research on comparative violence. With E. A. Duff, he wrote *Violence and Repression in Latin America: A Quantitative and Historical Analysis*.

DAVID PION-BERLIN is a doctoral candidate at the Graduate School of International Studies at the University of Denver. Previously, he served as a lobbyist in Washington, D.C., for the Chile Legislative Center, an organization concerned with human rights violations in the southern cone of Latin America. As a U.S. correspondent for Inter-Press Service, an international news agency, he has written extensively on political and economic issues pertaining to U.S.-Latin American relations.

JOHN W. SLOAN, presently Associate Professor at the University of Houston, received a Ph.D in political science at the University of Texas and has taught at North Texas State University, Purdue University, and the University of Houston. Sloan has published articles on Guatemalan elections, Colombian political parties, Mexican-U.S. relations, Inter-American relations, terrorism in Latin America, comparative public policy in Latin America, and public policy in Cuba and Brazil. He has just finished a book-length study of comparative public policy in Latin America.

MICHAEL STOHL is Associate Professor of Political Science at Purdue University, West Lafayette, Indiana, where he teaches courses on international relations and violence and politics. He is the author of *War and Domestic Political Violence* and articles on the nexus of civil and international conflict, political terrorism, and the U.S. role in the international economy. His publications also include (as editor and contributor) *The Politics of Terrorism* and, with Harry Targ, *The Global Political Economy in the 1980s*.

JIM ZWICK received a B.A. from Earlham College in 1981 and is currently a Ph.D. candidate in the Social Science Department of Syracuse University. He is a member of the International Peace Research Association and is currently coordinator of the Student Network of the Consortium on Peace Research, Education and Development (COPRED).